Rapidex
English
Convers____

Easiest way to improve
your spoken English

Rohit Gupta
B.E. Electronics

Kanchan Gupta
M.Sc. Electronics

PUSTAK MAHAL®

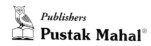

Publishers
Pustak Mahal®

Administrative office and sale centre

J-3/16 , Daryaganj, New Delhi-110002
☎ 011-23276539, 23272783, 23272784, 23260518
E-mail: info@pustakmahal.com • *Website:* www.pustakmahal.com

Branches
Bengaluru: ☎ 080-22234025, 40912845
E-mail: pustakmahalblr@gmail.com
Mumbai: ☎ 022-22010941, 22053387
E-mail: unicornbooksmumbai@gmail.com

© Pustak Mahal, New Delhi

ISBN 978-81-223-1660-5

Edition: 2021

Printed at : Ar Emm International, Delhi

Preface

Dear Learners,

Rapidex English Conversation is a successful journey you are going to enjoy. Carefully planned, every possible effort has been made to make it easy and useful. Hopefully, it would change you from an average learner of English into a fluent and flawless speaker of the language.

The book consists of three sections, viz, **Multiple Expressions Spoken in 90 Situations and Occasions, Sixty-day Course based on Conversation and Grammar** containing thirty days each and **Word Power.** In the portion based on grammar, basic but essential grammatical concepts have been taken up along with idiomatic sentences and some important sentence-structures. In the end of each chapter, some points have been given in boxes to be remembered.

We all know that *Practice makes a man perfect.* Therefore, ample **Tests** and **Exercises** have been given in the end of each expedition. These exercises have been assisted by their answers for your self-evaluation and to boost up your morale. Similarly, chapters on **Phonetics** and **Roman Script** are of special attention. Careful study of phonetics and its practice would certainly make your pronunciation and accent almost as natural as British and practice of Roman Script would shape up your personality with a legible and beautiful handwriting.

After the completion of this book, you would find out that English speaking is not really a tough job. However, before starting up, you shall have to–

- make a resolution;
- try hard to be firm in your resolution;
- and be consistant till you reach the goal.

So, fulfil these conditions and we guarantee to change you into a fluent speaker. *Well begun is half done* should be your motto of life and here we are to wish you all the best!

—Author

Contents

Section - 1
Multiple Expressions Spoken in 90 Situations and Occasions   1-50

1. Introduction   2-4
• To introduce someone for the first time, • To ask somebody about his business, • On meeting somebody for the first time, • To ask somebody how he/she is, • To ask about academic qualifications, • How to end a conversation?

2. Enquiry   4-9
• To ask somebody where he lives, • To tell somebody where he lives, • To ask for clarification, • To ask somebody for a good doctor, • To ask somebody for a drink, • To ask for directions, • On meeting a child, • To ask for permission, • To ask somebody about the future, • To ask somebody about washrooms

3. Favour/Help   9-17
• To agree with somebody, • To clear a point to somebody, • To have expectation from somebody, • To be ready to help somebody, • To give condolence, • To give somebody permission for something, • To ask somebody for a favour, • To invite somebody, • To ask somebody for legal advice, • To ask somebody for forgiveness, • To ask for time to meet, • To tell the way, • To ask for advice to buy something, • To tell somebody one's limitations

4. When getting disagreed   17-20
• To disagree with somebody, • To get disappointed, • When the time is bad, • To feel unhappy/sad

5. Obligation/Compliment   20-24
• To thank for help, • To appreciate somebody, • To compliment someone, • Thanks-giving, • On looking healthy, • Praising children, • To welcome somebody,

6. Mood/Feeling   24-29
• To calm somebody down, • To get a feeling, • To forgive somebody • To feel happy, • To get surprised, • To feel bored, • To feel hungry, • To meet somebody after a long time, • To feel something • To smell something, • To forget something

7. Request   29-30
• To ask somebody for help, • To ask somebody to sit, • Not being able to hear properly

8. **At Restaurant/Hotel** 31-35
• To ask somebody about his/her food preference • To ask the waiter to be quick, • To order for some drink, • To call a waiter, • To complain about the food, • When the food is not cooked properly, • When the waiter asks question, • To book a table, • When getting the wrong bill, • When the waiter asks for payment

9. **Telephonic Conversation** 36-37
• When receiving a call, • To make a call

10. **Conversation while Travelling** 37-38
• To start a conversation, • To continue a conversation, • To talk about the weather

11. **Announcements** 39-43
• Speech, • Some more sentences, • General announcements, • In public places, • In hospitals, • At airport, • At railway station

12. **Sentences about Time** 43-46
• To fix time, • To ask time, • Answer, • To ask the arriving time, • To tell the arriving time, • Related to home

13. **Miscelleneous** 46-50
• To stay positive, • Salesman services, • In office, • When calling, • To taste food, • To assure somebody, • To take leave of somebody

Section - 2
60-Day Course based on Conversation and Grammar 51-282

1st Expedition (Conversation) 52

Day 1. Invitation, Meeting and Parting, Gratitude, Congratulation and Good Wishes, Miscellaneous Sentences 52

Day 2. Refusal, Believing, Request 55

Day 3. Meals 58

Day 4. Time, Permission 61

Day 5. (A) Instruction/Order 64

Day 6. (B) Instrution/Order 67

Day 7. Encouragement, Consolation, Annoyance, Affection 70

Day 8. Negation, Consent, Sadness 73

Day 9. Quarrel, Apologies, Anger 77

Day 10. Tests 80

2nd Expedition (Conversation Contd...)   **84**

Day 11.	At Home	84
Day 12.	Out of Home, To servant	87
Day 13.	On Meeting	91
Day 14.	Shopping, Describing people/things	94
Day 15.	Study	97
Day 16.	(A) Health	100
Day 17.	(B) Health, Weather	103
Day 18.	Animals, Games	106
Day 19.	Person and Age, Character, Dress	109
Day 20.	Tests	112

3rd Expedition (Conversation Contd...)   **117**

Day 21.	Manners and Etiquettes, Signals	117
Day 22.	Office, Things	121
Day 23.	Law, Radio/TV/Post Office	124
Day 24.	Travel	127
Day 25.	Recreation, Dont's, Do's	130
Day 26.	Dealings, Business	133
Day 27.	Sayings, Miscellaneous Sentences	136
Day 28.	Attending a wedding, Cinema, On the playground, In the tourist office, In the hotel, With servent, With the Doctor, General topics	139
Day 29.	Idioms, Proverbs	145
	• Telephoning	149
	• Number, Date and Time	152
	• Health	155
	• Shopping	1158
Day 30.	Tests	162

4th Expedition (Grammar)   **173**

Day 31.	Greetings in Spoken Language	173
Day 32.	Good Manners in English	176
Day 33.	Exclamations	181
Day 34.	Phrases and Command Sentences	184
Day 35.	Present Tense	188
Day 36.	Past Tense	193
Day 37.	Future Tense	

Day 38.   Some Important Helping Verbs   201
Day 39.   Sentences of Order and Request   203
Day 40.   Exercises   206

5th Expedition (Grammar Contd...)   213

Day 41.   Alphabet of Roman Script   213
Day 42.   Vowels and Consonants in English   216
Day 43.   Pronunciation of English Vowels and Consonants   218
Day 44.   Pronunciation of English Consonants   225
Day 45.   Use of 'what', 'who', and 'how', in Interrogatives   228
Day 46.   Use of 'which', 'when', 'where', 'why', etc.   231
Day 47.   Miscellaneous Sentences   234
Day 48.   Negative Sentences and Question Tags   237
Day 49.   Use of he, she, it, this, that, you, I, each, none, etc.   240
Day 50.   Exercises   243

6th Expedition (Grammar Contd...)   249

Day 51.   Use of on, at, into, in, of, by, with, etc.   249
Day 52.   Co-relatives and Temporals   252
Day 53.   Prepositions with Verbs and Other Words   255
Day 54.   Active Voice and Passive Voice   258
Day 55.   Transformation of Senteces   261
Day 56.   Countable and Uncountable Nouns   264
Day 57.   Use of 'It' and 'There' as Subject   267
Day 58.   Some More Structures   270
Day 59.   Idiomatic Sentences   273
Day 60.   Exercises   276

Section - 3
Word Power   283-343

1. One-word Substitute   285
2. Foreign Words and Phrases   296
3. British vs American Words   307
4. Cliches   315
5. Idioms and Phrases   334

●●

SECTION - 1

Multiple expressions
spoken in
90 situations and
occasions

1. Introduction

1. To introduce someone for the first time

Let me introduce my friend Varun to you.

You know, Varun is my pal.

I'd like you to meet my friend, Varun.

This is my friend, Varun.

Have you met Varun?

He's my friend, Varun.

Meet my friend, Varun.

I'd like to introduce my friend, Varun.

2. To ask somebody about his business

What is your business?

What is your profession?

Which business do you deal in?

Where is your office (workplace)?

Where do you work?

What do you do?

What is your work/job?

3. On meeting somebody for the first time

Nice to meet you.

Nice to have met you.

Nice to know you.

It's a pleasure meeting you.

Good to meet you.

Glad to meet you.

A pleasure.

Pleased to meet you.

4. To ask somebody how he/she is

How are you?

How is it going?

How have you been?

How are you feeling?

How's life?

How are you keeping up?

5. To ask about academic qualifications

What did you study?

How much did you study?

What is your education?

Where have you passed out from?

Which school/college/academy you studied in?

What are your educational qualifications?

What's your academic profile?

What's your area of research?

Which school/college did you pass out from?

You are from which batch?

Where did you pass out from?

What is your area of interest?

How much did you score in college?

How many marks did you get in B.A.?

What are your strong subjects?

How were you as a student?

What was your pass percentage?

What graduation have you done?

In which subject are you graduated?

Where did you graduate from?

In what subjects have you done your masters?

When did you finish your masters?

6. How to end a conversation?

It was nice talking to you.
It's getting late.
I've to rush now.
I'm already late.
Can we talk later?
Can we keep this for later?
We'll discuss it later on.
Can I call you later?
Can I get back to you later?
I'll see you later.
Please give me permission to go now?
Well, I'll have to go now.
I think, I should move now.

2. Enquiry

7. To ask somebody where he lives

Where is your residence?
How far is your residence?
Any landmark helping me to locate?
Please guide me to the route to your place.
Where have you come from?
Where do you live?
To which place do you belong?

8. To tell somebody where you are going

I am going to London tomorrow.
I have to go to Mysore day after tomorrow.
My flight to Mumbai is at 10:30 a.m. tomorrow.
I will fly to Dubai next month.
I am leaving for Bengaluru tomorrow.

9. To ask for clarification

What do you want to say?
What is your opinion?
Do you have something to say/express?
What do you mean?
What is going on in your mind?
What is your point?
What are your intentions?
What is the point?
What exactly are you thinking?
What do you have in mind?
What are you talking about?
What is cooking in you mind?

10. To ask somebody for a good doctor

Do you know a good doctor?
Can you advise me a good doctor?
Who is your family physician?
Do you know some senior doctor for brain?
Are you aware of any good doctor?
Which doctor is most suitable for eye?
Which doctor is a specialist of lungs?
Which doctor is best in such a situation?
Can you guide me to an expert surgeon?
Is that doctor a specialist?
Under which doctor should a problem like this be treated?
Which doctor will you recommend?
Could you recommend me to a desired doctor?
Can you suggest a good doctor for heart?
Could you suggest an able doctor for teeth?

Whom should I consult for my problem of digestion?

Does he deal with problems similar to mine?

Please help me find an experienced doctor for T.B.

11. To ask somebody for a drink

What can I get for you?

Would you like something hot or cold?

What would you prefer, hot or cold?

Can I've something to drink?

What would you like, a small or large cup?

You prefer your drink chilled or at room temperature?

Would you like sugar separately?

Do you want a strong coffee?

Would you prefer to have milk separately or with it?

Coffee and milk separate?

How much sugar in your coffee?

Would you prefer espresso or black coffee?

Which tea would you like to drink/ have?

Flavoured or any special tea for you?

Do you want something other than coffee or coke?

Do you want a straw with your drink?

Regular tap-water or bottled water?

12. To ask for directions

How do I go there?

Do you know the direction towards post office?

Which is the shortest route to railway station?

How can I reach there easily?

What road should I take for going to Kanpur?

Can you tell me the right way to the market?

How far is the stadium?

Could you tell me a nearby landmark to the office?

What is the landmark near to bus stand?

Which road should I take to the zoo?

Where shall I find the sign for hospital?

How can I reach that place?

Where is the college located?

Which part of town is that ground?

After which crossing is it located?

On which road is it located?

Where is this area located?

Can you give me the exact location of the swimming pool?

What direction should I follow to reach the nearest hotel?

Are you familiar with that area?

Excuse me! where is hospital?

Excuse me! can you tell me where is bus stand?

Excuse me! where is this road going?

Could you tell me, how far is school?

Excuse me! do you know this address?

Could you please give me the direction to the temple?

Hello! can you please let me know how can I reach this address?

Excuse me! where is the house no A-300?

Kindly locate me this address.

Could you confirm me this address, gentleman?

13. On meeting a child

Hello!

How are you?

What's your good name?

How old are you?

In which class do you study?

What's your father's name?

Where do you live?

Which is your favourite subject?

What do you do in leisure?

Which class are you in?

Which school do you go to?

What game do you play?

Which movie did you watch last?

How many brothers and sisters do you have?

14. To ask for permission

May I come in?

Can I do it?

Excuse me, may I / can I help you?

If I may ask where are you going?

Do you mind, if I switch on the light?

I need your approval for journey.

Do I have your consent (permission) for shopping?

Would you allow me to ask a question?

Kindly permit me to speak.

Please approve for helping her.

15. To ask somebody about the future

What are your plans for the future?

Do you intend to study more in future?

What do you want to do after graduation?

Have you planned for the future?

Have you thought about your future?

Where do you see yourself in future?

What do you wish to do in life?
Have you set your goals for the future?
It's your time to think about your future.
Plan your future without wasting time.
A proper planning shall ensure a decent future.
Take your future seriously.
How do you see yourself in future?

16. To ask somebody about washrooms

Excuse me! where are the washrooms?
Can you tell me where the toilets are?
Can you tell me where's the loo?
Where is the public convenience?
Is there a toilet here?
Where can I find a toilet?
Could you guide me to the toilet?
Can I get access to the loo from here?
Can I use your toilet?
Where can I go for nature's call?
Can you guide me to the way to the toilet?

3. Favour/Help

17. To agree with somebody

I understand your point.
I got your point.
I accept your point.
I am fully (completely) agreed with you.
I follow you.
I understand what you mean.
Point well taken.
I'm with you.

Yes! you are right.

I clearly understand your point.

I believe you.

You have said it right.

We are together.

You couldn't be more correct.

You read my mind.

I got the message.

You seem to be correct.

What you said it is true (right/ correct).

I'm fine with it.

It suits me.

18. To clear a point to somebody

I'd like to make it clear.

Have you understood my point?

Do you follow me?

Do I need to repeat myself?

Have you got my point of view?

I hope you got the point.

I hope I need not repeat my point.

Let me put it once more.

I'll not remind you of this point again.

I hope I'm loud and clear.

Do I need say more?

I'm telling/saying this for the last time.

I won't talk about this again.

Did you get the point?

Treat this as writing on the wall.

19. To have expectation from somebody

Don't let me down, I am expecting a lot from you.

I want you to live upto my expectations.

I've high hopes from you.
I hope I'm not asking for too much.
I'm sure I can bank on you for everything.
Assure me, you will always be there for me.
I expect a lot from you.

20. To be ready to help somebody

I'm always there for you.
I'm by your side.
I stand by you.
You can count on me.
You've got my support.
You've got my backing.
I'm standing behind you.
You can lean on me.
You'll find me by your side.
I'm here if you need me.
I'll always be there for you.

21. To give condolence

Everything is planned.
This is God's wish.
It was destined to happen.
No one can predict, what happens?
Nobody can fight with destiny.
It's all governed by stars.
It was meant to be.
The fate is pre-defined.
There's little you can do to change the circumstances.
It's all in God's hand.
The Almighty wishes this way.
It's your karma.
Don't worry; what is gone, is gone.

We can't control our destiny (fate).

Nothing works against God's will.

22. To give somebody permission for something

You have my permission for travel.

I allow you to leave for Mumbai.

You can call me.

I give you my consent for the project.

I'll give you my clearance for loan.

You must seek my approval for your plan.

You need to take permission for living here.

You are permitted to stay.

You are allowed to leave.

I'm O.K. with you for company.

23. To ask somebody for a favour

Can you help me?

Can I ask you for help?

Can I ask you for a favour?

If I may ask, could you help me?

I need your help on this.

I request for your help.

Would you do me a favour?

I need your support.

Can I ask for your support?

I seek a favour from you.

I need your advice.

Could you please guide me on this?

I'd very much appreciate a favour from you.

Can I look forward for help from you?

If it's alright, would you consider a favour for me?

Do you mind helping me?

Can I expect a little help from you?

Can I look forward to your supporting?

24. To invite somebody

I'd like to invite you.

You are free to come.

May I request you to come in our function?

Kindly make it convenient to reach in time.

I hope to see you at the function.

I'm sure you'll take out time.

I'm glad to invite you for opening.

I'm pleased to invite you for lunch.

I'd like to extend this invitation for the family too.

Would you mind if I invite you for supper?

I hope you wont't mind if I invite you for cutting the ribbon.

I personally take this opportunity to invite you for some valuable suggestion.

I'd be grateful if you accept my invitation for a party.

25. To ask somebody for legal advice

I need your advice on rent.

I need your opinion on insurance.

Could you guide me on copyright?

I need your help on a legal matter.

I am looking for an expert advice on a dispute.

I need some legal consultation.

Could you advise me a legal expert?

Do you know a lawyer?

Can you please ask a lawyer to help me?

Can I ask for some legal opinion?

I have this legal point to discuss.

Can I discuss a legal matter with you?

Do you deal in such type of cases?

Do you have any experience in handling such matters?

Have you handled any similar cases?

Can I expect your services for my service?

I want you to handle this case for me.

Can you advise me on this legal matter?

How serious is this matter?

Can I bank upon you on this?

I hope the situation can be controlled.

I hope it isn't too late to approach the court.

What are the stakes involved?

What is our legal standing?

Do I stand a good chance of winning?

Will I get my due?

Can we settle this amicably?

Do you see a solution to this problem?

26. To ask somebody for forgiveness

Please, don't take my words or actions otherwise.

I'm really sorry.

I apologize.

I'm extremely sorry.

Accept my apologies.

I didn't mean it.

Please forgive me.

Kindly forgive me.

I ask for your forgiveness.

It's my mistake, I accept.

Pardon my actions.

Please excuse my rudeness.

I accept my mistake.

It's my fault.

I beg your pardon.

Pardon, please.

27. To ask for time to meet

I'd like to meet you.

Can I come to meet you?

Do you mind, if I come to see you?

Are you free to meet me?

Can I ask for some of your precious time?

Could you spare some time?

When would you be available?

What is the right time to meet you?

May I ask, if you are free to meet?

What time suits you?

Could you advise a suitable time?

When is it convenient for you to meet?

Is it a convenient time for you?

I hope it's not a problem to meet.

I hope it's not a botheration to ask you to meet.

28. To tell the way

It's just down the road.

It's a few metres ahead.

This place is just after the crossing.

You missed it behind.

Keep going straight and take right.

After a few yards, follow the house numbers.

It will be straight ahead on your right.

You need to take a 'U' turn and it will come on your left.
Follow the road sign on the roundabout.
Ask someone after entering the colony.
Keep on your left and you will soon reach there.
It's just a five-minute walk straight ahead.
Take first left and then immediate right, it's right there.
It's after the signal.
It's located just there.

29. To ask for advice to buy something

Can you tell me which is the best suitable colour for me?
Which according to you is best for me?
I am planning to buy a new coat.
I wish to buy a car, can you help me with it?
Can you help me buy a bike?
I intend to buy a new T.V., which one do you think is best?
Which is the most reliable company for radio?
Which brand is the best for mobile?
What makes it the best for summer?
Which company makes the best cooler?
Which company is the most trusted for oven?
Will you accompany me for buying a computer?
Let me know a good shop for buying sweet.
Which is a good market for buying woolen cloth?
What's the best I can buy in this budget of ₹ 5000?
What's your experience of buying second-hand things?
Could you tell me how to order online?

30. To tell somebody one's limitations

I must have to go now.
I have a compulsion.
I am bound.

I have a limitation.
Not everything is in my hands.
My hands are tied.

I am unable to help you.
I am afraid I cannot help you.
I must go by the book.
I can't cross my limits.
I have no control over the manager.
I am helpless.
I am feeling helpless.
There's little I can do about that.
I can't go beyond this point.

4. When getting disagreed

31. To disagree with somebody

I didn't get you.
What do you mean?
Pardon (say again).
I don't follow you.
I didn't understand what you meant.
I don't accept your point.
I differ from you on this.
We can't get along.
Can you be more clear?
What exactly do you mean?
It is not possible. / It is impossible. / It is unbelievable. / It is incredible.
That's not true.
It's your own opinion.
It's your perspective, not mine.
No chance.

32. To get disappointed

I'm not happy with you.
I'm disappointed with you.
I'm annoyed with you.
You have hurt me.
I didn't expect this from you.
You have let me down.
I don't feel like talking to you.
If only I knew your true intentions.
You should have been more sensitive.
You couldn't have done this to me.
You took me for a ride.
This was the least expected from you.
I should have known you better.
I misjudged you as a person.
I thought of you as a friend.
You back-stabbed me.
I don't believe you could do this with me.
You betrayed me.
You cheated me.
I took you lightly.
Watch your actions next time.
Let's call it quits.
We better part ways.

33. When the time is bad

Bad time will pass soon.
Don't loose hope.
Everything will be all right.
Things could be worse.
You did your best.
Have faith in God.

18

Look at the brighter side.
It will all be over soon.
Accept your fate. ´
This was destined.
Take it in your stride.
Make the most out of the situation.
It's not as bad as you think.
Leave it to God.
There are better days ahead.
It's part of life.

34. To feel unhappy/sad

I'm feeling bad today.
I am feeling dejected today.
I'm feeling low.
I'm depressed.
I've been feeling down today.
I'm not at all good today.
My heart is broken.
My heart bleeds.
I feel disgusting.
All just seems unwell.
I'm feeling dull.
I'm going through the worst.
My mind is tired.
I've a sinking feeling.
I am feeling helpless.
I feel like a loser.
Things just seem to slip out of my hands.
If only God was listening to me.
If only God was watching.
You can't even imagine my plight?

I'm stuck in life.
It couldn't get worse.
God knows! What more has to come?
God knows! How much more trouble?
Time has stopped for me.
I've lost faith in everything.
I've lost all the wisdom.
I don't know where's life going.
I don't know what to do.
I've no ideas left.
I wish someone is listening to my prayers.
Even God doesn't seem to listen.

5. Obligation/Compliment

35. To thank for help

Thanks.
Thank you very much.
Thank you so much for your help.
I'm indebted to you.
I owe you big-time.
I owe you one.
Thanks! So kind of you to help.
You are a true friend.
You proved your genuineness.
I'm grateful to you.
Thanks! you have been a support.
Thanks a lot.
Thanks a million.
I'd like to thank you.
I am heartily thankful to you.
I couldn't thank you more.
Thanks, I'm deeply moved.

Thanks, you will always be special.

I shall never forget your help, thanks a lot.

36. To appreciate somebody

Well done!

You did a good job!

You deserve an applause.

Great job!

Job well done!

You couldn't be better.

Good work.

You've done well.

This is beyond my expectations.

You've lived upto my expectations.

You've proved yourself capable (worthy).

You've done it like an expert.

You are brilliant (amazing/ splendid).

Very impressive!

Keep up the good work.

37. To compliment someone

Wow! you look breathtaking.

You look beautiful/charming.

You've done a great (wonderful/marvellous) job.

Very good going. Keep it up!

How come you manage to look so good everytime?

You look fresh.

You are looking very nice.

You look dashing (stunning/gorgeous).

You are looking very smart.

You look like a million bucks.

You are dressed to kill.

You look as fresh as a daisy.

You've left many hearts to flutter.

You look very attractive.

38. Thanks-giving

Thank you, everyone.

We hope you enjoyed the show (session/performance).

It was a pleasure to have you all here.

I'd like to thank Mr. Nath especially.

It was indeed an enlightening experience (show/ discussion).

Thank you all for taking out your precious time.

We sincerely appreciate your presence.

We look forward to seeing you again.

We are thankful to our penalists, participants, members and guests.

39. On looking healthy

He looks fit.

He looks great.

He's in top form.

He's in the pink of wealth.

He has a well-toned body.

She has a petite figure. He has a muscular body.

He's tall and athletic.

His energy never seems to dry.

He's an energetic person.

She has a glowing skin.

She's fit and healthy.

She looks like a teenager.

He can embarrass even a 16 years old.

She seems to grow younger with age.

She looks younger than her actual age.

40. Praising children

You are such a good boy.

You have grown really smart.

You look very pretty.

That's a smart dress you are wearing!

You have become intelligent.

You are growing up so fast!

Oh! you have done a very wonderful job.

You are so cute (adorable)!

Wow! your hand-writing is really beautiful.

41. To welcome somebody

Welcome!

Make yourself comfortable.

Pleasure (Nice/Glad) to meet you.

Feel yourself at home.

Please come!

It's a pleasure to have you here.

Delighted to have you here.

Please come, I was expecting you.

Feel free to ask for anything you need.

6. Mood/Feeling

42. To calm somebody down

Just chill.

Calm down.

Be patient.

Control yourself.

Get hold of yourself.

Relax.
Don't lose your cool.
Keep yourself cool.
Don't get all worked up.
Take it easy.

43. To get a feeling

I've a hunch that something wrong is going to happen.
I got a feeling of his coming.
I can smell that they are planning something.
I expect bright success from you.
I've an intention to go to him.
My sixth sense says he won't succeed.
My gut feeling is in your favour.
I won't be surprised if he returns.
I've this feeling that the train is on time.
My wisdom tells me that we will pass.
My mind rings a bell that the power is about to come.
This is a sign of success.
This is a signal for failure.

44. To forgive somebody

It's alright! It happens.
I am not blaming you.
Don't worry, it's over.
Forget it.
I won't hold it against you.
I accept your apologies.
Don't repeat the same mistake again.
I've already forgotten about it.
Move on. It's alright.

This won't come between us.
This won't spoil our relation.
Write it off.
No grudges!
I've no grudges against you.
Let's bury the hatchet.

45. To feel happy

I am so happy today.
It's a great day for me.
I am on the zenith today.
I feel on top of the world.
I'm high on life.
I'm really happy today.
I couldn't be happier.
I'm feeling amazing.
I'm in seventh heaven.
Life's good.
God is kind.
By the grace of God, life is running smoothly.

46. To get surprised

I'm amazed!
I can't believe my eyes.
Unbelievable!
Are you serious?
Are you pulling my leg?
Are you kidding?
You can't be serious.
It's the last thing I expected.
I'm shocked.
I can't imagine it.

Really?

Hey, is this really true?

I can't believe this!

Amazing!

Oh wow!

47. To feel bored

I'm bored.

I'm fully fed up.

I need a change.

I need a break.

When will this get over?

It's a waste of time.

It's getting overbearing.

I can't handle more.

It's enough.

It's more than enough.

I just don't know how to pass time.

Time doesn't seem to pass.

This sole time is getting on me.

Another chance and I'll run away.

Give me a break.

48. To feel hungry

I'm straining.

I'm famished.

My stomach is making a noise.

I've not had a slice of bread since morning.

I've not eaten anything since morning.

I just don't seem to get enough.

I'm full.

I've had enough.

I just overate.

I am feeling hungry.

I am unable to think of anything right now except bread.

I didn't have even a single slice of bread since morning.

I have taken my fill.

49. To meet somebody after a long time

It's been awhile since we met.

It's been long since we met.

It's great to see you after such a long time.

Long time no see.

Where have you been all these years?

How good to see you after so many years!

Where have you been lost all this while?

Where did you vanish?

Where were you hiding for so long?

Finally we meet again.

When was the last time we met?

Feeling so happy to catch you after a long break.

50. To feel something

It's soft like silk.

It's really very smooth.

It's like touching a feather.

It's as hard as rock/stone.

It's sharp on the edges.

This is blunt.

It's pointed.

51. To smell something

It smells rich/fresh.

What smells?

What's that scent?

These candles have good aroma.

These flowers smell brilliant.

It's a wonderful fragrance.

It stinks.

What's that stench?

That smells awful.

What's that odour?

Yakkk! It smells stinky.

Chhi ...... Its odour is very bad.

52. To forget something

I don't remember.

It slipped from my mind.

I've become forgetful.

I seem to be loosing memory.

I can recall.

It's difficult to remember.

I need to scratch my head.

I've become absent-minded.

I've too many grey hair.

I can't remember even a single thing.

My memory has begun to fade.

I forget things too often.

I don't recollect.

My brain has stopped recording.

She has become senile.

He's got a weak memory.

He always seems lost.

He just doesn't memorize.

He needs to be reminded every time.

It strikes him late.

She has a bad memory.

7. Request

53. To ask somebody for help

Please help me.

I need your help.

I request you to help me, please.

Your help in this matter is very necessary.

Please help me by lending some money to me.

54. To ask somebody to sit

Please have a seat.

Take your seat, please.

Please be seated.

Sit down.

Make yourself comfortable.

Pull a chair.

Make room for yourself.

55. Not being able to hear properly

I beg your pardon.

Pardon me!

Could you repeat what you said?

Say again! I didn't get you.

I didn't hear whatever you said.

Can you speak softly?

Can you be a bit louder?

Please speak slowly.

Could you please repeat?

You sound worried.

May I request you to repeat?

This speaker sounds unclear.

There is neutrality in her voice.

I am not getting across you.

Please repeat your words/what you said.

8. At Restaurant/Hotel

56. To ask somebody about his/her food preference

Are you vegetarian /non-vegetarian? or are you veg or non-veg?

Do you eat non-veg?

What diet do you follow—veg or non-veg?

Do you eat egg?

Do you relish non-veg?

Are you a pure vegetarian?

Do you prefer veg or non-veg?

Are you non-veg by choice?

Do you have non-veg often or occasionally?

57. To ask the waiter to be quick

Where's my order?

It's getting too long.

You should have told me before.

Can you get my order fast?

Who's the manager here?

Get my order fast or I'll complain.

You people seem to be casual.

You should not keep your customers waiting.

Please hurry up with our order.

The guests are getting angry.

This is really disappointing.

Your service seems really poor.

You must improve your service.

Who's responsible for service here?

Is this your regular practice?

Are you people always so casual?

You must take service-issues seriously.

I'll think twice before coming here again.

I won't suggest this place to anyone.

Do you have a complaint book?

Can you get me your feedback form?

This place has terrible service.

I'd never come to this place again.

58. To order for some drink

Could you get me some cold drinks?

Keep my drink small.

I'd like to place an order for a coffee.

What's new to drink?

What beverages do you serve?

No sugar for me.

I prefer regular tea without milk.

Don't put too much sugar in my coffee.

Get me sugar separately.

Get me milk separately.

59. To call a waiter

We are ready to order.

We'd like to order some food.

Could you please take our order?

What do you recommend?

What's the famous dish here?

What's your speciality?

What all cuisines do you serve?

What's the chef special item in your hotel / restaurant?

What's your signature dish?

What's popular with patrons here?

What do people normally order here?

What's other favourite here?

What's the dish of the day?

Is the non-veg fresh?

What is your menu?

Suggest some spicy/mild dishes.

Any new dish?

What's best here?

Do you have something that suffices us?

Anything complimentry?

60. To complain about the food

This does not seem like our order.

I don't think, I ordered this.

I think you've got my order wrong.

Please check, we didn't order this.

I think there is some confusion.

Just cross-check with the waiter.

I clearly remember not to order this.

Could you please replace my dish?

Could you get, what was ordered?

There's a confusion here, I didn't order this.

Could you tell me, what I ordered?

61. When the food is not cooked properly

It seems stale.

It's tasteless.

It's cold.

Its taste is really bad.

Can you replace my dish?

The crockery is not clean enough.

Your cutlery is dirty.

Don't you clean your cutlery?

Can you get me clean plates?

This food is too spicy.

The preparation is horrible.

62. When the waiter asks question

Sir, is everything alright?

Was this food fine?

Can I get you something else?

Would you have anything else?

I hope you enjoyed the meal.

Sir, how did you find our services?

Looking forward to having you back.

Please visit again.

63. To book a table

Are you calling from Maurya Hotel?

Is this Akbar Hotel?

Whom am I speaking to?

I'd like to make a booking for two persons in the evening.

I'd like to find out if there is any table vacant for four persons.

Do you have a place for four persons?

What time can I come for lunch?

Please note down my name and number.

Please reserve a table for 4 -5 people.

Please reserve a table for 7-8 persons.

Would it be O.K. if we reach by 7.30 p.m.?

64. When getting the wrong bill

Your bill is not correct.

You seem to overcharge me.

The prices here are exhorbitant.

There is some problem with your bill.

Can you correct and get me a new bill?

Get me the corrected bill.

The taxes are too high.

Not worth it.

The food is just not worth the prices.

You must mention the hidden charges.

Service charges are preposterous.

The calculation is incorrect.

Are you charging me whimsically?

65. When the waiter asks for payment

Sir, how do you prefer to pay, cash/card?

How would you like to pay?

Payment by cash or card?

Cash or card?

We only accept cash, sir.

You can pay anyway–either by cash or by card. We accept both.

Sir, kindly make your payment on the cash-counter.

9. Telephonic Conversation

66. When receiving a call

Hello!

How can I help you?

What can I do for you?

Can I take a message?

Whom would you like to speak to?

Would you like to leave a message?

May I know your name?

Who should I say is speaking?

Which department do you want?

Where should I transfer your call?

Can you please leave your name and contact number?

Can you hold for a moment?

Please be online.

May I know, whom am I talking to now?

Don't hang up.

Kindly wait for a moment.

Let me put you on hold, while I check whether Mr. Das is in or not.

What is the purpose of your call?

What is it regarding?

It is not regarding meeting.

It seems you've dialled a wrong number.

Sorry, I think I have dialled a wrong number.

You are mistaken, this is not 0000000000.

67. To make a call

Hello!

Is it L & T company/office?

Is this Mr. Suhel's number?

Can I speak to the manager?

Hello! Am I talking to Mr. Das?

Please call me online.

Hello! Are you Mr. Muneeb?

Hello! I am Jai speaking. May I know your good name / introduction?

Is Mr. Raju available?

When should I call back?

What is the right time to talk to you?

I'd like some information regarding postage.

What is your office / store timing?

I'd like to place an order for ice-cream.

I would like to update my personal information.

10. Conversation while Travelling

68. To start a conversation

Is somebody sitting here?

If you don't mind, can I join you?

Can I sit here?

Can I join you?

Would you mind if I sit here?

Do you mind if I sit here?

If I may ask, can I sit here?

I hope it's alright if I sit here.

69. To continue a conversation

Which place are you travelling to?

Where do you reside?

Are you going there for work?

How long is our journey?

How much time until I reach?

By moving at such a slow speed, shall we reach on time?

Have we started on time?

What place do you belong to?

Where is your hometown?

Do you travel on this route often?

How often do you travel?

Are you travelling alone?

Are you travelling for the first time?

Are you a first timer?

What makes you travel?

Which book are you reading?

Can I borrow the newspaper, please?

Shall we be served food?

Do these people also provide drinking water?

70. To talk about the weather

It's pleasant today.

Lovely weather.

Nice and pleasant outside.

It's really hot today.

It's burning outside.

It's pouring.

It's raining heavily.

It's drizzling.

It's very humid today.

It seems to be windy.

It's really cold.

Lousy weather.

It's cloudy outside.

It's hot as hell outside.

It's bright and sunny.

11. Announcements

71. Speech

Good morning / afternoon / evening.

Good evening ladies and gentlemen.

I'd like to welcome you.

May I welcome Mr. Rana?

Today we have with us our patron.

I'd like to welcome all my guests.

Allow me to welcome Mrs and Mr. Ashutosh.

It's an honour to all of us.

It's my honour to have lunch with you.

It's my pleasure to welcome the guest.

Before I start I'd request you to welcome our cheif guest.

First of all I'd like to thank you all for gathering here.

First and foremost I'd like to invite Mr. Jugal Kishor upon the stage.

72. Some more sentences

Today's gathering is for meeting new comers.

Today's function is meant for thanks-giving to our patron.

To grace the occasion I request Mr. Munib to come on the stage.

On our list of panelists today are Mr. A, Mr. B., Mr. C. and Mr. D.

We have with us this evening a lovely face.

We are honoured with the presence of our director.

Our esteemed guests are Mr. A, B, C and D.

I thank our guests for gracing the occasion with their persence.

Today amongst us we have our old friends.

Today's event is being held for our friends.

I'd request you to take seats.

May I ask you to take tea?

I'd request you to switch off your mobile phones.

Today's event is our annual function.

I am grateful to all of you to have come here.

It's a great pleasure to see all of you on this occasion.

We are indebted by your presence.

Your presence itself has made this event successful.

It is an encouragement to see so many participants.

We hope you enjoy today's programme.

I hope you will like the function.

Sit back and enjoy the event.

Sit back, relax and enjoy the show.

Please maintain silence.

We'll start with music.

First we have with us a dancer from Mumbai.

We shall begin in a while.

We are about to start the show.

We are now ready to announce the names of participants.

Let's begin with prayer.

Let me intruduce to you Mr. Panday.

Let me call upon Mrs. Archna Devi on stage.

May I request our chief guest to kindly step onto the stage?

May I request Mr. Salman Khan to hand out the prize?

May I invite Mr. chairman to announce the winner?

Over to my colleague, Mr. Arun.

My colleague will take you forward from here.

73. General announcements

This is to bring to your attention that the power supply is not sufficient.

May I have your attention please?

This announcement is for ladies only.

This is an announcement to inform you that we shall leave on Monday next.

Please pay attention to the announcements.

74. In public places

Please observe/maintain silence in the premise.

This building is under cctv surveillance.

Please locate the nearest exit.

This is a No Smoking zone.

Refrain from using your mobile phones.

In case of a suspicious object, inform the police.

Beware of pick-pockets.

Follow the signs along the aisles.

Maintain cleanliness in the premises.

Parking is not allowed here.

75. In hospitals

Please maintain the decorum of the hospital.

This announcement is for Mr Bachchan.

Mr Adeeb is requested to come to the reception.

This is to inform the relatives of the patient of cardiac surgery.

Attendants of the patient No. 255 kindly come to the main office.

Please observe / maintain silence in the hospital.

76. At airport

This is the final boarding call for flight number 05.

We are ready with boarding of flight number 10.

All passengers are travelling to America.

All passengers are booked on flight number 13.

This announcement is for passenger Mr Rakesh.

Kindly report to the service counter of the airlines.

Please check your exact gate number.

The gates for flight number 10 will close shortly.

We regret to inform the delay in arrival of flight number 15.

We are sorry to announce a delay in departure of flight no 07.

We regret the inconvenience caused to our passengers of flight number 03.

Kindly bear with us.

There's a delay in the departure of flight number 08.

Due to technical fault, flight number 02 is delayed.

77. At railway station

Train number 1665 is arriving on platform number 2.

Train number 1803 is delayed by one hour.

Please contact information counter for specific information regarding train no. 1774.

Please observe vigil around you.

In case of any suspicious object, inform/report to your nearest police booth.

Do not leave your belonging unattended.

Unidentified baggage will be removed and destroyed.

Keep your baggage with you at all times.

Pay only the published prices on the service counters.

Do not entertain any suspicious looking person.

Immediately report any suspicious event (object/ person).

In case of lost baggage contact railways police/ staff.

78. To fix time

I'll be there at 7:30 p.m.

Expect me by 7:30 p.m.

See you at half past seven.

I should be there by 7:30 p.m.

I hope to reach by 7:30 p.m.

I'll try and make it by 7:30 p.m.

I should reach by 7:30 p.m.

I will be coming by 7:30 p.m.

Hope 7:30 p.m. is alright by you.

7:30 p.m. sounds good.

7:30 p.m. seems convenient.

Be assured I'll be there by 7:30 p.m.

Don't worry I'll reach on time.

I'll be there by 7:30 p.m.

You will never have to wait later than 7:30 p.m.

79. To ask time

Excuse me! Do you know what time is it?

Excuse me! What's the time?

Excuse me ! What time is it?

Do you know what time is it?

Could you tell me what time is it?

80. Answer

It's 12 noon.

It's noon.

It's 12 o'clock.

It's twelve ten.

It's 10 minutes past 12.

It's quarter past 12.

It's twelve fifteen.

It's half past 12.

It's twelve thirty.

It's quarter to 1.

It's twelve forty-five.

81. To ask the arriving time

What time will you come?

When will you come?

When are you expected to come?

When should I expect you?

What time suits you?

When do I expect you?

Are you willing to come by 7 p.m.?

Should I assume you will be here by half past seven?

Could you confirm the exact time?

When are we meeting?

At what time are we catching up?

When is the right time for you to come?

When will you arrive?

What is the time of your arrival?

How much time you'll take to come?

82. To tell the arriving time

I should be there by 11:30 a.m.

I'll take about an hour to come.

It shouldn't be long before I come.

You can expect me by 7 p.m.

I'll see you at the right time.
I'll be there at the scheduled time.
I shall be there on time.
I'll be a bit late.
I'll be late by an hour.
I might be late by an hour.
I am running behind scheduled time.
Can I ask you to wait for me for a while?
It will be a while before I reach.
I'll surely be on time.
I am sure to be on time.
I don't think, I'll get late.
I won't keep you waiting.

83. Related to home

Set the alarm for 6:00 a.m.
Wake me up by 6:00 a.m.
I'll be up by 5:30. a.m.
I have to leave by 7:00 p.m.
Go to bed by 10 p.m.
Don't be too late.
What time is it?
When are they coming?
What time will they come?
How long until dinner?
What time did it start?
When do we have to reach there?
What time suits you?
What time he said, he was coming at?
Do you have time?
Follow your time-table.
Set things before time.
Don't waste time in these things.

I hope he will come on time.

I'll make it up to you next time.

It's not worth all the time.

13. Miscellaneous

84. To stay positive

Be punctual in life.

Make the most of your time.

Every moment is precious.

Hard work pays in the long run.

No one can control time.

You don't have any control over time.

Only we can walk with it or follow it.

Give it some time.

Be patient! wait.

Wait for the right time.

Let the right time come.

Take your time before you decide.

Punctuality is a trait of successful people.

Plan your time well.

Don't race against time.

Don't be in a hurry.

Wait! till proper time comes.

Save energy for the right time.

Take out time for yourself.

85. Salesman services

I would like to introduce myself as salesman.

I represent Pustak Mahal company.

I am a representative of Indian Oil company.

I would like to show you our new products.

May I show you the new product?

Kindly allow me to explain the features of this mobile.

This is a brand new product from our company.

Our company has introduced this new product.

This is the latest product of our company.

Our company specializes in mass-appealing books.

Our company deals in computers.

Our products are known for their quality.

May I give you the demo of this mobile?

Let me explain you the features of our new product.

I am sure it will add to your convenience.

You'll be glad to know about our product.

Our portfolio consists of many other things.

We deal in the following areas.

Our expertise is in medical field.

This will be really beneficial for you.

It will improve your efficiency.

This new product guarantees accuracy.

This new policy is most suitable for you.

Considering your requirements, may I recommend a set of books?

We have a special offer for you.

We have a scheme / plan.

Our company is offering discounts on this item till the end of this week.

86. In office

This is a time-bound project.

Submit the report on time.

Time is precious.

Don't waste time.

Value time.

Lost time won't come back.

I'm hard pressed with time.

This is a time-consuming job.

Go by the watch.

I don't have time for gossips.

Work over-time if needed.

Send in your over-time requirement.

Your timing is perfect.

You are always late.

You are always on time.

I'd appreciate if you follow time.

It's not time yet.

There's still time.

It won't take much time.

We don't have too much time.

How much time do you have?

Inform them timely.

We have a specified time frame.

I don't have any spare time for this.

Fast! Time is running out.

Watch out next time!

Be sure next time!

Mind it for future!

I'll get back to you in a bit.

Give me a minute.

Wait for a moment.

Follow your watch!
Don't delay! Finish it on time.
Reach office on time.
Don't go before time.
Make up for the lost time.
Give me some time.

87. When calling

You can come at 7:30 p.m.
You can come by half past seven.
Will you be able to come at 7:30 p.m.
I'll wait for you till 7:30 p.m.
Make sure you'll reach by 7:30 p.m.
Don't make it later than 7:30 p.m.
Try and make it by 7:30 p.m.
Don't keep me waiting after 7:30 p.m.
Let's catch up by 7:30 p.m.
Let's meet at half past seven.
Let's keep it for 7:30 p.m.
See you at 7:30 p.m.

88. To taste food

The recipe is perfect.
Everything just tastes great.
You are a great cook.
It's an authentic preparation.
This is very well cooked.
It's a bland dish.
This looks tasty.
It tastes too bitter (sour/sharp).
It's really spicy.

This is just lip-smacking.

It's a mouth-watering dish.

It's finger-licking dish.

89. To assure somebody

Time flies.

Times are tough.

These times are bad.

It's a really bad timing.

The time seems stuck for me.

I hope better time comes soon.

Lost time doesn't come back.

These are odd times.

This time too shall pass.

I don't have too much time.

90. To take leave of somebody

I'd like to take leave of you.

I'd like to wind up now.

Thank you for your visit.

I enjoyed meeting you.

I've to go now!

Can I take leave of you?

I hope it's fine, if I leave now!

I've got to go.

Time to go.

Time to push off.

I better get going.

I must say good night.

Though I don't want, I'll have to go now?
I hate it, but I must go now.
I'm quite late, I've to go.
If you permit, I must move now.
With your permission, I'd like to leave now.
Do I've your consent to leave?
Would you allow to let me go now?

●●

SECTION-2

60-Day Course

1-30 Days   — Conversation

31-60 Days — Grammar

1st Day

1st Expedition (Conversation)

This is your first expedition. This expedition starts with practical English based on sentences spoken on different occasions. On the basis of that, you have to proceed on. Learn the following sentences by heart and use them extensively in your daily talking. It will make you confident and a fluent speaker of English language.

1. Invitation

1. Come in please.
2. Please have something cold.
3. Will you please come over here?
4. Come for a walk, please. Let's have a stroll.
5. Would you like to come with us to the cinema?/Would you like to watch a film/movie with us?
6. Will you spend the whole day with us?
7. I will be glad to do so.
8. Let's go by bus.
9. Would you join me in the dance?/ May I dance with you?
10. No, I don't dance.
11. No, I don't know how to play cards.
12. Please spend next Sunday with us.
13. Thanks for your invitation to dinner.
14. I am sorry, I can't accept your invitation to dinner. Thank you for remembering me.
15. Will you come with us in Taxi to Fatehpur Sikri?
16. Many many thanks for your invitation. Your idea of a taxi tour is really grand. I'll surely join you.

2. Meeting and Parting

17. Good morning.
18. Hello, how are you?

19. Very well, thank you. And you?
20. I am fine.
21. I'm glad to see you.
22. It's my pleasure.
23. It has been a long time we met.
24. I've heard a lot about you.
25. Look, who is it?/who is here?
26. Are you surprised to see me?
27. Really I thought/was under the impression that you were in London.
28. I was there but I returned/came back last week.
29. O.K. see you again!/O.K. we will meet again!
30. Must you go/leave now?
31. Have a pleasant/nice journey!
32. God bless you!
33. Please convey my regards/compliments to your father.
34. May luck be with you!/Best of luck!
35. Good night.
36. Bye bye/Good bye.

3. <u>Gratitude</u>

37. Thanks a lot.
38. Thanks for your advice.
39. Thanks for the present/gift.
40. This is a costly/expensive gift.
41. I am much/very obliged/grateful to you.
42. Not at all. It is my pleasure.
43. You are very kind./ So kind of you.
44. This is no matter of kindness. It will rather please me.

4. <u>Congratulation and Good Wishes</u>

45. Wish you a happy new year!
46. Hearty felicitations on your birthday!
47. Congratulations on your success!
48. Congratulations on your wedding!
49. May you always be lucky! May luck always shine on you!

50. Hope you do well in your examination!
51. I congratulate you on behalf of all!
52. Many happy returns of the day!
53. Wish you all the best!

5. Miscellaneous Sentences

54. Let's have food now.
55. What would you like, tea or coffee?
56. I will come to the station to see you off.
57. Please look me up whenever you come to Delhi.
58. Let me introduce you to the family.
59. Please meet my wife, my daughter Kitty and Son Sumit.
60. You have lovely children.
61. I think we have met before.
62. What's the hurry? Please stay a little more.
63. I have no words to express my thanks to you.
64. You really saved my life.
65. May you have a long, happy and prosperous married life!

Points to Remember

1. 'Should' and 'Would' both are used together to show request and politeness, e.g., "Would you please lend me your car?"
2. Saying just 'Thanks' show a bit rudeness 'Thank you' is a little better. 'Thank you, sir' is more polite than 'thank you'.
3. 'On' is used with 'Congratulations' and 'Felicitations'.
4. Saying only 'Congratulations' or 'congrats' is also sufficient.

●●

2nd Day

6. Refusal

1. I won't be able to come.
2. I won't be able to do as you wish.
3. I don't want to come.
4. I am sorry to refuse.
5. They won't agree to this.
6. It's impossible/not possible.
7. I regret, I can't accept this proposal.
8. You don't agree with me, do you?
9. It can't be arranged.
10. She is averse to this idea/to it./She does not like it.
11. I wo'nt go with him.
12. She did not accept your proposal.
13. Your ideas are not as per our policy.
14. He is unable to cooperate.
15. I rejected his offer.
16. He denied that he assembled.
17. She regretted to not accept him.
18. They are not selected.
19. Sorry, I cannot help you.
20. He reufused to accompany me.
21. I rejected their offer.
22. They declined her proposal.

7. Believing

23. Don't you believe it?
24. It's only a rumour.
25. It's only a hearsay/ rumour.
26. Should/Can we trust this taxi driver?
27. You can trust them fully.

28. I have full faith in him.
29. Have faith in me.
30. He is a trustworthy person.
31. I believe in Allah.
32. Trust yourself.
33. Have confidence.
34. Seeing is believing.
35. Don't trust strangers in the first meeting.
36. Earn confidence by your hardwork.
37. You can trust me.
38. Don't give ears to rumours.
39. Be always faithful to your boss.
40. Be firm in your beliefs.
41. Confidence and trust are necessary for success.
42. I cannot believe him.
43. She is a confidant person.
44. Rumours are not to be believed.

8. Request

45. Please wait.
46. Please come back.
47. Let it be.
48. Please come here.
49. Please reply/answer.
50. Please wake him up.
51. Hope to hear from you.
52. Will you do me a favour?
53. Let me work.
54. Let me see.
55. Let me relax.
56. Please give me a pencil and paper.
57. Please do come day after tomorrow. Don't forget.
58. Please repeat./Pardon./I beg your pardon.

59. Could you move/shift a little?
60. Can you see me day after tomorrow?
61. Please forgive me.
62. Will you please open the window?
63. All are requested to reach in time.
64. Please arrange these sheets for me.
65. I request you to be kind.
66. May I request you to allow me to leave?

Points to Remember

1. The word 'please' is a very important word in English which shows politeness and request. Saying this word frequently during talking is considered to be good and a sign of civility. Frequent use of this word while asking somebody to do something makes one civilized. Therefore, instead of saying, "Give me a glass of water", always say, "Please give me a glass of water."

2. 'Let' is always used with either first person pronouns or third person pronouns, e.g., Let me read the book. Let them play foot ball first. Saying "Let you go to the market right now" is wrong. If second person and third person pronouns are used together, then we say 'Let us', e.g., Let us go to the market right now. It means 'you' and 'I' both should go to the market right now.

●●

3rd Day

9. Meals

1. I am feeling hungry.
2. What would you like to eat?
3. Which pickles do you have?
4. Have you had your breakfast?
5. Not yet, Roma.
6. Prepare/make the breakfast.
7. Let's take breakfast first.
8. Just taste it.
9. No, I have to attend a party.
10. What sweet dishes do you have?
11. Has Lata finished her meals?
12. Hurry up, food has been prepared.
13. Do you want a packet of cigarettes?
14. I prefer cigar to cigarettes.
15. You hardly ate anything. / You ate very little.
16. Have a little more. Please have some more.
17. Do you also smoke?
18. Would you have tea or coffee?
19. Bring/get me a cup of coffee.
20. Pour the coffee.
21. Waiter, the spoon is dirty/not clean.
22. Pass me the salt, please.
23. Give me some fresh butter, please.
24. Get/bring some more, please.
25. Help yourself, please.
26. Change the plates, please.
27. Are you a vegetarian?
28. No, I am not a vegetarian. I am a non-vegetarian.
29. I will dine out today. I will have my dinner out today.

30. Would you like some milk?
31. I have just sat down to have my meals.
32. I am not fond of rice. I don't eat/take rice.
33. What is there for dessert?
34. Two chapaties were not enough for me.
35. Alu-mutter is my favourite dish.
36. There is less salt in the vegetable/curry.
37. Don't take too much water on an empty stomach.
38. It is dinner time. Get ready.
39. What dishes are cooked today?
40. Bring a pinch of salt from your mother.
41. Potato is all we get here.
42. I am still thirsty.
43. They have invited me to lunch.
44. Please have your dinner with me.
45. Would you like to have boiled or fried eggs?
46. There were seven items/dishes at their party.
47. Naina is an expert cook.
48. May I have little/some more gravy?
49. I like tandoori/grilled chicken very much.
50. He is a glutton.
51. He is very thirsty.
52. He took pulses and salad only.
53. Do you like pickles?
54. When do you take breakfast?
55. Lay the table, Rekha.
56. Finish your dinner before leaving from here.
57. How many times did you taste this dish?
58. All the staff has gone to attend the party.
59. Sweet dishes are a must in marriage ceremonies.
60. When will you take lunch?
61. He prepared the breakfast before time.
62. She is an expert cook.
63. I have authored many books in cookery.
64. Who takes cold beverages after lunch?

65. What do you prefer after meals?
66. I hardly ate anything.
67. Ask him to take more.
68. Some people take tea after meals.
69. A cup of coffee after dinner is a good option.
70. Give me some potato.
71. Chicken chilly is his favourite dish.
72. Consumption of fatty food is discouraged these days.
73. High fatty food is harmful for heart.
74. Take protien-rich food.
75. Please add a little salt to my dish.
76. Rice is a good food.
77. Some people take rice daily.
78. Brown rice is considered good for health.
79. Vegetarian food is cheap but good.
80. Chinese food is easy to prepare.
81. South Indian dishes are tasty.
82. Idly is my favourite.
83. Dosa is also a tasty dish.
84. Chowmin is a Chinese dish.

Points to Remember

1. The word 'feel' is always followed by 'adjective' nor by 'noun', e.g., I feel thirsty (✓) not I feel thirst. (×)
2. For item of food, the generally use word is 'dish' though it has a different meaning which is a flat shallow container for cooking food in or serving it from.
3. 'Eat' and 'drink' are not commonly used in English is context of food and beverage. 'Take' is commonly used for both.
4. 'Drink' has a specific meaning in context of liqour. So, instead of saying 'drink water' say - 'take water.'

●●

4th Day

10. Time

1. What is the time by your watch?
2. It is half past seven.
3. When do you wake up?
4. I wake up early morning at half past six.
5. My sister has her breakfast around 8 o'clock.
6. When does the teacher come to school?
7. A little before nine.
8. When are the classes over in her school?
9. At quarter past three.
10. When do you have your dinner?
11. At half past seven.
12. I reached home at quarter to four.
13. It's ten past three now.
14. I have to go/leave at twenty-two.
15. By what time does your father usually come home every day?
16. At what time does he leave for office?
17. He leaves his office at 5 o'clock.
18. What is the date today?
19. It is fifteenth of December, nineteen seventy-six.
20. My birthday falls on .... (date).
21. I don't know, sir.
22. My watch gains two minutes daily.
23. Make the best of your time.
24. Now, he values punctuality/time. /Now, he knows the value of time.
25. He wastes his time.
26. He is punctual to the minute.
27. How fast time flies!
28. It's time to wake up.
29. My watch has broken.
30. He is quite in time. We have plenty of time.
31. He came at the right time.
32. You are late by half an hour.
33. We have enough time. We have plenty of time.
34. It is almost mid-night.

61

35. We are too early.
36. You are just in time. I would have left in another minute.
37. Better days will come. Good days are ahead.
38. I am trying to save each/every minute.
39. There is a time for everything.
40. Can you spare a little time?
41. Time once lost can never be regained.

11. Permission

1. Do we begin. Should we begin?
2. May I go/leave?
3. May I join you?/May I also come along?
4. Let me go.
5. You may go/leave now.
6. Please permit/allow me to go.
7. Can I use your phone?
8. Can I switch off the light?
9. May I play your video game?
10. May I come in, sir?
11. Can I leave my books with you?
12. Can we smoke in your room?
13. Of course, with great pleasure.
14. Will you please give me a lift? Will you please allow me in your car?
15. May I borrow your bike for a while?
16. Can I disturb you?
17. Can I stay in this room?
18. May we rest here for a while?
19. May I go to see a movie today?
20. May I accompany you to the Railway Station?
21. Can they clean the floor?
22. Should we log in the computer?
23. May we depart for Lucknow?
24. Should I remove the washing machine?
25. Can I help him unload the car?

Points to Remember

1. Interrogative sentences are of two kinds in English:
   (i) Simple Interrogative and (ii) Double Interrogative. Simple Interrogative is made by just putting the helping verb before the subject, e.g.,

   (a) Are you going to Kanpur tomorrow?
   (b) Have you taken food?

   This question is used to make confirmation regarding any thing.

2. Second kind of question is made with question words which are put even before helping verbs, e.g.,

   (a) Where are you going tomorrow?
   (b) What is your good name?

   This question is made to enquire about something.

2. Among helping verbs, there are two verbs which are used for seeking permission. They are 'may' and 'shall', e.g.,

   May I open the door? or
   Shall I open the door?

3. Difference between 'can' and 'may'. 'May' is used for permission and possibility whereas 'can' is used for 'capability' and 'permission'.

••

5th Day

12. (A) Instruction/Order

1. Do your work.
2. See him off at the station.
3. Speak the truth, don't tell a lie.
4. Try this coat on.
5. Work wholeheartedly.
6. Don't drink.
7. Fetch/get me a glass of water.
8. Talk politely./Be polite.
9. Reply by return post.
10. Check the accounts.
11. Sip the hot tea slowly.
12. Get a tonga from tonga stand.
13. Parking is not allowed here.
14. Squeeze two oranges.
15. Keep to the left.
16. Wake me up early in the morning.
17. Mend your ways.
18. Draw the curtain.
19. Take him around the city.
20. Bring the guest in.
21. Be polite to all. Speak politely with everybody.
22. Remind me of it at the proper time.
23. Keep pace with me.
24. Put the child to sleep/bed.
25. Remind me about it tomorrow.
26. Keep everybody ready.
27. Walk cautiously.
28. Come afterwards.
29. Wake me up at 5 o'clock.

30. Get ready if you want to come along.
31. Wait here until I'm back.
32. Don't speak like this.
33. Work carefully.
34. Do your own work.
35. You may go. I have some work to do.
36. Note this down.
37. Come back soon.
38. Come and see me some other time.
39. Please mind your own business.
40. Have patience.
41. Respect your elders.
42. You stay here.
43. Hope for good times.
44. Take care of the baby.
45. Hurry up, we are getting late.
46. Be punctual.
47. Save your time.
48. Read this book thoroughly.
49. Beware of pickpockets in crowded areas.
50. Walk to the left.
51. Be punctual in your office.
52. Attend all the workshops.
53. Don't speak to me when I am busy.
54. Devote yourself to work if you want to be successful.
55. Water the plants regularly.
56. Be polite in your behaviour.
57. Reply all the queries.
58. Take lukewarm water in winters.
59. Hire a taxi for me.
60. Park your vehicle on the allotted area.
61. Wash hands before eating.
62. Don't peal apples.
63. Concentrate on your work.

64. Pull the blinders.
65. Roam about this locality.
66. Go to bed early.
67. Stand straight.
68. Sit comfortably.
69. Do not lean on others.
70. Lie on your right side.
71. Usher in the guests.
72. Show me the plan.
73. Keep distance while driving.
74. Make yourself neat and clean.
75. Remember all the names.
76. Come to me.
77. Go briskly.
78. Bathe daily in the morning.
79. Don't waste your time.
80. Stay cheerful.

Points to Remember

1. In English, we use certain letters in the beginning of a word and the meaning of the base word gets changed, e.g.,
   Polite ⟶ *Im + polite = Impolite*
   (a) *Regular* ⟶ *Ir + regular = Irregular*
   (b) *Complete* ⟶ *In + complete = Incomplete*
   (c) *Developed* ⟶ *un + developed = Undeveloped*
2. Similarly, letters or words are added to the end of a word, e.g.,
   (a) *learn + er = learner*
   (b) *pressure + ise = pressurise*
   (c) *colony + ise = colonise, etc.*

These letters or words which are added are called **suffix**.

●●

6th Day

12. (B) Instruction/Order

1. Go yourself.
2. Be ready.
3. Light the lamp.
4. Switch on the light.
5. Put off the lamp.
6. Switch off the light.
7. Switch on the fan.
8. Send for him.
9. Let these people do their work.
10. Wash your hands.
11. Come soon.
12. Stop the car.
13. Go back.
14. Don't delay. / Don't be late.
15. Don't write with a pencil.
16. Write with a pen.
17. Don't copy others.
18. Hire a taxi.
19. Button up your coat.
20. Keep the fire going.
21. Feed the horse with grass.
22. Go and blow your nose.
23. Don't forget to inform me.
24. Tighten your shoe-laces.
25. Don't study at the cost of your health.
26. Write a detailed letter. Write a long letter.
27. Don't do so in future. Let this not happen in future.
28. Post this letter yourself.
29. Be punctual.
30. Don't beat about the bush.
31. Don't pluck flowers.
32. Give up bad habits.
33. Chew your food well.

34. Brush your teeth.
35. Don't chatter. Don't talk non-sense.
36. Arrange every thing in order.
37. Write in ink.
38. Don't be silly.
39. Look after the guests.
40. Mind your own business.
41. Hold with both hands.
42. Sacrifice your life for the motherland/country.
43. Don't hold up the work.
44. Be careful against bad habits.
45. Reset the computer.
46. Keep the change.
47. Keep your word.
48. Never deceive anybody.
49. Do your business honestly.
50. Don't look down upon others.
51. Meditate for five minutes daily.
52. Burn your fat by exercises.
53. Don't lose hope.
54. Stay confidence.
55. Have patiance.
56. Clear the road.
57. Put up the sign board.
58. Wash my clothes neatly.
59. Be aware of what's going around.
60. Take care of your relatives.
61. Be polite to your neighbours.
62. Treat the guests well.
63. Print my boi-data.
64. Show me the map of this city.
65. Drive in your lane.
66. Walk fast.
67. Breathe in and out.
68. Dictate me this page.
69. Recite the holy books over a day.
70. Listen to music.

71. Better your concentration by music.
72. Heal yourself naturally.
73. Jog with rope in the morning.
74. Brush your teeth twice a day.
75. Use towels after bath.
76. Polish my shoes.
77. Open your mouth.
78. Taste this syrup.
79. Consult a doctor now and then.
80. Keep your sorrounding neat and clean.

Points to Remember

Sometimes, prepositions like on, of, over, upon, into, off, in, down, etc. are used with verbs. This combination of Verb + Preposition is called phrasal verb.

If we change preposition with the same verb, each time the meaning will also change, e.g.,

1. *Please <u>put down</u> all that I say.* (note)
2. *He <u>put forward</u> his plan.* (presented)
3. *The meeting was <u>put off</u>.* (postponed)
4. *He <u>put on</u> new clothes.* (Wore)
5. *Let us <u>put out</u> the fire.* (extinguish)

In the above examples, we see that the verb 'put' has a simple meaning, 'to lay sth'. However, as the preposition changes, the meaning also changes.

To become a good learner of English, knowledge of phrasal verbs is a must. So, learn them by heart and speak English fluently and effectively.

●●

7th Day

13. Encouragement

1. Rest assured.
2. Stop worrying.
3. Don't cry like children.
4. What's bothering you?
5. Don't worry about me.
6. Don't be scared.
7. There is no need to worry.
8. I am not bothered about it.
9. You can ask me if there is any difficulty.
10. Take whatever you need.
11. You are unnecessarily worried.
12. I am proud of you.
13. Don't hesitate.
14. It doesn't matter.
15. Don't be discouraged.
16. Have faith.
17. Trust yourself.
18. Do not surrender.
19. Be steadfast.
20. Face the situation boldly.

14. Consolation

21. It is pity. It is very sad.
22. Console him.
23. That's the way things are.
24. It was God's will.
25. What cannot be cured must be endured.
26. Have faith in God, misfortune will fall.
27. May God give you strength to bear this terrible loss.
28. We offer our condolences.
29. We are deeply grieved at the death of her father.

30. It is not shame.
31. It was God's will.
32. Be always happy.
33. Never mind pitfalls.
34. Failures are ladders to success.
35. I emphatise with you.
36. My condolences are with you.
37. Bear all loss, God will give you more.
38. Loss and profit are routine in business.
39. Don't lose heart.
40. I sympathise with your loss.

15. <u>Annoyance</u>

41. Why haven't you begun/started the work yet?
42. Why do you contradict me?
43. Why do you stare at me?
44. You are angry for nothing. You are unnecessarily getting annoyed.
45. You just/simply waste your time.
46. Who is to blame?
47. Have I hurt you?
48. What a shame!
49. I could not believe that you are not an honest person.
50. Whom can I trust?
51. It was not my fault.
52. Actually, it was done by mistake.
53. He is a nuisance.
54. He has let me down.
55. He irritates me.
56. He has betrayed/cheated me.
57. He always calls late in the night.
58. Shut up!
59. Hold your tongue.
60. Are you in your senses?

16. <u>Affection</u>

61. That was very brave of you.
62. Well done! Good show! Keep it up!
63. That's wonderful.
64. Your work is praiseworthy.
65. You are so nice. How nice you are!
66. You have been a great help to me.
67. Bravo! that's so bold of you.
68. Congrats! we are proud of you.
69. I wish you more success.
70. How creative and original you are!
71. Bravo! you did well.
72. Really wonderful.
73. I appreciate your efforts.
74. My congratulations are with you!
75. Best of luck!
76. I wish you all success!
77. Long live, child!
78. Amazing!
79. Oh so nice of you!
80. Great! little master.

Points to Remember

In short forms or contractions, the letters which are omitted are replaced by Apostrophe'. So –

>*'Don't' is do not* ('o' is missing).
>*'Doesn't' is does not* ('o' is missing).
>*'Can't' is cannot* ('no' is missing).
>*'Shan't' is shall not* ('ll' and 'o' missing).
>'Won't' is would/will not ('uld' and 'o' are missing).

●●

8th Day

17. <u>Negation</u>

1. I can't accept what you say.
2. I know nothing in this connection.
3. Do not do such a mischief again.
4. It's not so/like that.
5. He could not manage to get leave.
6. I have no complaints./I do not have any complaints.
7. It's impossible. It cannot be so.
8. No, I could not go.
9. I don't know.
10. I don't want anything.
11. How can I do this?
12. I can't do this.
13. I don't agree/believe.
14. This is not true.
15. You should not allow this.
16. Don't find fault with others. Don't criticize others.
17. Don't be proud of your riches/money.
18. Don't cheat anybody.
19. Don't walk on the tall grass.
20. Don't be stubborn.
21. Sorry, I can't buy/afford it.
22. Sorry, I don't have any change.
23. I don't know how to sing.
24. Don't be angry./Don't lose your temper.
25. Don't be rude to anybody./ Don't speak harshly with anybody.
26. It is almost impossible.
27. No car is allowed.
28. It is not a thoroughfare.
29. I cannot believe the story he tells.

30. He is not a lawyer.
31. You are not suitable for this job.
32. She is not married.
33. His father cannot read without glasses.
34. Your mother does not agree to the proposal.
35. Karan is not my partner.
36. This shop does not open at 9 o'clock.
37. I am sorry, I can't do any thing.
38. They would not accept the invitation.
39. Raman is not a legal hair to this property.
40. I won't disclose the secret to anybody.

18. <u>Consent</u>

1. As you like/please.
2. You are right.
3. I have no objection.
4. No doubt!
5. It doesn't matter.
6. I would help you.
7. It will be so.
8. I agree with you.
9. I am with you.
10. You are correct.
11. Yes, it is true.
12. You are absolutely right.
13. I respect you.
14. She works hard.
15. I will accompany you.
16. Really, you need help.
17. I will follow your advice.
18. I accept your invitation.
19. I give my consent to you.
20. Do as your father does.

21. I am not trying to impose my will on you.
22. You don't seem to agree with me.
23. She is very cooperative. I will send her to you.
24. Your work is satisfactory.
25. My brother likes you, so do I.
26. You are a nice person.
27. I can understand your problem.
28. Nothing to worry about.
29. We have given our decision.
30. You may leave now.
31. Thirty persons can accommodate in this hall.
32. Yes, I have booked your room.
33. We are pleased to inform you.
34. Sarla is a nice girl.
35. Mr. Munib is the right person for this post.
36. The Taj Mahal is incredibly beautiful.
37. Your letter is well-drafted.
38. He is a man of authority.
39. Everyone likes me.
40. I support you.
41. He showed favour to me.
42. The judge is an honest man.
43. Dr. Shweta is my favourite.
44. I like everyone.
45. He has granted me special leave.

19. Sadness

1. Excuse me! I can't help you.
2. I am extremely sorry.
3. He is a total failure.
4. This machine is out of order.
5. Sorry, Mr. Malik is not present.
6. Excuse me, I do not agree with you.
7. Alas! we lost the match.
8. How sad it is!

9. It is a very bad presentation!
10. He cut a sorry figure in the competition.
11. Sorry for being late.
12. I beg your pardon.
13. Please excuse me.
14. I apologise for my behaviour.
15. He is in a very sorry state.
16. She lost her beauty in the accident.
17. I am helpless.
18. I can't do anything.
19. Nothing is in my hand.
20. It is out of my control.

Points to Remember

To express negation, consent, sadness or happiness, short and crisp sentences based on minimum one word are generally used in both writing and speaking. Long sentences are avoided as they mar the intensity of expression. So, keep in mind that while expressing your consent, negation, disapproval, surprise, sadness, happiness or doubt, use as short expressions as possible. If the need for long and complex sentence arises out of some particular situation, choosing appropriate and effective words is the rule.

9th Day

20. <u>Quarrel</u>

1. Why are you losing your temper?
2. Beware, don't utter it again!
3. You are very short-tempered.
4. He has got on my nerves.
5. Come what may!
6. What harm/wrong have I done to you?
7. You will have to mend your ways.
8. Why do you quarrel with him unnecessarily?
9. Don't get worked up/excited.
10. Now settle the matter somehow.
11. Are you in your senses?
12. Get out of my sight./Get lost.
13. How are you concerned with our affairs?
14. Now put an end to controversy. / Don't stretch the matter further.
15. Go to hell.
16. Let him mediate between the two parties.
17. The quarrel is settled. The matter ends here.
18. Now be friends.
19. Hold your tongue.
20. Mind you own business.

21. <u>Apologies</u>

1. Please don't mind this. Please don't feel bad about it.
2. I was just joking.
3. I am sorry, I got late.
4. I was pained to hear this.
5. Excuse me if there has been any mistake.
6. I beg your pardon.

7. Please excuse my incorrect pronunciation.
8. I am sorry for interrupting you.
9. I am sorry, I could not call you.
10. Apologize on my behalf.
11. Don't apologize. It does not matter.
12. It was merely done by mistake.
13. I am very sorry.
14. Don't worry, no harm is done.
15. I am very sorry if I have unknowingly hurt you.
16. It was done unknowingly.
17. It was not your fault.
18. I am really sorry to have kept you waiting so long.
19. That's all right.
20. I am sorry I can't hear you.

22. <u>Anger</u>

1. You should be ashamed of yourself. Shame on you.
2. You are too clever/smart.
3. You are an extremely cunning man.
4. Shame on you.
5. You are a mean fellow.
6. I don't want to see your face.
7. Don't talk nonsense.
8. Stop yapping.
9. Don't beat about the bush.
10. It's all because of you.
11. You can't get away like this.
12. You don't deserve forgiveness.
13. You are responsible for this loss.
14. Don't try to cheat me.
15. You are a bastered.
16. Your bad company has spoiled you.
17. There is still time for you to mend your ways.

18. Apologize to me.
19. Excuse her or go away from here.
20. I cannot bear your nuisance anymore.

Points to Remember

'Lose' and 'Loose' are two different words both in spelling, meaning and pronunciation. Lose is/ lu:z/ whereas loose is/ lu:s/. Take care.

In spoken language, tone of the speaker is very important. And it is tone or pitch of voice which determines whether the speaker is happy or sad, surprised or angry. So, besides learning the above sentences, you have to practise the fluctuation of voice, the expressions on you face and movement of your hands and head. A good companion in this path of yours is mirror. Sit before a mirror and scold as well as appreciate your 'self' as much as possible.

●●

10th Day

Test No. 1

From Day 1st-5th

I. **Correct the following sentences. For answer, match them with the sentences given from days 31st to 35th.**

1. Come at please. (1:1) 2. I will be glading to do so. (1:7) 3. Lets go by bus. (1:8) 4. No, I doesn't dance. (1:10) 5. Thank for your invitation to dinner. (1:13) 6. Hello, how is you. (2:18) 7. I've glade to see you. (2: 21) 8. Very well, thanks you. (2:19) 9. I am there but I returned last year. (2:28) 10. God blesses you. (2: 32) 11. Thank a lot. (3:37) 12. These is a costly gift. (3: 40) 13. I am grateful of you. (3:41) 14. Wishes you a happy new year. (4:45) 15. Congratulations over your success. (4:47) 16. May that you always be lucky. (4:49) 17. What would you like, tea either coffee. (5:55) 18. Please comes back. (8:46) 19. Do you also smoke too? (9:17) 19. Make the good of your time. (10:23) 20. Keep on the left. (12:15).

Test No. 2

From Day 6th-9th

II. **Correct the following sentences. For reference, Heading No. and Sentence No. are given against each sentence.**

1. Go yourselves. (12B:1) 2. Open the fan. (12B:7) 3. Write from a pen. (12 B:16) 4. Button your coat. (12B: 19) 5. Don't beat

about the bushes. (12 B:30) 6. Stop worry. (13:2) 7. Don't scared. (13:6) 8. We offers our condolence. (14:28) 9. Who is to be blame? (15:46) 10. How creative and original are you! (16:70) 11. I can't accept that you say. (17:1) 12. I don't knows. (17:9) 13. No cars is allowed. (17:27) 14. You are the correct. (18:10) 15. What sad it is! (19:8) 16. Comes what may! (20:5) 17. Don't get excite. (20:9) 18. I beg your pardons. (21:6) 19. Don't apology. (21:11) 20. I cannot bears your nuisance any more. (22:20)

Test No. 3

II. There is one or more mistakes in the following sentences. Correct the bold words and rewrite them.

1. Be careful not to **loose** your money. 2. Has the clerk **weigh** the letter? 3. Physics **are** not easy to learn. 4. You have a **poetry** to learn by heart. 5. My **luggages are** at the station. 6. You have five **thousands** rupees. 7. I saw a notebook on the **grounds.** 8. Let us see a **theatre** tonight. 9. Which is the **street** to the village? 10. He is five feet **high.** 11. Are you **interesting** in your work? 12. I have **now** left cricket. 13. She **puts on** red shoes. 14. My **goods** are costly. 15. There **is** a lot of flowers on this tree. 16. How **many** tea do you want? 17. What **does** elephants **eats**? 18. He has given up smoking, **isn't it**? 19. I **has** a car. 20. You need not **to** cry.

Answer: 1. lose, 2. weighed, 3. is, 4. poem, 5. luggage is, 6. thousand, 7. ground, 8. movie, 9. which road, 10. tall, 11. intrusted, 12. remove 'now', 13. put on, 14. items of goods, 15. are, 16. much, 17. do, 18. hasn't he?, 19. have, 20. remove 'to'.

Test No. 4

IV. Fill in the blanks in the following sentences with the correct word from the bracket in each sentence.

1. .....(Shall/will) you please help me out of this difficulty? 2. She was overjoyed...(to/into) see her lost baby. 3. Thanks....(to/for) your good wishes. 4. We congratulated him...(at/on)

his success. 5..... (Get/Let) me go. 6. Are you feeling...(thirst/ thirsty)? 7. Do you... (drink/take) milk or tea? 8. What... (is/ are) the news? 9. Remind me... (on/of) his promise to post this important letter. 10. Switch... (out/off) the light. 11. Go... (on/in) person to post this important letter. 12. Give....(in/up) smoking; it is harmful. 13. Is there any need... (for/to) worry? 14. Don't find fault... (on/in/with) others. 15. Are you angry... (on/with) me? 16. I know very little... (of/in/on) this connection. 17. Get out...(from/of) my sight. 18. You are...(loosing/losing) your temper. 19. We...(may/shall) have some coffee. 20. We must avoid...(smoking/to smoke).

Test No. 5

V. (i) Look up a dictionary and write meanings of the following verbs:

1. Fetch, 2. Enjoy, 3. Meet, 4. Burst, 5. Bring, 6. Enter, 7. Chew, 8. Cheat, 9. Want, 10. Amuse, 11. Agree, 12. Obey, 13. Move, 14. Forget, 15. Forgive, 16. Hire, 17. Abstain, 18. Fire, 19. Wear, 20. Attire.

(ii) Read the following pairs of words and note down their difference.

1. Believe-Belief, 2. Check-Cheque, 3. Speak-Speech, 4. Agree-Agreement, 5. Cool-cold, 6. Invite-Invitation, 7. Pride-Proud, 8. Accept-Except, 9. Angry-Anger, 10. Thirsty-Thirst, 11. Allow-Allowance, 12. Admit-Admission, 13. Fire-Furious, 14. Lose-Loss, 15. Prove-Proof, 16. Clear-Clarity, 17. Suspect-Suspicion, 18. Noise-Noisy, 19. Kind-Kindness, 20. Grow-Growth.

(iii) Write the opposite words for the following:

1. Come, 2. Accept, 3. Clean, 4. Improper, 5. Without, 6. Switch off, 7. Back, 8. Early, 9. Disagree, 10. Many, 11. Able, 12. Empty, 13. Soft, 14. Rich, 15. Happy, 16. Tall, 17. Quiet, 18. Clever, 19. Active, 20. Pitiful.

Answers V (i) 1. to go to where somebody/something is and bring them/it back, 2. to get pleasure from something, 3. to come together face-to-face, 4. to break open or apart especially because of pressure from inside, 5. to provide with something, 6. to go inside, 7. to bite food into small pieces in your mouth with your teeth, 8. deceive, 9. desire, 10. entertain, 11. to give consent, 12. to do what somebody asks you, 13. to change position, 14. to be unable to remember, 15. to stop feeling angry with somebody who has done something wrong, 16. to pay money to borrow something, 17. stop, 18. flames, 19. put on, 20. garments.

(ii) 1. Verb–Noun, 2. Verb-Noun, 3. Verb-Noun, 4. Verb-noun, 5. Adj-Noun + Adj, 6. Noun-Adj, 7. Verb-Prep + conj + verb, 8. Adj-Noun, 9. Adj-Noun, 10. Adj-Noun, 11. Verb-Noun, 12. Verb-Noun, 13. Noun-Adj, 14. Verb-Noun, 15. Verb-Noun, 16. Adj-Noun, 17. Verb-Noun, 18. Noun-Adj, 19. Adj-Noun, 20. Verb-Noun.

(iii) 1. go, 2. reject, 3. dirty, 4. proper, 5. with, 6. switch on, 7. front, 8. late, 9. agree, 10. few, 11. unable, 12. full, 13. hard, 14. poor, 15. sad, 16. short, 17. noisy, 18. fool, 19. passive, 20. cruel.

11th Day

2nd Expedition (Conversation Contd...)

In the 1st expedition, you learnt sentences spoken about/on Invitation, Meeting & Parting, Gratitude, Congratulations & Good Wishes, Miscellaneous sentences, Refusal, Believing, Request, Meals, Time, Permission, Instruction/Order, Encouragement, Consolation, Annoyance, Affection, Negation, Consent, Sadness, Quarrel, Apologies and Anger. In this expedition, you will learn sentences spoken– At Home, Out of home, To servant, On meeting, While shopping, On describing people/things, On study, On health, On weather, about animals, Games, Person and age, Character and Dress. Go ahead, Good luck!

23. <u>At Home</u>

1. Look, make the bed over here.
2. The milk has turned sour.
3. Let me tether the cow.
4. Keep the room clean/dusted.
5. The coals were burnt to ashes.
6. How many children do you have?
7. We cook potatoes everyday for our meals.
8. What new dish is cooked today?
9. When did the washerman last take the clothes for washing?
10. Get this coat ironed again.
11. Put wet clothes in the sun.
12. Let me get ready.
13. You are talking too long.
14. We will reach there before time.
15. Her mother-in-law is good-natured.
16. You are welcome.
17. You should not go back on your words.
18. He behaved very rudely.

19. Get your utensils tinned.
20. I can't wait any longer.
21. I have been out since morning.
22. I am feeling sleepy.
23. I had a sound sleep last night.
24. There is nobody inside.
25. Now go to sleep/bed.
26. You took a long time.
27. I will be ready in a moment.
28. Why did you not wake me up?
29. I did not think it proper to wake you up.
30. I will relax/rest for a while.
31. Pull a chair, please.
32. You are still awake.
33. Who is knocking at the door?
34. I woke up late this morning.
35. There is someone to see you.
36. Please come in.
37. Please be seated. Please have a seat. Please sit down.
38. Where is Anupam?
39. I don't know where he is.
40. What's it?
41. Who's it?
42. It's me, Munib.
43. Is Arun in?
44. The day is far advanced.
45. I'm hard up/tight these days.
46. Engage some expert cook.
47. I am deadly tired these days.
48. Let us have a chat.
49. Bolt the door.
50. It's time to depart now.
51. Keep the household things in their place.
52. Take rest here tonight.
53. You are dozing.
54. Make my bed.

55. Your nose is running.
56. We kept talking till very late.
57. Ring up the doctor.
58. My maternal uncle has come to see me.
59. This gentleman has some work with you.
60. I have a shower bath everyday.
61. Wash the doors of the house.
62. Wipe them well with cotton cloth.
63. He checked all the taps of the house.
64. Let us paint the house green.
65. They are getting the house repaired.
66. Thanks for visiting our house.
67. His house is located on road.
68. I want a house facing sea.
69. They visit us once a month.
70. I bought every necessary article for the house.

Points to Remember

In English language, plural is generally made by adding 's' or 'es' to the singular. When there is a compound noun, 's' or 'es' will be added to the main word, e.g.,

> *(a) Father-in-law* ⟶ *fathers-in-law*
>
> *(b) Commander-in-chief* ⟶ *Commanders-in-chief, etc.*

●●

12th Day

24. Out of Home

1. The shoe is very tight.
2. Where does this road lead to?
3. This road leads to Bijnor.
4. Just hold my cycle/bike.
5. I have to keep awake/ wake up at night.
6. Always keep to the left.
7. Always walk on the footpath.
8. Beware of pickpockets.
9. I am not fond of theatre/seeing plays.
10. I have changed my house. I have shifted from the old place.
11. Can anyone get a texi/cab here?
12. Come what may, we must reach the meeting in time.
13. This road is closed to the public.
14. No entry without permission.
15. The boss is inside the parlour.
16. Park the car in that ground.
17. To walk in the morning is useful to health.
18. Cricket is an outdoor game.
19. Drain system in our city is excellent.
20. Stop while people are on the zebra crossing.
21. My bike gives an average of 60 km/l.
22. Too much traffic leads to air pollution.
23. Never overtake from the left side.
24. Road accidents are frequent these days.
25. Low-floor buses are automatic and comfortable.
26. Let's have dinner or lunch outside once in a month.

27. Children should not play on the roads.
28. Avoid from mingling with strangers.
29. If you make a promise, keep it.
30. Beware of street food.
31. Don't consume open and dusty food.
32. I like swimming.
33. He made a jump from a hillock.
34. The tiger hunted a deer.
35. Animals are also important for us.
36. The sky looks lazy.
37. The sun is the hottest star of the solar family.
38. The atmosphere is getting changed by degrees.
39. Neighbours are an asset to us.
40. Help that old man cross the road.
41. Walk on foot as much as possible.
42. Where is the fruit market?
43. I want to go to the post office.
44. How far is the railway station?
45. There are many good doctors in this city.

25. <u>To servant</u>

1. Come here, boy.
2. Bring the food.
3. Get me a glass of water.
4. Go and post these letters.
5. Wash the clothes.
6. Hurry up/make haste.
7. Lift/Pick up/Carry the bundle.
8. Give me half a bread.

9. You go now, I have to do some work.
10. Show the way.
11. Show him around.
12. Don't interrupt.
13. Just listen.
14. Don't worry.
15. Wait a bit.
16. Switch on the fan.
17. Don't make a noise.
18. Go and see why the child is weeping.
19. Give me a pencil and a piece of paper.
20. Wait here until I am back.
21. You may go now.
22. Wake me up at 4 o'clock.
23. Light the lamp.
24. Switch on the light/switch off the light.
25. Move aside.
26. Use your mind.
27. Don't forget to come early tomorrow.
28. Go and relax for a while.
29. Clean the floor well.
30. Unload this vagon.
31. Get the letter signed before I come back.
32. Avoid direct contact with your boss.
33. Stay alert regarding any queries from the office.
34. Keep an eye on every visitor.
35. Don't phone me before 11 a.m.
36. Wash and clean my car.
37. Welcome the guests warmly.
38. Call a rickshaw for me.

39. Prepare my tiffin.
40. Are all the shoes mended?
41. Keep the door open all day.
42. Let not strangers enter my office.
43. Take regular training of your work.
44. Attend the workshops.
45. Follow the discipline strictly.

Points to Remember

1. Words ending with '–able' are adjectives. So, you can make adjectives by adding '–able' to verbs and nouns, e.g.,

    Comfort + able = Comfortable

    Eat + able = Eatable

    Sale + able = Saleable

    Agree + able = Agreeable

2. To some verbs and nouns, '–al' is also added to make them adjective, e.g.,

    Brute + al = Brutal

    Centre + al = Central

    Continue + al = Continual

    Term + al = Terminal, etc.

●●

13th Day

26. <u>On Meeting</u>

1. It has been nice/pleasing seeing you.
2. When do I see you again?/When shall we meet again?
3. I am glad to see you.
4. There is something important to do.
5. Why did you not come that day?
6. You are mistaken./you are at fault.
7. Long time no see. (Informal)/I did not see you for long.
8. He has asked for you.
9. My work is not yet over.
10. I have come to seek your advice.
11. I wish to talk to you.
12. I waited long for you.
13. You are late by half an hour.
14. We have come too early.
15. How are you?
16. Introduce me to him.
17. Wire about your welfare./Send SMS about you health.
18. Take exercise daily.
19. I have not heard about him for long.
20. Let's have some good breakfast.
21. Your letter has just been received.
22. Write immediately on reaching the hotel.
23. Don't forget it. Keep it in mind.
24. Let me know when he comes.
25. See you again.
26. Give/Convey my regards to him.
27. Do write to me sometimes/on and off.
28. Please give me your address.
29. Meet me next Monday.
30. Have you arranged a meeting with him?

31. It was nice meeting him.
32. You are always welcome.
33. There is no need for formality./Don't be formal.
34. I am not on good terms with him.
35. We have an excellent relationship with each other.
36. Thanks for a pleasant/wonderful/lovely evening.
37. Please give me your address and contact number.
38. How many states of India have you visited so far?
39. I take particular interest in interacting with foreigners.
40. English is one of the international languages.
41. He was very much pleased to see you.
42. Can we meet soon?
43. Nice to meet all the members of your family.
44. Our meeting is of crucial importance.
45. What were the obstacles to join the meeting?
46. I think, he has been mistaken in the meeting.
47. Where have you been for a year?
48. This shirt suits you very well.
49. Let us wait for him.
50. I'll ask him when he comes back.
51. When did you arrive here?
52. How was your journey?
53. Did you attend the meeting?
54. Are you interested in joining our group?
55. You spoke very well.
56. Your voice modulation is good.
57. Come, they are waiting for us.
58. What you see him, convey my compliments.
59. Did you recognize me?
60. How is your boss?
61. When are you learning from here?
62. What are the sights you visited so far?
63. Can you tell me about some of your forest experiences?
64. Did those people behave amicably?
65. I am pleased to welcome you.

66. You are always welcome.
67. Lay yourself wherever you want.
68. I want/like to accompany you next time.
69. She is a good fellow traveller.
70. I would like to brief you after lunch.
71. The meeting was postponed due to storm.
72. Stay alert while interacting with strangers.
73. Do you remember the minutes of the meeting?
74. The meeting was a grand success.
75. Reply my questions thoughtfully.
76. I need the agenda of the meeting.
77. The participants have come.
78. Please confirm the meeting.
79. Take all your documents while going for meeting.
80. I meet almost one hundred new people daily.

Points to Remember

In English language, there are some nouns which have different meanings in singular and in plural forms, e.g.,

(a) 'Rich' means wealthy, 'Riches' means property.
(b) 'Good' means nice, 'Goods' means luggage.
(c) 'Glass' means transparent and hard substance, 'Glasses' means spectacles.
(d) 'Colour' means hue, 'Colours' means flags, etc.

●●

14th Day

27. <u>Shopping</u>

1. He is a petty/ordinary shopkeeper.
2. The hankers are shouting at the top of their voice.
3. The rice is of an inferior quality.
4. This article is selling at a throw-away price.
5. There is a depression in trade these days./There is a slump.
6. This book is selling like hot cakes.
7. I am short by fifty rupees.
8. This confectioner sells stale stuff/things.
9. You have given me one rupee less.
10. This cloth shrinks on washing.
11. This mango is over-ripe.
12. Everything is closed because of the strike.
13. All varieties of cloth are available at this shop.
14. This book is very popular.
15. The prices are falling.
16. This coat is tight for me.
17. This chair is quite cheap for sixty rupees.
18. Don't cut the hair too short.
19. Don't buy on credit.
20. Clear my accounts.
21. Bring flour for twenty rupees from the market.
22. My trousers are loose/tight.
23. My watch needs cleaning and oiling.
24. Does your shoe pinch you?
25. This cloth is enough for a coat.
26. Take my measurements.
27. Give me some good books.
28. The doctor has a large practice.
29. Charge a reasonable price for this shirt.
30. Is the stuff good?
31. Is the colour fast?
32. How far is the market from here?

33. It's quite far.
34. If you wish to buy everything from one place, go to Super Bazar.
35. This shopkeeper sells adulterated stuff/things.
36. Do you accept cheques?
37. It is soiled/dirty.
38. It is torn.
39. It is brand new.
40. "Big Bazar' offers good discounts.

28. <u>Describing people/things</u>

1. He is tall.
2. She is short.
3. He is of medium height.
4. Mamta is fat.
5. Kitty is thin.
6. Nitin is well-built.
7. Neha is pretty/beautiful.
8. Vipin is handsome.
9. Simi is fair.
10. Saurabh is dark.
11. His complexion is wheatish.
12. Nitin has moustache and beard.
13. Pradeep is clean shaved.
14. This box is heavy.
15. This packet is light.
16. This table is round.
17. My purse is square.
18. This basket is oval.
19. This book is circular.
20. This well is very deep.
21. This pond is shallow.
22. This route is long but safe.
23. This route is short but risky/dangerous.
24. This chapati is stale and hard.
25. The bread is soft and fresh.
26. This food is delicious.

27. There is a high wall between the two houses.
28. This room has a low ceiling.
29. He has bulging eyes.
30. His shoulders are stout.
31. Twins are a common phenomenon these days.
32. Dwarfs entertain people in circuses.
33. She is always worried for her complexion.
34. Youths are fond of gyms these days.
35. Keep all your documents safe and secure.
36. He has a good sense of making presentations.
37. Guards have to be alert.
38. Media should never be biased.
39. My receptionist is dutiful.
40. Receptionist should be smiling and enduring by nature.

Points to Remember

1. Words ending with '–ant' or '– ent' are either nouns or adjectives, e.g.,

<u>Nouns</u>	<u>Adjectives</u>
Applicant	*Abundant*
Servant	*Ignorant*
Ascent	*Important*
Comment	*Excellent*
Content	*Intelligent*
Supplement	*Violent*

2. Words ending with '–ful' are also adjectives, e.g., *Powerful, Beautiful, Awful, Colourful, Truthful*, etc.

●●

15th Day

29. <u>Study</u>

1. As we labour, so shall we be rewarded./Reward depends on labour.
2. Which books in English have you read?
3. I' m too tired to attend the class.
4. When does her examination begin?
5. I'll pass my B.A. this year./ I'll be graduate this year.
6. I could not study anything today.
7. He failed in the B.A examination.
8. The question is very easy.
9. Neither Asha nor her sister comes to school regularly.
10. I will definitely pass/get through.
11. I read a very interesting book last night.
12. He is weak in Hindi.
13. Classes start early nowadays/ these days.
14. We have completed or finished our studies.
15. Either you beg his pardon or pay the fine.
16. He does not know anything. He is good for nothing.
17. She has been absent since Wednesday.
18. I had no time to finish my work.
19. What does it mean?
20. She takes keen interest in her studies.
21. The students will know the result tomorrow.
22. You have passed the examination.
23. Why don't you let me read/study?
24. If you pass, your parents will be happy.
25. I know how to speak English.
26. In which college do you study?
27. How are you getting on your studies?
28. I have been in this college since 1980.
29. Your school is good.
30. Keep the book with you for the present.

31. He often runs away from the school.
32. What are you looking at? Why don't you pay attention?
33. Don't you have any influence on the head master?
34. Our school will be closed for vacations from tomorrow.
35. Boys, time is over, hand in your papers.
36. The new time-table will come into force from Ist May.
37. Why do you chatter non-sense?/Hold your tongue./Keep quiet.
38. I don't have a spare pencil.
39. We are not on speaking terms.
40. We are not on visiting terms.
41. I have been in this college for two years.
42. She is doing M.A. in English.
43. You are a good educationist.
44. I love books on education.
45. This boy won't be able to get on in the class X.
46. Stop yapping./Shut up./Hold your tongue.
47. Has the roll been called?
48. Mathematics is my bugbear.
49. English is my favourite subject.
50. I like comparative study of languages.
51. All the efforts failed.
52. He did his level best.
53. I respect Mr. Munib Ahmed.
54. He is senior to me by 8 years.
55. A good boy brings credit to his class.
56. He is ahead of me in class.
57. Who is the paper-setter?
58. It is time for school.
59. He is not a punctual student.
60. Punctuality and discipline are necessary for students.
61. He is slow in Mathematics and Physics.
62. He is a voracious reader of Biology books.
63. The bell is about to go.
64. Now, you should leave for school.
65. I recited a poem in the class.
66. Do you have a spare exercise book?

67. I need an extra pen.
68. The college is a moulding place for students.
69. The headmaster exempted my fee.
70. I have offered English, Biology, Chemistry and Physics.
71. Private schools take high charges these days.
72. C.B.S.E. is a good board.
73. NCERT books are available everywhere.
74. Note down main points in the class.
75. Schooling has become very expensive.
76. Children reamain tense due to early schooling.
77. School teachers should be properly trained.
78. He runs five schools.
79. Play schools are common these days.
80. Study and sports are inseperable.

Points to Remember

'Re' is a prefix which is added in the beginning of a verb. 'Re' means 'again'. In this way, we can make new words having the sanse of 'again', e.g.,

$$Re + Pay \rightarrow Repay$$
$$Re + turn \rightarrow Return$$
$$Re + call \rightarrow Recall$$
$$Re + join \rightarrow Rejoin$$
$$Re + mark \rightarrow Remark$$
$$Re + mind \rightarrow Remind$$
$$Re + cycle \rightarrow Recycle, etc.$$

●●

16th Day

30. (A) Health

1. I had got fever last night.
2. Take medicine from a doctor.
3. I am worried about my health.
4. He is an eye specialist.
5. He is run down in health.
6. I have hurt my big toe.
7. All his teeth are intact.
8. He is blind in one eye.
9. He is lame.
10. I often suffer from constipation.
11. My digestion is bad. My stomach is upset.
12. Press my head gently. It's comforting.
13. His eyes are sour and watering.
14. His body is covered with boils.
15. These days cholera has spread in the city.
16. Exercise is a panacea for all diseases.
17. He is a heart-patient.
18. Medicine is bitter but it cures the patient.
19. Nowadays fever is raging violently and doctors are minting money.
20. Can you read the thermometer?
21. Dengue and cholera are raging these days.
22. How long has your brother been suffering from fever?
23. Quinine is an effective remedy for Malaria.
24. I am feeling feverish.
25. Consult a doctor.
26. He has chronic fever.
27. His fever is down.
28. The lady recovered from fever.
29. Workload has ruined his health.
30. He has indigestion.
31. You should exercise regularly.

32. Laughter is the best medicine.
33. He possesses a very good health.
34. We should eat fresh fruit and vegetable.
35. Keep your food covered.
36. She is in her periods.
37. She is in her fiftees but she looks beautiful.
38. She is trying to reduce her weight.
39. He is very weak in health.
40. Try to reduce your weight.
41. He has a frail body.
42. His complexion is yellow.
43. Black hair is the mark of youthfulness.
44. We should consult the dentist over in three months.
45. There are wrinkles all over his face but he is energetic.
46. Constipation is the root of all diseases.
47. Walking in the morning is very beneficial.
48. We should take plenty of water daily.
49. Too much spicy food is harmful for health.
50. He always takes rest after lunch.
51. I am accustomed to walking after dinner.
52. An apple a day keeps the doctor away.
53. Always wash your hands before and after meals.
54. Milk is a complete diet.
55. She is fond of honey.
56. Influenza is a common disease here.
57. Do not take medicine without doctor's advice.
58. He does not care for his health.
59. Consult an opthalmologist.
60. Excessive work has deteriorated his health.
61. He is suffering from tooth decay.
62. Clean your big toe.
63. Colour blindness is curable.
64. The accident made him lame.
65. Take sufficient water to cure constipation.
66. Walking after supper is good for digestion.

67. Headache has made him restless.
68. Why are your eyes watering so much?
69. Avoid cholera by taking watermelon on empty stomach.
70. Swift inhaling and breathing out is a good excercise.
71. We have no cardiologist in our area.
72. Injection is a fast reliever.
73. Medicine has become a business these days.
74. Measure your fever by thermometer.
75. Dengue is caused by mosquitoes.
76. Malaria is caused by female mosquito.
77. He has been suffering from mouth ulcer far a mouth.
78. Curd is a very good medicine in summer.
79. Lack of apetite is a matter of concern.
80. Keep checking your weight.
81. Excessme weight should be reduced soon.
82. Herbalite products are effective is losing weight.
83. We all should be health-conscious.
84. Body weight and body mass should match.
85. Eating less and taking much water is good for health.

Points to Remember

We can make lots of nouns by adding '-ion' to the end of verbs ending with '-t', e.g.,

(a) Act + ion → Action
(b) Protect + ion → Protection
(c) Collect + ion → Collection
(d) Correct + ion → Correction
(e) Eject + ion → Ejection
(f) Reject + ion → Rejection
(g) Select + ion → Selection
(h) Inject + ion → Injections, etc.

Exception: Adjustment, Assortment, Allotment, Investment, etc.

••

17th Day

31. (B) Health

1. I feel like vomiting./I am feeling sick.
2. Take a dose of medicine every four hours.
3. Fresh air is rejuvenating.
4. I am not feeling very well today.
5. His feet are swollen because of walking.
6. My health is down.
7. Take a purgative.
8. He is fed up with his illness.
9. Beware of quacks.
10. His diagnosis is very good.
11. Your nose is running.
12. His leg is fractured.
13. I am extremely tired.
14. How is he today?
15. His hand was dislocated while playing volley ball.
16. Today he is better than yesterday.
17. This medicine will bring your fever down.
18. He has a headache.
19. She is suffering from irregular menses.
20. I shall get myself checked up early.

32. Weather

1. It kept drizzling all the night.
2. The sky is overcast.
3. It is terribly cold today.
4. The heat has made me giddy.
5. Even an umbrella is of no use in stormy rain.

6. It is getting colder day by day.
7. It is biting cold outside.
8. Punctuality is a must in the treatment of T.B.
9. 'Eat slowly and chew thoroughly' is a good principle.
10. I am proud of my younger brother.
11. I am shivering with cold.
12. I did not get drenched.
13. It is raining cats and dogs.
14. Moon is the nearest satellite to the earth.
15. Ponds, rivers, lakes and oceans are necessary for rain.
16. The wind is icy.
17. It is very sultry.
18. The rain prevented me from going outside.
19. Humidity is increasing day by day.
20. There is a silver lining in dark clouds.
21. There are four seasons in India.
22. Flowers bloom in the spring season.
23. Heavy rains cause flood.
24. If winter comes, can spring be far behind?
25. Winter is the season of heavy diets.
26. We are going to the U.S. in the summer vacations.
27. Floating clouds in the sky is a beautiful scene.
28. Frogs come out in the rainy season.
29. If hot wind blows, stay in your houses.
30. Nights are cold when the sky is cloudless.
31. Rainy season has its own charm.
32. People wait for rains desperately.
33. Rains have rejuvenating effect on the earth.
34. Weather in Delhi is almost identical to that in UP.
35. Save water profusely during summer.

Points to Remember

Adverbs are generally made by adding '-ly' to Adjectives, e.g.,

(a) Able + ly	= Ably	(b) Aimless + ly	= Aimlessly
(c) Bad + ly	= Badly	(d) Calm + ly	= Calmly
(e) Efficient + ly	= Efficiently	(f) Wrong + ly	= Wrongly
(g) Glad + ly	= Gladly	(h) Humble + ly	= Humbly
(i) Kind + ly	= Kindly	(j) Honest + ly	= Honestly
(k) Right + ly	= Rightly	(l) Neat + ly	= Neatly
(m) Active + ly	= Actively	(n) Grave + ly	= Gravely
(o) Beautiful + ly	= Beautifully	(p) Harsh + ly	= Harshly
(q) Amazing + ly	= Amazingly	(r) Amicable + ly	= Amicably
(s) Forceful + ly	= Forcefully	(t) Time + ly	= Timely
(u) Correct + ly	= Correctly	(v) Effective+ly	= Effectively

●●

18th Day

33. Animals

Q1. Which animals give us milk?

Ans. Cow, buffalo and goat, etc.

Q2. Which animal barks?

Ans. Dog.

Q3. Which animal has long neck?

Ans. Giraffe.

Q4. Which animal gives us wool?

Ans. Sheep.

Q5. Which animal has a bushy tail?

Ans. Squirrel.

Q6. Which animal is a cross between horse and donkey?

Ans. Mule.

Q7. What do mules do?

Ans. They carry load.

Q8. Which animal has a trunk?

Ans. Elephant.

Q9. Which animal has a hump on its back?

Ans. Camel.

Q10. Which animal has horns?

Ans. Cow, buffalo, goat, bull, ox, etc.

Q11. Which animals pull wagon?

Ans. Horse, mule, ox, bullock, camel, etc.

Q12. Which insect lives in a hive?

Ans. Bee.

Q13. Which bird hoots at night?

Ans. Owl.

Q14. Which animal resembles human beings?

Ans. Ape.

Q15. Which insect weaves web?

Ans. Spider.

Q16. Which animals are the beast of prey?

Ans. Lion, tiger, wolf, leopard, hounds, hyena, etc.

Q17. Do all animals give us milk?

Ans. No.

Q18. What is a dog popularly known for?

Ans. Faithfulness.

Q19. Are giraffes herbivorous or omnivorous?

Ans. Only herbivorous.

Q20. Squirrel is a bird or mammel?

Ans. Small animal.

Q21. Which is taller - horse or mule?

Ans. Horse.

Q22. What is the use of elephant's teeth?

Ans. Many an article of daily use or decoration is made of them.

Q23. For how long can a camel remain without water?

Ans. For more than ten days.

Q24. Which fly is known to be the busiest?

Ans. Honey bee.

Q25. Which bird possesses the sweetest voice?

Ans. Nightingale (male).

34. Games

1. Rama is playing cricket.
2. Hope, you are not hurt badly.
3. I prefer riding to walking.
4. I am flying a kite.
5. We all shall play chess today.
6. Who won the game?
7. What games do you play?
8. Come, let us play cards.
9. You shuffle the cards and I'll cut.
10. Our team has won.
11. Can you wield a lathi?
12. Come, let us play.
13. The game has started.
14. Games are as important as studies.
15. I sprained my ankle while jumping.
16. He has set a record in high jump.
17. He is a fast sprinter/racer.

18. Do they teach you exercise/gymnastics in your school?
19. Our school has a big playground.
20. Who is the captain of your baseball team?
21. Can I play badminton with your racket?
22. Is your team also playing in the national football tournament?
23. I like rowing.
24. She plays regularly for the team.
25. We do drills once a week.
26. Cricket is one of the most played game.
27. Some people like cycling as a sport.
28. Kite flying was once a game of Nawabs.
29. Chess is useful for sharpening memory.
30. He enjoys playing chess before going to bed.
31. Sports are now part of business.
32. Shuffling cards is not easy.
33. Sports are also necessary for mental health.
34. Rope jumping is also an interesting game.
35. Milkha Singh is a renowned athlete.
36. Every school has a playground.
37. Azhar has been a well-known captain of Indian Cricket Team.
38. Badminton is both an indoor and outdoor game.
39. Ludo is an indoor game.
40. Football is an outdoor game.

Points to Remember

Adjectives which end with '-ful' are positive and those which end with '-less' are negative Adjective in most of the cases, e.g.,

(a) *Colourful (Positive)*	*Colourless (Negative)*
(b) *Pitiful (Positive)*	*Pitiless (Negative)*
(c) *Needful (Positive)*	*Needless (Negative)*
(d) *Powerful (Positive)*	*Powerless (Negative)*
(e) *Shameful (Positive)*	*Shameless, etc. (Negative)*

Exception: *Hateful, doubtful, painful, etc.*
Hateless, doubtless, painless, etc.

●●

19th Day

35. Person and Age

1. What is your good name?/Your name, please.
2. Please introduce yourself.
3. What is your age? How old are you?
4. I have just completed twenty.
5. You are older/younger than me.
6. I am a bachelor.
7. She is married.
8. She has only two daughters.
9. What is your father?/ What does your father do?
10. He is retired from government service.
11. He looks aged.
12. He has gray hair.
13. Does she dye her hair?
14. Do you have a joint family?/Is yours a joint family?
15. Yes, it is.
16. How many brothers do you have?
17. Our eldest brother lives separately.
18. He is just a kid.
19. You look younger than your age.
20. My brother is sixteen years old.

36. Character

1. To get angry is to show weakness.
2. An idle man is as good as half-dead.
3. Neither borrow nor lend.
4. You must come out with the truth.
5. There is great joy in selfless service.
6. He has atoned for his sin.
7. Neither deceive nor be deceived.

8. The virtuous alone are happy.
9. An empty mind is a devil's workshop.
10. Life is for others' service.
11. Don't ask anything from anybody.
12. My conscience does not permit.
13. To rest is to rust.
14. He who eats without earning has no choice.
15. She always keeps on talking.
16. She is very jealous for her sister.
17. We are sure of your honesty.
18. He pretends to know everything.

37. Dress

1. This cloth is fifty rupees per metre.
2. Please don't wear sweater in summer.
3. This cloth is extremely warm.
4. Indian women usually wear sarees.
5. Don't put on wet clothes.
6. Wear old coat, buy new book.
7. I will come after changing my clothes.
8. Nowadays the youth wear clothes of the latest fashion.
9. She was wearing/clad in a silk sari.
10. My clothes have gone to the laundry.
11. He was wearing a blue uniform.
12. It is a waterproof coat.
13. These dresses are for you.
14. A man is judged by his clothes.
15. This dress is a little tight for me.
16. This coat is loose at the waist.
17. Do you have shirtings?
18. Yes, we have good suitings also.
19. My suit is different from yours. Your suit is not like mine.
20. His shirt is not similar to mine.

21. People prefer light colour in summer.
22. Cotton is very comfortable to wear.
23. Fashion designing has good scope.
24. Tie is also a part of male dress.
25. There are many types of frocks.
26. Frill frock suits well to children.
27. Clothing is a part of culture.
28. Design and fabric of clothe are as per climate.
29. Males generally use Dhoti in South.
30. Ladies generally use Saree in Assam.
31. Rajasthani clothes are very heavy.
32. Kurta and pyjama is a comfortable clothing.
33. Shorts are in vogue these days.
34. Contrasting clothes look good.
35. People used to wear matching clothes earlier.

Points to Remember

1. In the previous chapter, you learnt how to make adverbs from Adjectives. Now, you would learn how to make Adverbs from nouns. Technique is the same. You have to add 'ly' to the end, e.g.,

   (a) Father + ly ⟶ Fatherly

   (b) Body + ly ⟶ Bodily

   (c) Man + ly ⟶ Manly

   (d) Scholar + ly ⟶ Scholarly, etc.

2. Another way is by adding '–y' to the end of nouns, e.g.,

   (a) Greed + y ⟶ Greedy; Rain + y ⟶ Rainy

   (b) Hand + y ⟶ Handy; Sun + y ⟶ Sunny, etc.

●●

20th Day

Test-1

From Days 11th-15th

Total Marks: 20

Rating: 'Very good' for 16 or above.

'Fair' for 12 or above.

I. **Correct the following sentences. The mistakes are given in italics in each sentence.**

1. The milk has *became* sour.
2. Why didn't you wake me *on*?
3. You should not go back *from* your word.
4. Sonia is taller of *a* two girls.
5. Wait *the* bit.
6. I saw the woman *whom*, the boss said, was away.
7. This rice is *on* inferior quality.
8. I am short *for* fifty rupees.
9. This chair is quite cheap *at* sixty rupees.
10. Do not buy *at* credit.
11. Does your shoe *pinches* you?
12. Show me a shoe with *an* narrow toe.
13. As we labour, so shall we be *reward*.
14. I am *so* tired to attend the class.
15. The question is *so* easy.
16. He is *week* in Hindi.
17. She has been absent *for* Wednesday.
18. *Should* you pass, your parents will be happy.
19. I have been in this college *since* two years.
20. He is junior *than* me by one year.

112

Test-2

From Days 16th-19th

Total Marks: 20

Score: 'Very good' for 16 or above.

'Fair' for 12 or above.

II. **Correct the following sentences. Thereafter, check them by matching the italic words with the given answer.**

1. He is *a* eye specialist.
2. All his *tooth* are intact.
3. He is blind *from* one eye.
4. Nothing *for* worry.
5. Can you *see* thermometer?
6. He is *bad* hurt.
7. Prevention is better *to* cure.
8. Happiness is *a* best tonic.
9. I am not feeling *good*.
10. How are your getting *of* in your business?
11. My health has gone *for* on account of hard work.
12. The patient is shivering *from* cold.
13. Many people died *from* malaria.
14. It is getting *cold* day by day.
15. *Sheeps* give us wool.
16 I prefer riding to *walk*.
17. Who *did won* the match?
18. Is *your* a joint family?
19. My brother is sixteen *year* old.
20. We are quite sure *for* your honesty.

Total Marks: 20

Score: 'Very good' for 16 or above.

'Fair' for 12 or above.

III. **In each of the sentences, given below, are two options. Choose the right option and fill in the blanks. Also try to understand the rule or principle hidden therein.**

1. I...(passed/have passed) the B.A. examination in 1976. 2. How... (many/much) letters did she write to me? 3. They have not spoken to each other... (for/since) two weeks. 4. She has been looking for a job... (for/since) July 1975. 5. I... (had/have) already bought my tickets, so I went in. 6. He was found guilty...(for/of) murder. 7. They are leaving (for/to) America soon. 8. She was married... (to/with) a rich man. 9. This shirt is superior... (than/to) that. 10. Write the letter...(with/in) ink. 11. She can't avoid...(to make/making) mistakes. 12. The train... (left/had left) before I arrived. 13. She... (finished/had) finished her journey yesterday. 14. You talk as if you... (know/knew) nothing. 15. She is... (taller/tallest) than her sister. 16. It will remain a secret between you/and...(me/I). 17. A girl friend of... (his/him) told us this news. 18. Mr. Munib and ... (myself/I) were present there. 19. Amitabh played a very good... (game/play). 20. I played well yesterday, ... (isn't it?/didn't I?)

Answer: *1. passed, 2. many, 3. for, 4. since, 5. had, 6. of, 7. for, 8. to, 9. to, 10. in, 11. making, 12. had left, 13. finished, 14. knew, 15. taller, 16. me, 17. his, 18. I, 19. game, 20. didn't I?*

Total Marks: 20

Score: 'Very good' for 20 or above.

'Fair' for 12 or above.

IV. Fill in the blanks with the help of options given in bracket.
1. How...(much/more/many) children do you have? 2. Custard is my favourite...(food/dish) 3. Where does this road... (lead/go) to? 4. Is he a ... (dependible/dependable) person? 5. Is he an... (important/impotent) minister? 6. When does your examination... (begin/commerce)? 7. ... (If/should) you pass, your parents... (will/shall) be happy. 8. The boy is so weak in Mathematics that he will not be able to get... (up/on/in) with the class. 9. Good boys bring credit.. (to/for) their school. 10. A little girl...(recalled/recited) a beautiful poem. 11. The squirrel has a...(wooly/hairy/bushy) tail. 12. The sun is bright because the sky is...(cloudy/cloudless). 13. As he is a (shameful/shameless) person, he pays for a good deed with a bad one. 14. She had... (wore/worn) a simple sari. 15. Children need... (protection/defence) from traffic hazards. 16. ....(Quietly/Quitely) he went out of the convention hall. 17. Munib and Majid help... (each other/one another). 18. Small children help...(each other/one another). 19. Minakshi has not come... (too/either). 20. They went for a...(ride/walk) on their bicycles.

Answer: 1. many, 2. dish, 3. lead, 4. dependable, 5. important, 6. commence, 7. if-will, 8. on, 9. to, 10. recited, 11. bushy, 12. cloudless, 13. shameless, 14. worn, 15. protection, 16. Quietly, 17. each other, 18. one another, 19. either, 20. ride.

Score: 'Very good' for 20 or above.
'Fair' for 12 or above.

V. **Change the following words into new words by adding some letters/a letter on your own, e.g., old– gold, etc.**

now, he, ox, our, an, how, hen, ear, all, refer, and, on, low, bear, me, able, ill, up, at, bus.

Answer: snow, she, box, hour, pan, show, then, year, ball, reference, land, upon, blow, beard, men, table, bill, cup, rat, bush.

Score: 'Very good' for 20 or above.
'Fair' for 12 or above.

VI. **Write the plural forms of the following words:**

Man, knife, journey, city, woman, ox, tooth, sheep, deer, foot, child, brother, church, fly, day, brother-in-law, wife, proof, news, key.

Answer: Men, knives, journeys, cities, women, oxen, teeth, sheep, deer, feet, children, brothers, churches, flies, days, brothers-in-law, wives, proofs, items of news, keys.

Score: 'Very good' for 20 or above.
'Fair' for 12 or above.

VII. **Write the present, past and participle forms for the following verbs:**

Light, lose, mean, pay, say, write, throw, win, beat, begin, lie, lay, know, hurt, put, cut, hold, forget, shut, take.

Answer: light-lighted-lighted, lose-lost-lost, mean-meant meant, pay-paid-paid, say-said-said, write-wrote-written, throw-threw-thrown, win-won-won, beat-beat-beaten, begin-began-begun, lie-lied-lied, lay-laid-laid, know-knew-known, hurt-hurt-hurt, put-put-put, cut-cut-cut, hold-held-held, forget-forgot-forgotten, shut-shut-shut, take-took-taken.

●●

21st Day

3rd Expedition
(Conversation Contd...)

You have completed two expeditions so far and you have learnt much. Still, there are some important topics which should be covered. These are related to– manners and etiquette; signals or instructions at public places; conversation in office; sentences on general things; law; radio/T.V./ post office; travel; recreation, some Dont's; Some Do's; dealings; business; sayings; attending a wedding; cinema; playground; tourist office; hotel; servant; doctor; general topics; idioms; proverbs; telephoning; numbers, date and time; health; and shopping.

Manners and Etiquette

Etiquette are the formal rules of correct or polite behaviour in society, in business and profession. In our day-to-day life– be it at home or at office, while travelling, in social gatherings like marriage, birthday party, inaugural functions, educational debates, meetings and political sessions– certain rules have to be followed.

Learn them by heart, use them frequently and turn yourself into a civilized and well-mannered person.

38. Etiquette

1. That will do. This/it is enough.
2. Don't bother, please.
3. No trouble at all.
4. Don't worry about me.
5. So kind/nice of you.
6. It would be very kind of you.
7. How can I help you?
8. Why did you trouble yourself?
9. This is sufficient.

117

10. Please don't be formal.
11. Please stay a little more.
12. Please excuse me.
13. May I say something?
14. Don't mind.
15. I am at your service/disposal.
16. We couldn't entertain you properly.
17. May I sit here?
18. Thanks for your help!
19. We are grateful to you.
20. No question of thanks. It would rather please me.
21. Thank you for your sensible/good advice.
22. With love and best wishes–yours sincerely, Munib.
23. Kindly excuse me for the trouble.
24. Regard to sister and love to children!
25. What can I do for you?
26. Please drop in sometime.
27. Please make yourself comfortable.
28. Pleased to meet you!
29. Your lecture enlightened me.
30. No noise, please.

39. <u>Signals</u>

At public places, we generally come across short but meaningful phrases or terms which either guide us to a particular destination, for example, traffic signals, placards, signboards, and banners, etc or they instruct us what to do and what not to do.

We give below some important instructions for you.

1. Drive slowly.
2. Keep to the left.
3. Dangerous turn ahead.
4. No parking, here.
5. Cross from here.
6. Dogs not permitted.

7. No entrance.
8. Exit.
9. Entrance.
10. Keep off the grass.
11. No entry without permission.
12. No smoking.
13. Pull the chain.
14. To let.
15. School ahead.
16. Road closed.
17. Dead end ahead.
18. W.C./Gentlemen's/Men/Ladies/Women.
19. Waiting Room.
20. Please stand in a queue.
21. For ladies only.
22. Heavy vehicles are not allowed.
23. Photography is prohibited.
24. Beware of dogs!
25. Reserved parking.
26. Tow-away zone.
27. Accident-prone Area.
28. No horn.
29. Man at work.
30. Danger!
31. Drive slow.
32. Roads merge ahead./Merging roads ahead.
33. Narrow lane.
34. For Handicapped.
35. No Thoroughfare.
36. Guard your Belongings./Take care of your luggage.
37. Sale/For sale.
38. No credit.
39. Fixed Price.
40. Self-Service.

Points to Remember

1. Etiquettes and manners should necessarily be followed as they reflect our society and culture. The purpose of rules is to make life easy and trouble free. That's why, it is said, "Discipline is beauty."

2. Similarly, short instructions, guiding maps, indicators and signal plates are meant to make life easy-going and smooth. Ignoring them is equal to offence. Respect them and be cheerful.

3. Sometimes, it is very easy to identify a noun. For example, if a word ends with '-ness' it is a noun, e.g., Goodness, Illness, Sadness, Thickness, etc.

4. Another identity is '-ance', e.g., Allowance, Alliance, Clearance, Pursuance, etc. Similarly, some nouns end with '-ence', e.g., Absence, Preference, Difference, Presence, Audience, etc.

●●

22nd Day

40. Office

1. This is a Punjab National Bank Cheque.
2. This clerk is a favourite of the officers.
3. For how many days, would you have to take leave?
4. Work pressure is very heavy these days.
5. I want to make a call.
6. Put up the notice on the Notice Board.
7. Is the boss in?
8. Please sign here.
9. My application has been accepted.
10. He didn't/couldn't get leave.
11. He has been warned.
12. I'll think over this matter.
13. He has resigned.
14. This point was not touched.
15. I'll surely keep this in mind.
16. I follow all what you say. I am following whatever you are saying.
17. The head clerk is all in all in this office.
18. His resignation has been accepted.
19. No smoking.
20. Can you make this graphic design on computer?
21. My watch has stopped.
22. Is it late?
23. You are late by an hour.
24. Type this letter fast.
25. What's the date today?
26. She has joined only today.
27. Is there any phone call for me?
28. I have fixed an appointment with the Director at 3 o'clock.
29. Are you working in that office?

30. It's better if you resign.
31. What post do you hold?
32. Success has gone to his head.
33. I'm very busy today.
34. What is the salary you draw?
35. How is the office atmosphere?

41. <u>Things</u>

1. This is a very fine/nice/beautiful picture.
2. Please give change.
3. You have not shown me your photograph.
4. Please deliver the goods at my hotel.
5. I have to get my spectacles changed.
6. I need another blanket.
7. My watch has been sent for repairs.
8. I want rice, pulses and curry.
9. I want one dozen of cigars and two dozens of cigarettes.
10. The mirror was broken by him.
11. Please have something cold.
12. I haven't seen your book.
13. This box is very heavy.
14. Bring/get all these things.
15. Pack these things/articles.
16. Please carry your holdall.
17. He left his house bag and baggage.
18. You should travel light.
19. He is fond of beautiful things.
20. This cloth appears durable.
21. Put the utensils back on the shelf.
22. Get your room painted green.
23. Get your house whitewashed.
24. I have to get my furniture repaired.
25. This is a comfortable sofa.

26. This pen gives a smooth writing.
27. I like oval shape of office.
28. Make/paint circular patterns on the wall.
29. I bought first class bricks for my house.
30. He likes transparent glass in the window.
31. Don't sip too hot coffee.
32. I am about to buy a 5G SIM soon.
33. There are many types of rotating chairs.
34. Online transaction is easy.
35. Let's make India a digital India.

Points to Remember

1. Office is a place where formalities are followed strictly. There is a specific decorum to be maintained in an office. Hierarchical differences among various office-holders and lower-grade employees are necessary for smooth running of an office. Above all, humanity can never be compromised at the cost of rules and regulations.

2. There are some nouns in English which are always written in singular but they are used both as singular and plural, e.g.,

     (a) I saw a deer in the forest.
     (b) Deer are beautiful animals.
     (c) There is a hair on his nose.
     (d) His hair is black.
     (e) Sheep give us wool.
     (f) A sheep is an innocent animal, etc.

●●

42. Law

1. He was accused of murder.
2. He was in the police lock-up for two days.
3. He reported this incident to the police.
4. The accused was acquitted.
5. He absconded from his house.
6. He was released on bail.
7. Lawlessness prevails in the city.
8. Your act is illegal.
9. Justice demanded it.
10. You are my witness.
11. This is against the law.
12. He is innocent.
13. It is for you to judge.
14. These are all forged documents.
15. He filed a suit against me.
16. The lawyers cross-examined the witness.
17. Nowadays, litigation is on the increase.
18. The police is investigating the matter.
19. I have filed a criminal case against him.
20. The magistrate convicted the accused.
21. At last, the plaintiff and the defendant reached a compromise.
22. He got a death sentence.
23. The jury gave its verdict in favour of the accused.
24. The murderer has been hanged.
25. Ignorance of law is no excuse.
26. The judge punished the thief.
27. What was the judgement in the case?
28. He is an eye-witness.
29. He is a law-abiding man.
30. Justice delayed is justice denied.
31. Murders have become common these days.
32. The police arrested the murderer.

33. I lodged an FIR in the police station.
34. Why do you accuse him of theft?
35. Bail is not easy to get.
36. There is lawlessness everywhere these days.
37. Avoid illegal acts.
38. Justice may be delayed.
39. He can judge the matter better.
40. He filed a suit against his friend.

43. Radio/TV/Post Office

41. I have bought a colour television.
42. You T.V. is on.
43. My radio is off.
44. News bulletin is broadcast simultaneously from all radio stations.
45. I am very fond of watching T.V.
46. Now switch on/tune in to channel Zee.
47. The postman is sorting out the letters.
48. The next clearance is due at 4:30 p.m.
49. The mail is delivered thrice a day.
50. I sent ₹ 50/- by money order.
51. The registered packet needs more stamps.
.52. Please acknowledge the money order.
53. The television plays an important role in our life.
54. My radio has a very clear reception.
55. Have you weighed the parcel?
56. I have to buy some envelops and postcards by the post.
57. This channel is disturbed.
58. You haven't tuned it properly.
59. Two workers in the postal department are on strike.
60. What will the stamp on this letter cost?
61. Use of television is getting lesser day by day.
62. Connect your mobile to the T.V.
63. Radio is almost out of use now.
64. Simultaneous broadcast of radio is possible from many stations.
65. Couch potato is one who spends maximum time before T.V.
66. Multiple channels are available.
67. Use of postal correspondence is minimum these days.

68. When will this mail reach the destination?
69. Send me Rs. 1000/- by money order.
70. Get it registered before dispatching.
71. I have received the money order.
72. Television revolutionised the world.
73. F.M. radio has a very clear reception.
74. Please buy me stamps for Rs. 100/-
75. Speed post is fast and safe.
76. Courier service is also fast.
77. In this basement, network of mobile is not working.
78. Turn the modem on.
79. The postman is a very hardworker.
80. Stamp duty has increased lately.

Points to Remember

1. There are some terms which are strictly used in legal context, e.g., status quo, sub judice, de jure, etc. These terms are called legal jargon. So, be cautious while using them in your speech or writings.

2. Radio-broadcast is now a thing of the past. Rapidly advancing technology has replaced this gadget of yester years. FM is the only existing means to spread information in the form of radio technology.

3. Some nouns are made by adding '-ment' to the verb, e.g.,

agree+ment	=	agreement;
amaze+ment	=	amazement;
amend+ment	=	amendment;
argue+ment	=	argument;
employ+ment	=	employment;
excite+ment	=	excitement;
settle+ment	=	settlement, etc.

4. Some nouns end with '-ant', e.g.,

servant, applicant, accountant, consonant, defendant, merchant, etc.

●●

24th Day

44. Travel

1. Hurry up, please.
2. We have lost our way.
3. It's a long journey.
4. I have to go to Agra.
5. Why did you come back so soon?
6. Where are you staying?
7. Have you bought the ticket?
8. Is the Jodhpur Mail arriving on time?
9. I will go to Kolkata by 10:30 train.
10. We'll go together.
11. Badrinath temple will reopen in June this year.
12. When does the Punjab Mail leave?
13. We will reach in time.
14. On which platform will the train arrive?
15. How far is the railway station from here?
16. Hurry up, otherwise you will miss the train.
17. The train is out of sight now.
18. I am going to the station from here.
19. It's no thoroughfare.
20. The road is closed for repairs.
21. They could not catch the train.
22. The front wheel has less air.
23. I am going to the railway station to see off my uncle.
24. It is only 10 minutes walk.
25. I am going to the station to receive them.
26. The tyre of the car burst.
27. I am fond of cycling.

28. I changed the train at Saharanpur.
29. The booking office remains open twenty-four hours.
30. Is this the direct train to Chennai?
31. I will accompany you to the station.
32. I will be in Kalagarh next week.
33. Crossing the railway tracks is prohibited.
34. The next station is Allahabad.
35. There is still half an hour for the train to leave.
36. Hurry up, the train stops here for a short while.
37. The train is due at half-past eleven.
38. If you don't make haste, you will miss the train.
39. Hire a giude so that you may not lose the way.
40. He undertook a long journey.
41. Did you buy the return ticket also?
42. When are you going to depart?
43. Who will stay with you?
44. Tickets are selling in advance.
45. When the flight is scheduled?
46. Have you bought all the necessary things for your journey?
47. Keep some books for your travel.
48. Before leaving, make necessary search.
49. Food on the way is costly.
50. How many stations are there in the way?
51. How many people are allowed for the tour?
52. Travelling is a good experience.
53. Platform ticket is available.
54. Speed of trains is tremendous.
55. Be alert while travelling.
56. It is a general parking area.
57. Don't park here.

58. It is a reserved parking.
59. Our destination is two stations far.
60. I can never forget the time I passed with you.
61. How many countries of the world have you visited?
62. Travelling is a very good experience.
63. I have travelled by rail, road and air.
64. Cost of air travelling has reduced a lot.
65. Journey by ship is an adventurous experience.
66. He does not get travelling allowance from the office.
67. There are many tourist spots in India.
68. There are many opportunities of growth in the tourism sector.
69. Travelling in the first class is very expensive.
70. We learn many things by travels too.
71. Always reach the station by half an hour in advance.
72. Enquire about the arrival time to Chandigarh.
73. Photography is also a part of travelling.
74. Please buy my a travel charger of mobile.
75. How much do you charge for Delhi-Darshan?
76. Travellers usually keep eatable with them.
77. Don't litter the parks.
78. Use binoculars while sight-seeing.
79. Be humble and courteous to the forein travellers.
80. Assist the old and physically challanged during travels.
81. Metro is also a fast and cheep means of travel.
82. Before boarding, collect information about your destination.
83. The more knowledge you have, the easier the travel.
84. Don't tease your fellow-travellers.
85. Take care of your luggage while travelling.

25th Day

45. <u>Recreation</u>

1. We were listening to music.
2. She will wait for you at the Cinema Hall.
3. She can play the piano but not the violin.
4. I used to go to watch a film every Sunday.
5. Stamp collecting/philately is my hobby.
6. I showed some of my stamps to Amitabh.
7. It was a sweet/melodious song.
8. It was a very interesting story.
9. Is today's play worth-seeing?
10. The film 'Karma' will be released soon.
11. Music has a soothing effect on mind.
12. Cinema is a means of amuzement as well as education.
13. He is a master of piano.
14. Violin is his favourite pastime.
15. He used to see two films every month.
16. Stamp collection is also a good hobby.
17. Amitabh gave a number of hit films after 'Zanjeer' film.
18. Lata Mangeshkar is a melodious singer.
19. His way of story-telling is very good.
20. Comic story books used to be a good pastime in the past.
21. All plays written by Shakespeare are worth-washing.
22. In summer holidays, we went to Shimla.
23. There is a good water park in Moradabad.
24. Crystal World is also a good water park in Haridwar.
25. A magician entertains people by his tricks.
26. Go for a sunbath on some beach for recreation.
27. There are many beaches in Goa.
28. Dancing is a good art of entertainment.
29. He likes watching comedian's performance.
30. 'Laughter Challenge' is a good source of entertainment.

46. Dont's

31. Don't shirk work.
32. Don't be in a hurry.
33. Don't speak ill of others.
34. Don't quarrel with others.
35. Don't depend upon others.
36. Don't laugh at others.
37. Don't go out barefoot.
38. Don't waste your time.
39. Don't steel others' things.
40. Don't lose your temper.
41. Don't sit idle.
42. Don't doze while working.
43. Don't pluck flowers.
44. Don't spit on the floor.
45. Don't disturb others.
46. Don't turn the pages.
47. Don't write anything on your books.
48. Don't disturb the queue.
49. Don't forget to remember me.
50. Don't hesitate in telling me your problem.
51. Don't consume too much fatty things.
52. Don't look down upon others.
53. Don't ill-treat your guests.
54. Don't waste your time in gossiping.
55. Don't walk in the centre of the road.
56. Don't overtake anybody from wrong side.
57. Don't beat about the bush.
58. Don't interface with other's matters.
59. Don't make your uniform dirty.
60. Don't spend too much money on your classmates.

47. Do's

61. Write as neatly as you can.
62. Handle a book with neat hands.
63. Keep to the left.
64. Always shake hands with right hand.
65. Cultivate the habit of working hard.
66. Always keep the idiots off.
67. Talk respectfully to others.

131

68. Sink your differences.
69. Wake up early in the morning.
70. Go out for a walk in the morning and evening.
71. Brush your teeth in the morning and before going to bed.
72. Wash your hands before and after meals.
73. Stand upright, don't bend.
74. Patch up your differences.
75. Mend your ways.
76. Obey your elders.
77. Love your youngsters.
78. Give your regards to your elders.
79. Be punctual and attentive.
80. Chew your food properly.
81. Hold firmly.
82. Be respectful to elders.
83. Trim your nails once a week.
84. Litter your drawers once a month.
85. Take sufficient sleep.

Points to Remember

1. Travelling is not only a good means of recreation but it also offers us opportunities to learn new things about the world while travelling, try to mingle with new people, make new friends, try to know about new places, its flora and fauna, history, culture, language, etc. Simultaneously, share your knowledge with them, too.
2. Observe Do's and Dont's of the places you visit.
3. Some words are made opposite by adding '-dis' to the beginning of words, e.g.,
   - (a) able ⟶ disable.
   - (b) agree ⟶ disagree
   - (c) obey ⟶ disobey
   - (d) count ⟶ discount
   - (e) respect ⟶ disrespect
4. But all the words beginning with '–dis' are not necessarily opposite, e.g., *distance, disturb, distort, distinct,* etc.

••

26th Day

48. Dealings

1. Keep the accounts clear.
2. How is the grain market?/What is the current price of grain?
3. Please count the money.
4. I got duped by him.
5. This is a base coin.
6. He invested all the money in trade/business.
7. Settle the wages.
8. How is your business going on?
9. Give the boys hundred rupees each.
10. Did you get your wages?
11. Now I am square with you.
12. Advance money will have to be paid.
13. How much money can you spare for me?
14. Don't spend more than you earn.
15. Has he paid your salary?
16. That's all, please make the bill.
17. I am hard up/tight these days.
18. Don't deceive anybody.
19. I don't have any cash.
20. We will deposit all our money in the bank.
21. There is a shortage of funds/cash.
22. How much is the cash in hand?
23. I am not after money.
24. I'll invest everything in the business.
25. All the money has been spent.
26. Can you lend ₹ one lac?
27. I have to pay several bills.
28. He charges high rate of interest on the lent money.
29. Don't be spendthrift.
30. Never hesitate in helping the poor and needy.
31. He opened a new account in the State Bank.
32. Price of gold is constant for some time.
33. Money begets money.

34. Duping others is not a good thing.
35. Deposit all the base coins here.
36. I always settle the wages.
37. His business is flourishing these days.
38. Distribute this money among the children.
39. Dress your wound properly.
40. I never lose time in paying electricity bills.

49. <u>Business</u>

41. Do you have any dealings with him?
42. Are you in service or business?
43. Business is flourishing these days.
44. Get the parcel delivered from the station.
45. Let us have a deal.
46. Please arrange for the payment of my wages.
47. Money begets money.
48. Kindly give us five thousand rupees in advance.
49. Are you in business?
50. I am under debt.
51. How much is the bill?
52. How much does it cost?
53. This cheque is to be encashed.
54. Post these letters.
55. There is a slump in business these days.
56. What is your profession?
57. How many shareholders are there in this company?
58. He is in the import-export trade.
59. We are brokers.
60. Have you sent an invoice for the goods?
61. He is not fair in his dealings.
62. You are a good businessman.
63. These days, there is a great dipression in business.
64. He has delivered all the parcels.
65. Think over well before striking a deal.
66. Pay his wages without delay.
67. Ask for some advance money.

68. He has been running this business for ten years.
69. She is under huge debt.
70. Can you calculate my bill?
71. How much did you pay for your breakfast?
72. Issue me a post-dated cheque.
73. Bring all the assignments to me.
74. Become a good professional.
75. Your company holds a respectable position.
76. He is interested in export business.
77. Brokers are in plenty here.
78. I have seen the invoice.
79. It is a trade secret.
80. Devote maximum time for your business.

Points to Remember

1. When we talk of social or public life, 'dealing' is considered an important benchmark. The more we are fair in our dealings, the more we prosper is business and society. In our private life too, fair dealing cannot be ignored.

2. There are words which end in '-ship', e.g., membership, lectureship, scholarship, etc. These nouns are Abstract Nouns. We add '-ship' to a common noun and a new noun, which is abstract, comes into being.

3. Similarly, we can make Abstract Nouns by adding '-hood' to common nouns, e.g.,

father+hood	=	fatherhood,
child+hood	=	childhood,
Man+hood	=	manhood,
boy+hood	=	boyhood,
girl+hood	=	girlhood,
parent+hood	=	parenthood, etc.

●●

27th Day

50. <u>Sayings</u>

1. Truth is bitter.
2. Hard work always pays.
3. Idleness is the rootcause of all ills.
4. A divided house cannot stand.
5. Truth always wins.
6. Familiarity breeds contempt.
7. Prosperity gains friends, but adversity tries them.
8. Honesty is the best policy.
9. Extolling/Praising you at your face is flattery.
10. Learning breeds controversy.
11. All are not alike.
12. Nothing is permanent in this world.
13. Experience teaches the unskilled.
14. Man is slave to his stomach.
15. A base coin seldome runs.
16. All is fair in love and war.
17. Perseverance prevails.
18. Courtesy costs nothing.
19. Death pays all debts.
20. Every ass loves its bray.
21. Give a dog a bad name and hang him.
22. Handsome is that handsome does.
23. When the cat is away, the mice will play.
24. To caste pearls before swine.
25. His senses have taken leave.
26. Fools to others, to himself a sage.
27. Penny-wise pound-foolish.
28. Fools argue, wisemen discuss.
29. Keep away from fools.
30. All happiness is in the mind.
31. An apple a day keeps the doctor away.
32. Don't jest if you cannot bear a jest.
33. Happiness invites envy.
34. A fear of words is no proof of wisdom.

35. A little knowledge is a dangerous thing.
36. Empty mind is devil's workshop.
37. A cold lover is a faithful friend.
38. A good son makes a good husband.
39. Love conqueres all.
40. Love is not to be found in market.

51. Miscellaneous Sentences

41. The gas has finished.
42. The situation in the city is tense.
43. There is pindrop silence in the room.
44. Computer knowledge is essential these days.
45. Munib is a simple and straightforward man.
46. He was elected unanimously.
47. How long will you take to get ready?
48. The law and order situation is deteriorating day-by-day.
49. Never underestimate the enemy.
50. There is a slump in the share market these days.
51. She is grumbling all the time.
52. Petrol is highly inflammable.
53. He is a man of good taste.
54. Don't look at me like this.
55. Indra Gandhi had an impressive personality.
56. Make the most of the opportunity.
57. Talking to him is below my dignity.
58. The two countries signed a peace treaty.
59. Always respect your elders.
60. Don't beat children.
61. Truth always prevails.
62. Proud brings shame.
63. Don't trust everybody.
64. Parents deserve the highest regard.
65. Slow and steady wins the race.
66. Failures are ladders to success.
67. Life is a combination of joys and sorrows.
68. Hard work always pays.
69. Keep your word.
70. Friendship is an excellent gift from god.

71. Water is a combination of Hydrogen and Oxygen gases.
72. A tense mind is restless.
73. Silence is half consent.
74. Computer has revolutionised the twenteeth century.
75. Election should be fair.
76. He has full control over law and order.
77. He committed mistake by underestimating his enemy.
78. He who keeps grumbling is never happy.
79. Make best out of the worst.
80. Proud is not a good thing.

Points to Remember

1. 'Sayings' are short sentences or phrases which carry loads of meanings and significance. Handed down to us for centuries, they still hold good. They are based on experience. In short, they are 'Ocean in cup'. Make your speech and writing effective and forceful by including one or some of them.

2. To make Adjective from Nouns and Verbs, we add '-ive' and '-ous', e.g.

Attract + ive	=	*Attractive;*
Prevent + ive	=	*Preventive;*
Act + ive	=	*Active;*
Cooperate + ive	=	*Cooperative;*
Elect + ive	=	*Elective;*
Select + ive	=	*Selective;*
Danger+ous	=	*Dangerous;*
Fame+ous	=	*Famous;*
Mountain+ous	=	*Mountainous;*
Poison+ous	=	*Poisonous;*
Prosperity+ous	=	*Prosperous;*
Humour+ous	=	*Humorous*, etc.

28th Day

52. Attending a Wedding

1. Where has the barat come from?
2. Where will the barat go?
3. Do you have the dowry system?
4. When is the muhurat for wedding?
5. I want to/would like to see the bride and groom.
6. The wedding/party was very good.
7. Please accept this small/little gift.
8. The function was well-organised.
9. How did you enjoy the party?
10. I enjoyed to the full.

53. Cinema

1. Which movie/film is running in this cinema hall?
2. Is this a good movie?
3. What is the star cast of this film?/Who are the characters in this movie?
4. For how much is the ticket for dress circle?
5. How much is for balcony?
6. When will the film start?
7. What is the duration of this film?/When will the movie end?
8. Is this a cine complex/Multiplex?
9. How many screens are there in this PVR?
10. The sound system in this hall is good.

54. On the Playground

1. I want to see a cricket/football/hockey match today.
2. How far is the stadium?
3. For how much is the entry ticket?/What is the price of the ticket?
4. For how long will the match go?

5. How many teams are participating?
6. What are the games which are played on this stadium?
7. The stadium is vast and impressive.
8. Who won the match yesterday?
9. Who won the toss today?
10. Which are the games you like to see/play?

55. In the Tourist Office

1. Which are the worth-seeing places in this city?
2. I would like to see/visit/tour the Ajanta and Ellora caves.
3. What is the best transport to Mathura – train or bus?
4. Where should I stay in Agra?
5. I have visited Delhi five times.
6. I want a tourist guide. Where will I get one?
7. Tourism business is good in our city.
8. The Taj Mahal was built by Emperor Shah Jahan.
9. The Red Fort and Jama Masjid were also built by the Emperor Shah Jahan.
10. Hundreds of tourists visit these historical monuments daily.

56. In the Hotel

1. Is there any room available in this hotel?
2. What do you charge for a single/double bed room?
3. Take my luggage to Room No. 6, please.
4. Please send my breakfast/lunch/dinner in my room.
5. I am going out for an hour.
6. Was there a call for me?/Is there any call for me?
7. Please send my visitors to my room.
8. Get me some cold/hot water.
9. The washerman/laundryman has not come yet.
10. When is the last order received?/What time is the last delivery?

57. <u>With Servant</u>

1. Get some vegetables from the market.
2. Get the stuff or things from the cooperative store.
3. Wake me up at 5 o'clock.
4. Go and post this letter.
5. Are the clothes back from the laundry?
6. Make me a cup of tea.
7. Is the food/lunch/dinner ready?
8. Go and dust the room.
9. Carry this luggage to the platform.
10. Wait here until I come back.

58. <u>With the Doctor</u>

1. I have got some temperature/fever and also cough.
2. How many times a day should I take this medicine?
3. What all can I eat?
4. You should keep a monthly record of your weight.
5. Your blood pressure is normal.
6. Cut down on your sugar and salt.
7. You should eat green and fresh vegetables.
8. Where should/does one go for X-ray?/Where is the X-ray department?
9. This is a free dispensary. Medical care is free here. There is no consultation fee. We don't charge the patients anything.
10. This clinic also provides the facility of pathological tests.

59. <u>General Topics</u>

1. His work was quite disappointing.
2. I'll be glad to get rid of him.
3. Your coat is not like mine.
4. You cannot correct the mistakes.
5. He's the one who won the match.

6. Who is taller of the two girls?
7. Most of the people would agree with it.
8. I asked her whether she was going to the market or not.
9. Will you speak to her if she comes?
10. The unfortunate/poor man was shot dead.
11. He resembles his mother.
12. Silver is a precious metal.
13. I got/received eight hundred and forty-two rupees.
14. She goes to Church on Sunday.
15. I go for a walk in the morning.
16. I got this book for three hundred rupees.
17. They will study German besides English.
18. I am determined to go.
19. I have made up my mind to send him to Allahabad.
20. We hang the picture on the wall.
21. The murderer was caught red-handed.
22. Will you please lend me your pen for a while?
23. Can I borrow a pen from you?
24. The meeting will start early.
25. I'll attend the meeting.
26. I went to bed early last night but couldn't sleep.
27. When do you go to bed?
28. Does she keep her money in the bank?
29. It's very hot here in the summer.
30. It's too hot here to play hockey.
31. Chennai is farther than Kolkata.
32. We will collect/get/gather more information.
33. You came here later than I.
34. Delhi and Mumbai both are big cities, the latter is situated by the sea.
35. This grocer has good business.

36. This lawyer has many clients.
37. The mother gave me a good piece of advice.
38. This keyboard is not functioning well.
39. Shagufta has long and pitch black hair.
40. I don't have enough fruit.
41. Do you want to buy two dozens of bananas?
42. This floppy is virus-infected.
43. Here is a sheep and there is a deer.
44. The shepherd has twenty sheep and two deer.
45. Her wages are low.
46. Suman and Rita are coming here.
47. The number of students is decreasing year by year.
48. Many students are absent today.
49. We will eat fish/chicken at dinner tomorrow.
50. This book took me one and a half.
51. Lend me a hand.
52. He will always honour his word.
53. Are you spying on me?
54. You have done wonders/marvels.
55. She is a touch-me-not.
56. Why don't you listen to me?
57. Munib hates backbiting.
58. We should always help the needy.
59. Our boss is Mr. Ram Avtar Gupta.
60. He is a noble and large-hearted man.
61. I have an experience of eight years.
62. Write beautifully as well as correctly.
63. India is one of the powerful countries of the world.
64. I love my country.
65. A man is known by the company he has.
66. Pustak Mahal is an established name in Industry.

67. Mr. Rohit Gupta is its Director.

68. The publishing industry is passing through a tough time.

39. We are still hopeful.

70. Fluctuation is natural in life.

Points to Remember

1. Apostrophe s ('s) is used in English language to show Possessive case in case of living things, particularly human beings, e.g.,

    (a)   Rakhi's brother is an engineer.

    (b)   My father's office is very splendid.

2. Sometimes, 's is also used for non-living things, e.g.,

    (a)   Please grant me one day's leave.

    (b)   In today's world, everybody is busy.

3. But in case of lifeless objects, preposition 'of' is generally used for possessive case, e.g.,

    (a)   Colour of this wall is very attractive.

    (b)   Design of the house is very impressive.

    (c)   The back of this chair is very comfortable.

4. In case of 's, if the noun is plural and ends in 's' then we use only apostrophe (') at the end of the noun, e.g.,

    (a)   This is boys' hostel.

    (b)   Girls' dress is light-coloured.

5. 'Apostrophe s' is also used in some idiomatic expressions, e.g., *to their heart's content, in my mind's eye, a hair's breath, a stone's throw, sun's rays,* etc.

●●

29th Day

60. Idioms

An idiom is a group of words whose meaning is different from the meanings of individual words.

1. In this world, everyone wants to *grind his own axe*.
2. *Practice makes a man perfect*.
3. *Let bygones be bygones*, take care in future.
4. They *exchanged hot words*.
5. It appears he is *off his wits*.
6. Their shouts *rent the sky*.
7. I *praised* him *to the skies*.
8. Nowadays your *bread* is *buttered*.
9. He is a *jolly fellow*.
10. Pack up your *bag* and *baggage*.
11. We are *poles apart*.
12. You have given *a long rope* to this boy.
13. Nowadays, T.V. sets are *selling like hot cakes*.
14. Ratnakar deceit *turned out a new leaf* and became a saint.
15. *Take* the time *by the forelock* and success is yours.
16. Opportunists never hesitate to *pray the rising sun*.
17. He is *making merry*/thriving these days.
18. Mohan is *on the right side* of forty.
19. The thief was caught *red-handed*.
20. The child is *under* his *uncle's care*.
21. The station is *within a stone's throw* from my village.
22. The boy is *in the good books* of the Principal.
23. He is *an apple of* my *eye*.
24. *Whom God loves die young*.
25. *One beats the bush, another takes the bird*.

26. *The older the goose, the harder to pluck.*

27. He *died in harness.*

28. They are always *at daggers drawn.*

29. Seing his painting, I was *on my wit's end.*

30. I am *all in all in* the family.

31. He invited *all and sundry* in the marriage party.

32. He *left no stone unturned* to appease his boss.

33. When I invited him, he *turned down* the offer.

34. Great people used to *burn midnight oil.*

35. *To call a spade a spade*, he is very hardworking.

36. He had to *eat humble pie* in the end.

37. You should not *eat your words.*

38. He agreed to *meet me half way.*

39. His wrong deeds *put his* father *on his mettle.*

40. You are not *worth your salt.*

41. Increasing prices have made it difficult to *make both ends meet.*

42. The opposition party *set their face against the bill.*

43. He was *within an ace of dropping* when I held him.

44. He *won his laurels* in the village.

46. I *received* her with *open* arms.

47. Don't *turn a deaf ear to* what I say.

48. I achieved my object *by hook or by crook.*

49. *Flesh and blood* is of little importance in politics.

50. I *take exception* to your remark.

61. Proverbs

A proverb is a well-known phrase or sentence that gives advice or says something that is generally true.

1. While in Rome do as Romans do.

2. As you sow, so shall you reap.

3. A thing is valued where it belongs.

4. To the good, the world appears good.
5. An empty vessel makes much noise.
6. Health is wealth.
7. No pain, no gain.
8. Time once lost cannot be regained.
9. Society moulds man.
10. Union in strength.
11. Fools praise fools.
12. Many heads, many minds.
13. Too many cooks spoil the broth.
14. There is no use of crying over spilt milk.
15. A bad man is better than a bad name.
16. Make hay while the sun shines.
17. Opportunity knocks at the door but once.
18. Man is mortal.
19. Honesty is the best policy.
20. Spare the rod and spoil the child.
21. Barking dogs seldome bite.
22. It is of no use building castles in the air.
23. Penny wise, pound foolish.
24. Give loan, enemy own.
25. Laughter is the best medicine.
26. Birds of a feather fly together.
27. Where there is a will, there is a way.
28. A bad workman quarrels with his tools.
29. Strike iron while it is hot.
30. Silence is half consent.
31. A man is a slave to his stomach.
32. Haste makes waste.
33. Look twice before you leap.
34. A honey tongue, a heart of gall.

35. All is well that ends well.
36. First impression is the last impression.
37. Cut your coat according to your cloth.
38. Speech is silveren, silence is golden.
39. If winter comes, can spring be far behind?
40. Every dog has its day.
41. Once bitten, twice shy.
42. Style makes the man.
43. Society moulds man.
44. One nail drives another.
45. Familiarity breeds contempt.
46. Diamond cuts diamond.
47. Truth lies at the bottom of a well.
48. There is a black sheep in every society.
49. There is something black in the bottom.
50. One lie leads to another.
51. It takes all sorts to make the world.
52. It takes two to make a quarrel.
53. A friend in need is a friend indeed.
54. Rome was not built in a day.
55. Failures are ladders to success.
56. Sweet are the uses of adversity.
57. A rolling stone gathers no moss.
58. Tit for tat.
59. A drop of water in the ocean.
60. Happiness is short-lived.
61. Much cry, little wool.
62. Every shining object is not gold.
63. Practice makes a man perfect.
64. Slow and steady wins the race.
65. Life is a combination of joys and sorrows.

66. Old is gold.

67. Experience is the best teacher.

68. Boss is always right.

69. Baggers are not choosers.

70. Give respect and take respect.

Points to Remember

Proverbs are sentences short in length but great in meanings and significance. They are handed down to us from ages and they hold good in all times. Metaphorically, they are 'oceans in cups'. Therefore, learn them all by heart as well as ponder over them. Also use them on and off in your writings and speeches.

---

62. Telephoning

Telephonic or mobile conversation is a very important part of today's life. Effective and natural conversation with people in various disciplines of life on mobile or writing e-mails is considered to be a key to success.

When you want to make a call

1. I need to make a call.

2. He needs to phone his boss.

3. She needs to call her brother.

Asking for a mobile number

4. Do you know Mr. Anand's mobile number?

5. Do you have the number of the hospital?

6. Do you have any contact number?

7. What is your mobile number?

8. What is the S.T.D. code for London?

9. What number do I have to dial for tea?

10. What is your extension number?

Starting Conversation

11. Hello, it is Gyan speaking.
12. Hello, it is Rama, here.
13. Is Dr. Rathore in? I am his client.
14. I am speaking from Pustak Mahal, New Delhi.

To confirm the right person

15. Is that Mr. Anand?
16. Am I speaking to Dr. Gulathi?
17. Hello, is it Mrs. Ranawat?

Asking for somebody

18. Is Mr. Kishore in?
19. Is your Dad there?
20. Can I speak to Mr. Shahrukh?
21. Can I speak to one of your parents?
22. Can I speak to someone in the Accounts Department?

    Note: If the person you want to talk to is absent, the following reply may be given:

23. Sorry, he is not here.
24. Sorry, I don't know anything about it.
25. I'm afraid, he is not available.
26. Who is calling? I am afraid, he is out of the station.

    • If the person we are calling to is familiar to us, we generally start conversation by asking about their health.

        Hello, Danish. *How are you?*

        Hi, it's Charu. *How are you?*

    • In response to the above question, we say—

        I am fine, thanks. or

        Not great, really.

- Purpose of calling—

  I am phoning *about evening tea.*

  I am calling *regarding your ad.* in the newspaper.

- To ask whether you can do something.

  Can I leave a message?

  Can I call back later?

  Can I give you my number?

- To ask someone else to do something.

  Could you *ask her to call* me, please?

  Could you *put me through* to Mr. Akash, please?

  Could you *give him a message*, please?

Note: In English, telephone numbers are said separately even if there are two same digits. They are said double five, double three, etc. The number 0 (zero) is said as letter 'O'. So, the number 2055 would be said as two o double five.

- To give details of where somebody can contact you, say, you can contact me on...; e.g.,

  You can contact on 20553766.

  You can contact on my mobile.

  You can contact on my sister's number.

Ending a telephone call

- When you end a telephone call, say Goodbye or See you..., e.g.,

  Thanks for your help, *goodbye.*

  O.K. then, *good bye.*

  Bye darling, *see you!*

- When you say goodbye, you may want to send your best wishes to someone else. In an informal situation, use 'say hello to...' and in a more formal way, use 'Give my best wishes to····', e.g.,

  Say hello to your friends.

  Give your father *my best wishes.*

63. Numbers, Date and Time

In the following lines, you will learn how to say number, date and time in English. If you want to speak English correctly, you must study this section and practise the points discussed below.

1. When you want to say how much something costs using the unit of money ₹, use... *rupees* and to talk about the smaller units used with rupees, use... *paise*, e.g.,

   This watch cost me eighty-seven *rupees* twenty. (₹ 87.20)

   This ticket cost nine *rupees* fifty-five (*paise*). (₹ 9.55)

2. When you want to talk about how heavy something is, using the units of measurements written as k and g, use *kilos* and *grams*.

   Please give me 1 *kilo* of sugar.

   I want 20 *grams* of salty butter.

   Please put five *litres* of petrol in the car.

3. To talk about how long something is, using the units of measurements written as *km, m* and *cm*, use *kilometres*, *metres* and *centimetres*. ('ft' for *feet*, 'yd' for *yard*, 'in' for *inches*) e.g.,

   We are twenty *kilometres* away from Bijnor.

   This pencil is twenty *centimetres* long.

   He is over six *feet* tall.

152

4. To talk about amounts as parts of a hundred (%) use *per cent*, e.g.,

> Fifty *per cent* growth has been reported.
>
> Rate of interest is two point five *per cent.*

5. To talk about temperature, written as °C, use *degrees*, e.g.,

> It is over thirty-five *degrees* today.

6. To talk about the order in which something happens or comes, use *first, second, third,* etc, e.g.,

> It is their *third* wedding anniversary.
>
> I stood *first* in the college (topper).

7. To say what the date is, use *first, second, third,* etc of *March/April/November,* etc. e.g.,

> It is the *first of July* today.
>
> Tomorrow is the *tenth of March.*
>
> It is *September the fifth* today.
>
> It's *April the twenty-second.*

8. To say what date something is happening or happened on, use *on* before the date.

> He was born *on the fifth of July*, 1990.
>
> He died on *April the twenty-sixth*, 1980.
>
> We are going to France on the *third of October.*

9. To ask date, use – What's the *date* today?

10. To say what day of the week it is, use it's..., e.g.,

> 'What day is it today?'   'It's Tuesday'.
>
>   It is Sunday today.

11. To say what time of a particular day something happens, use on... morning/afternoon/evening/night, e.g.,

> We will meet *on* Sunday *afternoon.*
>
> She visited me *on* Saturday *night.*

12. To say that you do something all Mondays, Tuesdays, etc, use *every*, e.g.,

    I call her *every Sunday*.

    She calls me *every Friday*.

13. To say that you do something on Saturday, then *not* on next Saturday and then on next Saturday and then it continues in this way, use *every other*..., e.g.,

    I play football *every other Sunday*.

    She cooks food *every other Friday*.

14. To ask what day something is happing, use what day....?

    What day's the conference?

    Tell me *what day* you will leave?

15. To say when something happened, use...ago, e.g.,

    She called me a *week ago*.

    He was born *three years ago*.

16. To say what time it is when the clock shows the exact hour, use... o'clock, e.g.,

    I get up in the morning at 5 *o'clock*.

    It's four *o'clock* in the afternoon.

Note: *Midday* is used to mean 12 o'clock in the middle of the day. *Midnight* is used to mean 12 o'clock in the middle of the night.

17. To say that it is thirty minutes or less after a particular hour, use, past...,e.g.,

    It is *twenty past six*.

    It is *five past seven*.

    It is *quarter past three*. (3:15)

    It is *half past three*. (3:30)

18. To say that it is a particular number of minutes before a particular hour, use, to..., e.g.,

    It is *five to three*. (2:55)

    It is *quarter to seven*. (6:45)

19. To ask how much time something lasts or how much time you need for something, use How long..?

> *How long* is the film?
>
> *How long* does the meeting usually last?
>
> *How long* will the tour take?

In response to the above question, you say—

> *It's three* hours long.
>
> *It takes one* hour for the meeting to last.
>
> *The tour takes* about four days.

20. To say which part of a month something happens in, use at the start of...in the middle of... or at the end of··· e.g.,

> I go to college *at the start* of January.
>
> The summer holidays start *in the middle* of May.
>
> They are leaving *at the end* of game.

64. <u>Health</u>

Health and illness is an issue which we often talk about in our daily life. If we become ill or unfortunately have an accident, the following phrases and expressions will allow us to talk to a doctor. Use them to get the advice or treatment that you need.

Describing a problem

- If you need to describe a medical problem, you can use, I've got..., e.g.
  > *I've got* a cold.
  >
  > *I've got* a temperature.

- If you want to say which part of your body hurts, you can use *my.... hurts*, e.g,
  > My *back hurts.*
  >
  > *My feet hurt.*
  >
  > *My neck hurts.*

- If the pain you have is an ache, you can say which part of your body it is in by using *I've got..ache*, e.g.,

  I've got stomachache.

  She's got toothache.

- You can talk about more general problems that you are having using *I feel ...*, e.g.,

  I feel sick.

  I feel better now.

Saying what happened

- In case of an accident, you will have to describe what happened. You will need to use past tense, such as *I fell...* or *I burnt...*

  I had an accident.

  I fell down the stairs.

  He burnt his hands.

- If the problem is that you are unable to do something that you should be able to do, you can use *I can't...* e.g.

  I can't breathe properly.

  She can't bend her arm.

- If the accident is serious and you have broken a bone in your body, use *I've broken...*e.g.,

  I think *I have broken* my arm.

  I think *she has broken* a tooth.

  Note: In English, we don't say 'I have broken the leg'; the correct expression is, 'I have broken my leg.'

Asking for information

- When you are asking for information you may need to get someone's attention before you can ask them a question. To do this, first we say *excuse me*.

  Excuse me, is there a hospital near here?

  Excuse me, how do I make an appointment?

- To ask whether something exists near to where you are, use *Is there...?*

     Is there a dentist near here?
     Is there a pharmacy on this street?

- When you need to get information about someone or something, start your question with *what...? which...? How...? Who...?* and *When...?*

     What is this medicine for?
     What number do I call for an ambulance?
     What do I ask the pharmacist for?
     Which doctor did you consult last time?
     Which street is the clinic in?
     How often do I take this medicine?
     How long will he be in the hospital?
     When will my operation be?
     When does visiting time start?
     What time do I need to be at the hospital?

- To ask what to do about your problem, use *Should I...?*
     Should I make another appointment?
     Should I keep taking the tablets?

- To ask for something, use *can I have...?*, e.g.,
     Can I have a packet of aspirins, please?
     Please *can I have* a plaster?

- If you want to be very polite, you can use *Is it possible to...?* e.g.,
     Is it possible to see a different doctor?
     Is it possible to see his surgeon before operation?

- To buy something from a pharmacy, use *Can I have...?* or *I would like...*, e.g.,
     I would like some cough medicine.
     I would like cream for dry skin.
     Can I have a strip of asperine?

- To ask someone whether they can do something for you, use *Could you...*, e.g.,

Could you call a doctor?

Could you give me some advice on how to get fit?

- When you want to do one thing and not another, use *I would prefer to...*, e.g.,

    I would prefer to go to the local hospital.

    I would prefer to see a female doctor.

Note: It is more polite to say *I would like to...* than simply *I want to...*

Making suggestions: The most simple way to make a suggestion is to say *we could..* or *you could...*, e.g.,

    You could ask the pharmacist.

    We could phone his family.

- If you want to suggest doing something with something else, use *shall we...?*, e.g.,

    Shall we call a doctor?

    Shall we give him some money?

- A slightly informal way of making suggestions of things to do or use is *How about...*, e.g.,

    How about changing your diet?

    How about walking to work instead of driving?

Note: '*How about*' is always followed by 'ing' form.

65. <u>Shopping</u>

Shopping has its own attraction in life. On the one hand, people are very excited, particularly children and women; on the other hand, there are some who get tense on the mention of shopping especially poor, low-salaried and daily wagers, etc. Anyway, there are some etiquette which have to be kept into mind while shopping. These polite expressions help build cordial relationship between shopkeepers and their customers. To ask for something in a shop, use *I'd like to...* or *could I have...* e.g.,

    I'd like two kilos of tomato, please.

    I'd like a bottle of water, please.

    Could I've a kilo of mangoes?

    Could I've a dozen of bananas?

- If you are looking for something, you can say *I'm looking for* or *I need...*, e.g.,

  I'm looking for a camera for my daughter.

  I'm looking for a white shirt.

  I need a new umbrella.

  I need a new travel bag.

- To ask if the shop sells the thing you want, use Do you sell..or *Have you got...?*,e.g.,

  Do you sell light bulbs?

  Do you sell newspapers?

  Have you got raincoats?

  Have you got dinner-sets?

- When you have decided what you want to buy, use *I'll have...* or *I'll take...*, e.g.,

  I'll take these books.

  I'll take two pineapples.

  I'll have a blue shirt.

  I'll have a new pair of shoes.

Saying what you have to do

- If you need to buy something, use *I've to...* or *I've got to...*, e.g.,

  I've to buy some exercise books.

  I've to buy two tickets of the movie.

  I need a new umbrella.

  I need a new travel bag.

- We can also use *I need to...*, e.g.,

  I need to buy some items of golden jewelery.

- If shopping is very important and it cannot be avoided, use *I must...* e.g.,

  I must take some chairs from the market.

  I must buy a bicycle.

Talking about your plans

- If you're going to tell someone what you are going to do, use *I'm going to...*, e.g.,

  I'm going to buy a new pair of shoes.

  I'm going to buy a new T.V. set.

- To talk about what you're thinking of buying or where you're thinking to go, use *I'm thinking* of..., e.g.,

   I'm thinking of going to the market tomorrow.

   I'm thinking of buying some pillows.

- For something you would like to do, but that's not certain, use *I hope to*..., e.g.,

   I hope to meet her in the market tomorrow.

   I hope she will buy a shirt for me.

Expressing opinions

- When you look at things in shops, you may want to say what you think of them, use *I think*... or *I don't think*..,e.g.,

   I think this tie would go with blue shirt.

   I don't think you need any more pens.

- To agree with someone else's opinion, use *I agree* or *you're right*, e.g.,

   I agree with you, we should go for shopping.

   You're right, you don't need another pair of jeans.

- If you're shopping with someone else and you want to know about their opinion regarding something, use *what do you think*? e.g.,

   What do you think of these trousers?

   What do you think of blue goggles?

- While making a choice, when you want to know of your friend's opinion, use *which*...?,e.g.,

   Which one of these dolls do your think to be the best?

   Which spectacles do you think suits me well?

- To ask for the price of something, use *How much*...?, e.g.,

   How much is this bottle of soft drink?

   How much is that green coat?

- To say what you like or don't like, use *I really like* or *I quite like*..., e.g.,

   I really like mangoes very much.

   I really like listening to light music.

   I quite like ice cream in winters.

160

Note: When *like...* is followed by a verb, it is generally in the –ing form.

- To express that you like something more than another, use '*I prefer....to*, e.g.,

    I prefer white drinks *to* the black ones.

    I prefer sleeping *to* gossiping here and there.

- *Asking for permission*: To ask the shopkeeper in a shop if you do something, use *Can* I..., *Do you mind if...*, *Is it O.K. to....*, e.g.,

    Can I try on this jacket?

    Do you mind if I taste another apple?

    Is it O.K. to try these trousers on?

●●

30th Day

Test No-1

From Day 21st-25th

Total Marks: 20

Scoring: 16 or above – Very good

12 or above – Fair

I. Correct the following sentences either by making corrections or by replacing the bold words.

1. Please don't trouble **myself**.
2. Please stay **for** little more.
3. Put up the notice **at** the notice board.
4. He is very proud **for** his promotion.
5. He was accused **for** murder.
6. He has been released **at** bail.
7. He was sentenced **for** death.
8. My radio **is** stopped.
9. Now switch on **for** Vividh Bharti.
10. Have you **weighted** the parcel?
11. You can **new** your driving licence from the transport office.
12. We have **loosed** our way.
13. Why did you **came** back?
14. The road is **close** for repair.
15. The train is due **on** half past eleven.
16. We were listening **at** music.
17. It was a very **interested** story.
18. Do not depend **on** others.

162

19. Do not spit **at** the floor.
20. Go for **an** walk in the morning and evening.

Test No - 2

From Day 26th-27th

Total Marks: 20

Scoring: 16 or above – Very good
12 or above – Fair

II. Correct the bold words in the following sentences:

1. Have the account **clear**.
2. Did you **got** your wages?
3. There is storage **on** money.
4. How is he getting **at** with has work?
5. Honesty is **a** best policy.
6. The man is **the** slave to his stomach.
7. Your coat is cleaner **to** mine.
8. Will you speak to her if she **come**?
9. Will you please **borrow** me your pen?
10. Come home **behind** me.
11. The number of the students **are** decreasing.
12. I read this book in **a** hour and a half.
13. Sita and Rita **is** coming here.
14. My mother gave me some good **advices**.
15. The unfortunate was **shoot** dead.
16. They will study German **beside** English.
17. The murderer was caught and **hung**.
18. A dog is a **wolf** in his lane.
19. All's well that **end's** well.
20. A **crow** in hand is worth two in the bush.

Total Marks: 20

Scoring: 16 or above – Very good
12 or above – Fair

III. Correct the bold words in the following sentences:

1. He **speak** English very well.
2. This film will be **played** shortly.
3. Your elder brother is five and a half feet **high**.
4. The player plays very **good**.
5. Many **homes** have been built up.
6. She is **an** coward girl.
7. We had a nice **play** of football.
8. I have **no any** mistakes in my dictation.
9. Strong **air** blew my clothes away.
10. I hurt a **finger** of my right foot.
11. She does not look **as** her brother.
12. I have a **plenty** work to do.
13. She spent the **rest** day at home.
14. His father was **miser**.
15. **After** they went home for dinner.
16. I have **came** to know about your health.
17. She has **the** heart filled with the milk of human kindness.
18. She is junior **than** me.
19. English is **very** fovourite to me.
20. Learn these sentences **from** heart.

Answers: 1. speaks, 2. released, 3. tall, 4. well, 5. houses, 6. a coward, 7. game, 8. haven't any, 9. wind, 10. toe, 11. like, 12. lot of, 13. the rest of the day, 14. a miser, 15. afterwards, 16. come, 17. a, 18. to, 19. remove 'very', 20. by.

164

Total Marks: 20

Scoring: 16 or above – Very good
12 or above – Fair

IV. Fill in the blanks with correct article a, an, the.

1. ......wheat grown in this area is of a good quality.
2. Is lead.....heavier than iron?
3. I like to have/eat.....apple daily.
4. This is .... cheque drawn on the Overseas Bank.
5. This is ....very fine picture.
6. ....murderer has been hanged.
7. She is .... honest lady.
8. All ...... letters have been stamped.
9. She will wait for you at .... cinema hall.
10. Make .... habit.
11. .... Quran is a holy book.
12. I have .... umbrella.
13. There is .... man outside of .... gate.
14. My father is .... doctor.
15. She is .... iron lady.
16. This is ...... book I was searching for yesterday.
17. Many ...... man works hard for their livelihood.
18. Be .... courageous person.
19. I saw .... fish in the net.
20. Rapidex English Conversation is ..... famous book.

Answers: 1. the, 2. nil, 3. an, 4. the, 5. a, 6. the, 7. an, 8. the, 9. the, 10. a, 11. the, 12. an, 13. a, the, 14. a, 15. an, 16. the, 17. a, 18. a, 19. a, 20. a.

Total Marks: 20

Scoring: 16 or above – Very good
12 or above – Fair

V. Fill in the blanks with the correct form of the words given in brackets in each sentence.

1. What is the cause of your .... (sad)?
2. His .... has turned grey though he is still young. (hairs).
3. This .... not enough (be).
4. Rama .... not get leave (do).
5. Your watch .... stopped (have).
6. There are more a dozen .... in the zoo (deer).
7. Has he .... your salary? (pay).
8. Let .... strike a bargain (we).
9. You can avoid .... mistakes (make).
10. Yesterday, I .... the letter in an hour and a half (write).
11. How many brothers do you .... (has)?
12. How many ...... (sheep) are there in the field?
13. She has not ...... (keep) her promise.
14. I ...... (enjoy) a lot yesterday.
15. Diwali .... (be) a big festival.
16. I .... (love) my India.
17. Children .... (be) playing in the field.
18. What is the ...... (grow) rate of your company?
19. Sorrow and .... (happy) are part of life.
20. We should .... (respect) our elders.

Answers: 1. Sadness, 2. hair, 3. is, 4. did, 5. has, 6. deer, 7. paid, 8. us, 9. making, 10. wrote, 11. have, 12. sheep, 13. kept, 14. enjoyed, 15. is, 16. love, 17. are, 18. growth, 19. happiness, 20. respect.

Scoring: 16 or above – Very good
12 or above – Fair

VI. Fill in the blanks with the words given. Chose the correct word.

for, into, of, in, by, with, to, from, besides, after, at, upon,

1. What was the judgement .... the case?
2. He is fond .... cycling.
3. The road is closed .... repairs.
4. Who will pay .... the repairs?
5. I fell.............his trap.
6. I am not short ....money.
7. Right .... his childhood, he has been very kind to others.
8. They will study German .... English.
9. Your coat is not similar .... mine.
10. The letter is sent .... post.
11. I prefer tea .... coffee.
12. You have to opt .... a subject.
13. .... how long, are you working here?
14. Birbal was a man .... intelligence and wit.
15. I have paid .... the meal.
16. My house is closed .... the station.
17. He threw flowers............ me.
18. What would you like to take .... curd?
19. .... you.
20. .... where are you coming?

Answers: 1. in, 2. of, 3. for, 4. for, 5. into, 6. of, 7. from, 8. besides, 9. to, 10. by, 11. to, 12. for, 13. for, 14. of, 15. for, 16. to, 17. upon, 18. besides, 19. After, 20. From.

Total Marks: 20

Scoring: 16 or above – Very good
12 or above – Fair

VII. Complete the following sentences with the help of proverbs given on page no 146.

1. An empty vessel makes ....
2. Society moulds ....
3. Union ....
4. As you sow, so ....
5. To the good, the ....
6. Too many cooks ....
7. A bad man is ....
8. Make hay while ....
9. Honesty is ....
10. Spare the rod ....
11. Penny wise ....
12. Birds of a feather ....
13. Strike while ....
14. Silence is ....
15. Look twice ....
16. Cut your coat ....
17. Diamond cuts ....
18. There is a black sheep ....
19. A friend in need...........
20. Rome was not...........

Answers: 1. much noise, 2. man, 3. is strength, 4. shall you reap, 5. whole world looks good, 6. spoil the broth, 7. better than a bad name, 8. the sun shines, 9. the best policy, 10. and spoil the child, 11. pound foolish, 12. fly together, 13. the iron is hot, 14. golden, 15. before you leap, 16. according to your cloth, 17. diamond, 18. in every society, 19. is a friend indeed, 20. built in a day.

VIII. Use the following idioms in your own sentences:

1. bag and baggage, 2. at daggers drawn, 3. die in harness, 4. on one's wit's end, 5. to sell like hot cakes, 6. turn over a new leaf, 7. poles apart, 8. all and sundry, 9. to eat humble pie, 10. To meet someone halfway, 11. put someone on one's mettle, 12. worth one's salt, 13. to make both ends meet, 14. within an ace of something, 15. won one's laurels, 16. with open arms, 17. turn a deaf ear, 18. by hook or by crook, 19. flesh and blood, 20. take exception.

IX. Correct the following sentences.

1. I **needs** to make a call.
2. She needs to **calling** her brother.
3. Do you **knew** Mr. Anand's mobile number.?
4. **Can** you have the number of the hospital?
5. What **are** your mobile number?
6. What **are** the S.T.D. code for London?
7. What number do I have **for** dial for tea?
8. What is **yours** extension number?
9. Hello, **I am** Gyan, speaking.
10. I'm speaking **in** Pustak Mahal, New Delhi.
11. **Are you** Mr. Anand?
12. Is Dr. Gulathi **talking**?
13. Hello, **who are you**?
14. **Do** I speak to Mr. Shahrukh?
15. **No, he** is **not** in the office.
16. **I don't knew.**
17. **He is not** available.
18. Who are you **talking**?
19. **Let me talk** to someone in the **Economics** Department.
20. Give me Mr. Lokesh' mobile number.

Test No - 10

Scoring: 16 or above – Very good
12 or above – Fair

X. Correct the following sentences.

1. This watch **costed** me eighty-seven rupees.
2. Give me 1 **kilo** sugar.
3. We are twenty **kilometre** from Bijnor.
4. He is over six **foot hight**.
5. It is **more than** 35°C.
6. It is their anniversary **three**.
7. I stood **one** in the class.
8. It is July **one** today.
9. He was born on **five** July, 1990.
10. **Which** date is it today?
11. **Which** day is it today?
12. I call her **all** Sunday.
13. She cooks food on **Sundays but not every Sunday**.
14. **On which** day is conference?
15. **Which** day **you will** leave?
16. She called me **one week before**.
17. I get up in the morning **on** 5 a.m.
18. He came to me **at 12 p.m.**
19. What is the time **in** your watch?
20. It is **five hour twenty minutes**.

Test No - 11

Total Marks: 20

Scoring: 16 or above – Very good
12 or above – Fair

XI. Correct the bold part in the following statements.

1. I **have cold**.
2. My back **pains**.
3. **I have stomach pain**.
4. I **am** sick.
5. I **am** better now.
6. I **got** an accident.
7. I fell **from** the stairs.
8. **His hands burnt**.
9. **I am feeling difficulty** to **breathe**.
10. **Her arm cannot bend**.
11. **It looks I have broken the arm**.
12. **Where** is hospital **here**?
13. **I want to take** an appointment.
14. **Where is the near dentist**?
15. **Which is this medicine**?
16. **Which** ambulance number do I call?
17. **What I say** to the pharmacist?
18. **How many times** do I take this medicine?
19. **When is his operation**?
20. **When I need to come** in hospital?

171

Test No - 12

XII. Correct the following statements:

1. I have to buy a camera for my daughter.
2. Give me a new umbrella.
3. Can you give me electric bulbs?
4. Is there any raincoat in your shop?
5. I need to want some exercise books.
6. I want to purchase two movie tickets.
7. I have to buy some chairs definitely.
8. I am planning to go to buy new shoes.
9. I am going to buying a new TV set.
10. I am going to think to go to the market.
11. I expect so.
12. According to me, this tie would go with blue shirt.
13. You do not need any more pens.
14. I am agreeing you.
15. What is your idea about these jeans?
16. How is this trouser in your opinion?
17. Which doll of these do you like?
18. How much cost is of this bottle?
19. In fact, I like mangoes very much.
20. I like more white cold drink.

Answers: 1. I need a camera for my daughter. 2. I need a new umbrella. 3. Do you sell electric bulbs? 4. Have you got rain coat? 5. I've to buy some exercise books. 6. I've to buy two tickets of the movie. 7. I must buy some chairs. 8. I'm going to buy a new pair of shoes. 9. I'm going to buy a new T.V. set. 10. I'm thinking of going to market. 11. I hope so. 12. I think this would go with blue shirt. 13. I don't think you need any more pens. 14. I agree with you. 15. What do you think of these pairs of jeans? 16. What do you think of these trousers? 17. Which one of these dolls do you like? 18. How much is this bottle? 19. I really like mangoes very much. 20. I prefer white cold drink.

172

31st Day

4th Expedition (Grammar)

Let us start our fourth expedition with greetings. In India, most commonly used greeting is **Namastay** or **Namaskaar**. Muslims say **Assalam 'alaykum** and Sikhs use **Sat Sri Akal**, etc. However in English language, different greetings are used based on different times.

Greetings in Spoken Language

From Dawn to 12 Noon–
1. Good morning, Grandpa!
2. Good morning, Dad!
3. Good morning, Sir!

From 12 to 5 p.m.–
4. Good afternoon, Grandpa!
5. Good afternoon, Mummy!
6. Good afternoon, Dear!

After 5 p.m.–
7. Good evening, Uncle!
8. Good evening, Auntie!
9. Good evening, Dear!

While going to bed at night–
10. Good night!
11. Sweet dreams!

After meeting somebody–
12. Pleased to meet you!

Any time with people of your rank–
13. Hi!, Hello! ('Hi' or 'Hello' can also be used with elders).

While parting with somebody–
15. Goodbye, children!
16. See you again.

173

17. Good day to you.
18. Bye, bye!
19. Farewell, dear!
20. Bye, see you later!

Points to Remember

1. 'Grandpa' is the short form of 'grandfather'.
2. 'Grandma' is the short form of 'grandmother'.
3. 'Dad' or 'Daddy' is used for 'father' in spoken language.
4. 'Mom' or 'Mummy' is used for mother in spoken language.
5. Uncle is commonly used for 'Chacha', 'Taya', 'Mausa', 'Phoopa', etc. Apart from these, the word 'uncle' can be used for any older person except father, grandfather, teacher, employer, boss, senior officers, brother, brother-in-law, etc. Similarly, the word 'Auntie' can be used for any older woman except mother, sister, grandmother, sister-in-law, senior officers, employers, boss, etc.
6. You can use the word 'uncle' for any unknown elder/older person to invite his attention. For example, you go astray. You can interrupt any elder person and ask him the way by saying, "Uncle, could you please tell me where this road leads to?" or "Uncle, what is the route to station, please?
7. You can also use the word 'Uncle' for the relatives of your wife or husband.
8. 'Aunt' 'Aunty' or 'Auntie' are different spellings of the same word.
9. 'Sir' can be used for any older person to show respect.
10. 'Madam' can be used for any woman to show respect.
11. 'Cousin' is used for uncle's son or daughter. 'Cousin brother' or 'Cousin sister' is wrong usage.
12. 'Mrs' is used for married woman, 'Miss' is used for unmarried woman. But if any woman does not want to show her marital status, she can use 'Ms'/miz/. It means, this title can be used for both married and unmarried women.

13. Besides Hindi, English, Urdu and Punjabi languages, there are varied equivalents of 'Namaste' in various states and Indian languages. They are as follows—

*   In Nagaland, Arunachal Pradesh and Meghalaya– '*Hello*' is used.
*   In Utterakhand, Uttar Pradesh, Madhya Pradesh, Chhattisgarh, Jharkhand, Haryana and Himachal Pradesh– '*Namastey*' is used.
*   In Jammu and Kashmir– '*Assalam alaykum*' is used.
*   In Punjab– '*Sat sri akal*' is used.
*   In Gujrat– '*Namastey*' is used.
*   In Rajasthan– '*Khammaghani*' is used.
*   In Maharashtra– '*Namaskar*' is used.
*   In Karnataka– '*Namaskara*' is used.
*   In Goa– '*Dev Boro Dis Dium*' is used.

*   In Bihar– '*Prannam*' is used.
*   In Keral– '*Namaskaram*' is used.
*   In Tamil Nadu– '*Vanakkam*' is used.
*   In Andhra Pradesh and Telangana– '*Namaskaram*' is used.
*   In Orissa– '*Namaskara*' is used.
*   In West Bangal and Tripura– '*Nomoshkara*' is used.
*   In Sikkim– '*Namaste*' is used.
*   In Assam– '*Nomoskaar*' is used.
*   In Manipur– '*Khurumjari*' is used.
*   And in Mizoram– '*Chibai, Ekhai*', is used.

●●

32nd Day

A

There are certain broad language-specific differences in English and Hindi. For example, in Hindi, we use 'ji' in general after any name, as– Pathakji, Gandhiji, Bhayaji, etc. In English, there is no equivalent of 'ji'. Similarly, in Hindi, we use 'Aap' 'Tum' or 'Vay', etc. But in English, there is only one word, i.e., 'you'. It does not mean that in English, there is no mannerism. It is there, but the way we express good manners in English is totally different from that of Hindi.

English people frequently use the following words to express their gratitude, humility and so on. These words are:

1. Please	5. Allow me	9. Pardon
2. Thanks	6. After you	10. That's all right
3. Welcome	7. Sorry	11. It's all my pleasure
4. Kindly	8. Excuse me	

1. 'Please' is used for making request. If you want to ask time, borrow something from somebody, give your consent and make some enquiry, etc., using 'please' is necessary. Dropping 'please' in the above cases is regarded as a very rude way of talking and full of vanity.

Polite way	**Impolite way**
1. Please give me your pen.	Give me your pen.
2. What's the time, please?	What's the time?
3. Please go ahead?	Go ahead.
4. Yes, please.	Yes.
(Replying somebody's question).	

2. (a) If somebody has done even a little favour to you – like, you asked somebody an address, or time and you get the answer, never forget to thank him/her saying **'Thanks'** or **'Thank you'**. You can say **'Thank you so much'** for greater emphasis.

(b) If somebody offers you something and you are not interested in taking that, don't say, **"I don't want to take."** Instead of that, say, **"No, thanks"**.

3. If you have done a favour to somebody and he says 'Thanks' to you, you need not remain silent. Say any one of the following words:

   1. No mention.
   2. It's fine.
   3. My pleasure.
   4. Welcome/You are welcome.

Remember, if you don't say any of the above phrases, you would be regarded as 'proud' or 'ill-mannered'.

4. If somebody borrows something from you and you want to give it, don't say **"Take it"** because this expression is somewhat rude. The proper and correct way is **"Yes, you are welcome"** or **"With great pleasure."**

5. If you want to help somebody, there is a different expression used on this occasion. For example, you want to help some elderly person lift a bag or you want a child to cross the road, say, **"Allow me."** or **"May I help you?"** **"What help can I offer?"**

6. While entering a room or crossing a road, we generally keep our olders or elders in the front position. In this case, you have to say **"After you,"** meaning, you would follow him/her.

177

7. Expressing grief in English is very common even on petty things. To do this, **"Sorry"**, **"Excuse me"** and **"Pardon"** are generally used.

(a) If you touch somebody's hand by mistake, say instantly **"Sorry"**.

(b) If you want to pass between two persons who are talking do that saying **"Excuse me"**. Similarly, you are sitting with some people and you have an urgent requirement of going somewhere, say **"Excuse me"** and go away.

(c) If you are on telephone line and the incoming voice is not clear, you say **"Pardon me"** or **"I am sorry"** rather than **"I can't hear you."**

(d) If you go to see somebody without prior information, don't enter the room or house without saying **"May I come in, please?"**

The reply will be, **"Yes, come in please,"** or **"With great pleasure"** or **"Of course"**.

Above are some of the expressions of good manners in English. We should keep them in mind while making conversation.

B

Some expressions expressing politeness:

1. I am sorry, I could not make it that day.
2. I am sorry, I could not make it in time.
3. I am sorry, I got a little late.
4. Please convey my apologies.
5. It was all by mistake. Please excuse me.
6. I am very sorry.
7. Sorry to have disturbed you.
8. I beg your pardon.
9. Allow me to say.
10. May I have your attention, please?
11. It's all yours.
12. Will you please permit me to speak?
13. Let me also help you.

14. Will you please move a bit?

15. Will you please speak slowly?

16. Will you mind speaking a bit softly?

17. Will you please let me sit?

18. Could you spare a few moments for me?

19. As you please.

20. Please make yourself comfortable.

21. Sorry for the inconvenience.

22. That is very kind of you.

23. Please help yourselves.

24. Glad to meet you.

25. Thank you for your valuable/kind advice.

26. I will try my level best.

27. Hope you are enjoying yourself/yourselves.

Points to Remember

A

1. In every country, there is a specific way to express mannerism and civility. In Hindi, 'ji' is added to names of elders to show respect. Sometimes, plural pronoun is used with singular noun for this very purpose. But in English, singular remains singular even if the pronoun is used for a highly respectable person, for example.

Hindi	**English**
Gandhiji hamare rashtrapita hain.	*Mr. Gandhi is our father of nation.*

2. In Hindi, there are different words for second person personal pronoun in nominative case, as Tu, Tum, Aap; but in English, there is only one word 'You'. For example:

(a) Tu Kahan gaya tha?	*Where did you go?*
(b) Tum Kahan gaye the?	*Where did you go?*
(c) Aap kahan gaye the?	*Where did you go?*

Similarly, plural number is used in Hindi for third person singular noun to show respect. For example:

Vay raat ko aa sakte hain.　　　　*He may come at night.*

B

To beg pardon, there are many expressions in English which are frequently used while making conversation. They are:

1. Excuse (V*) – *Excuse me.* (Simple and general way)
2. Forgive (V) – To remove from mind for ever the feelings of revenge.
3. Pardon (V) – To free somebody from the punishment got due to some mistake or fault.
4. Mistake (V) – Confusion or misunderstanding for somebody, e.g., *Please don't mistake me for his father.*
5. Sorry (adj) – To express grief, e.g., *Sorry for being late.*

Nowadays, '*I beg your pardon*' or just '*pardon*' is very common. People generally use this expression when they are not able to hear the incoming voice over phone properly. In that case, the meaning is '*please repeat, I can't hear.*'

*V– It stands for verb.

●●

33rd Day

Expressions	When to use
1. Marvellous!	to show admiration.
2. Well done!	to show admiration for the work done.
3. Beautiful!	to show admiration or praise.
4. Hey!	to attract attention; to show surprise, anger or interest.
5. Wow!	to express great admiration.
6. My God!	to show surprise plus annoyance.
7. Wonderful!	to show admiration.
8. Of course!	to show your consent.
9. Thank God!	to convey thanks to Almighty.
10. By God's grace!	to express kindness from Almighty.
11. May God bless you!	to give blessings to somebody.
12. Same to you!	to reciprocate what has been said!
13. Excellent!	to express great admiration.
14. How sad!	to express grief.
15. This is a good news!	to show happiness.
16. What a great victory!	to express joy and surprise.
17. Good heavens!	to show wonder.
18. Hello! listen!	to attract somebody's attention.
19. Hurry up, please!	to express urgency or shortness of time.

20. How terrible!	to express grief.
21. How disgraceful!	to express shame.
22. How absurd!	to show illogic and insensibility.
23. How dare he!	to express anger.
24. How sweet!	to express happiness.
25. How lovely!	to express admiration.
26. How dare you say that!	to express surprise with anger.
27. Oh dear!	to express love.
28. Quiet, please!	to express that you want silence.
29. Yes, it is!	to express confirmation.
30. Really!	to express wonder.
31. Is it!	to stress your consent or confirmation.
32. Thank God!	to thank Almighty.
33. Many happy returns of the day!	to congratulate somebody on his/her birthday.
34. Hurrah!	to express happiness.
35. Congrats/ Congratulations!	to congratulate somebody.
36. What nonsense!	to express anger.
37. What a pleasant surprise!	to show great surprise.
38. How tragic!	to express sorrow.
39. How disgusting!	to express disgust.
40. Beware!	to alert somebody.
41. What a pity!	to show sorrow.
42. What an idea!	to express surprise.
43. Welcome, Sir!	to greet somebody.
44. Cheers!	to express happiness while lifting up glass to drink.
45. Watch out!	to ask somebody to be alert.

46. Touchwood!	to avoid bringing bad luck.
47. Come what may!	to express 'no concern' for the result.
48. Hurry up!	to ask somebody to be fast.
49. Thanks! Thank you!	to show your obligation.
50. For your good health!	to wish somebody good health.
51. What a shame!	to show your dislike or disgust.
52. Wonderful!	to show wonder.
53. What a bother!	to show your worry/discomfort.

Points to Remember

1. Exclamatory sentences or expressions end with the mark of exclamation (!).
2. Affirmative sentences end with full stop.
3. Interrogative sentences end with the mark of interrogation (?).
4. Exclamatory sentences beginning with 'What' and 'How' end with 'Verb' for example–
   (i) What a beautiful building the Taj is!
   (ii) How beautiful the Taj is!
5. While speaking exclamatory sentences, there should be rise and fall in tone to express happiness, sorrow, surprise, etc.

●●

34th Day

Phrases and Command Sentences

A phrase is a group of words which does not have any verb and which has a particular meaning when used. In simple terms, phrases are incomplete sentences which convey full sense. We give, in this chapter, a list of phrases commonly used in day-to-day conversation. Learn them by heart and enjoy!

A

Phrases	Usage
1. Just coming!	I am just coming.
2. Very well!	You did your job very well.
3. Fine!	I am fine.
4. As you please/like.	Do as you please.
5. Anything else?	Do you need anything else?
6. That's enough?	Stop please, that's enough?
7. Thanks?	Thanks for your favour?
8. O.K.	Everything is O.K.
9. Why not?	"Can I join you?" "Why not?".
10. Not a bit.	Are you uncomfortable?" "Not a bit."
11. Take care.	Take care. Every thing will be O.K. soon.
12. See you tomorrow.	O.K., I leave. See you tomorrow!
13. By all means.	I will help you by all means.
14. That is too much.	That is too much. I cannot bear any more.
15. Yes, Sir!	"Did you attend the meeting?" "Yes, sir!"
16. No, not at all.	"Are you worried?" "No, not at all."
17. Never mind.	"I am obliged to you." "Never mind."

18. Does not matter.	"You have suffered much loss." "Does not matter."
19. Nothing else.	I need nothing else.
20. Nothing special.	"Is there anything special?" "Nothing special."
21. Welcome!	"Thank you very much." "Welcome!"
22. Rest assured!	"Would you please get me a ticket?" "Rest assured."
23. Long time no see!	"Long time no see. Perhaps he has left".
24. Goodbye!	Take care, sir! goodbye!
25. Not the least!	"Any problem?" "Not the least."
26. Exactly!	"Pollution is increasing day by day." "Exactly."
27. Anyway!	Anyway! you have to join your duty.
28. Last but not least!	Last but not least, today's children are tomorrow's nation builders.

B

Sentences of Command or Order

Though the sentences that follow are short but they are not phrases. These are Imperative or Command sentences which begin with a verb in most of the cases. Since the command is generally given to a person who is present before us, we don't mention him. So, the subject 'you' is understood. But when we want to give stress, we use 'you', for example–

(i) *Go to market.* (Here, 'you' can also send somebody else in his place.)

(ii) *You go to market.* (Nobody else would go except 'you'.)

Some Command Sentences

1. Stop here.
2. Speak loudly.
3. Listen to me.
4. Wait here.
5. Come here.
6. Look here.
7. Take it.
8. Go there.
9. Wait outside.
10. Go upstairs.
11. Come downstairs.
12. Get off.
13. Be ready/Get ready.
14. Keep quiet.
15. Be careful/Be cautious.
16. Go slowly/walk slowly.
17. Go at once.
18. Get away.
19. Chew thoroughly
20. Speak slowly.
21. Write beautifully.
22. Turn to the right.
23. Talk to him.
24. Post this letter.
25. Practise writing.
26. Read loudly.
27. Walk regularly in the morning.
28. Eat slowly.
29. Sit straight.
30. Call him in.
31. Go to market.
32. Be patient.
33. Show mercy.
34. Kill insects.
35. Wash your hands.
36. Drive carefully.
37. Aspire for success.
38. Compete with others.
39. Muster up courage.
40. Face challenges.
41. Go to bed.
42. Wake up.
43. Move fast.
44. Talk to me.
45. Offer your prayer.
46. Sit straight.
47. Have a nap.
48. Reply my question.
49. Roam around the city.
50. Contact him early.
51. Don't cheat anybody.
52. Be faithful.
53. Don't spit on the walls.
54. Wash your hands before meal.
55. Practise reading loudly.

56. Work hard.

57. Don't waste time.

58. Think before you talk.

59. Be punctual in your duty.

60. Don't postpone your work.

Points to Remember

1. All the sentences in group B are command sentences. They can be changed into request sentences just by putting 'please' before each sentence. For example–
   (i) Open the door. (command)
   (ii) Please open the door. (request)

2. When a request is made to a boss or senior official, 'kindly' is used in place of 'please'. For example—
   Kindly allow me leave for two days.

3. 'Don't' is the short form of 'Do not', 'Can't' is the short form of 'Cannot'. 'Cannot' is written one word. No space between 'Can' and 'not'.

4. 'For more information about command sentences, refer to 9th Day.

••

35th Day

Present Tense

In English language, there are twelve types of tense. The three basic tenses –Present, Past and Future– have been divided into four sub-types– Indefinite, Continuous, Perfect and Perfect Continuous. Today, we shall study Present Tense in detail.

A
Present Indefinite Tense

Affirmative
1. He reads a book.
2. She cooks food.
3. I play hockey.
4. They make a noise.

To show a simple truth or some habitual action or a simple statement.

Negative
5. He does not read a book.
6. She does not cook food.
7. I don't play hockey.
8. They don't make a noise.

Simple statement in the negative.

Interrogative (Simple)
9. Does he read a book?
10. Does she cook food?
11. Do I play hockey?
12. Do they make a noise?

Used just to get confirmation.

Interrogative (Double)
13. What does he read?
14. Where does she cook food?
15. How do I play hockey?
16. When do the boys make a noise?

Used to enquire about something.

B

Present Continuous Tense

(a)

Affirmative

1. He is playing hockey.
2. I am reading a book.
3. We are watching T.V.

To show an action, going on at the time of speaking.

Negative

4. He is not playing hockey.
5. I am not reading a book.
6. We are not watching T.V.

Used to show that action is not going on at the time of speaking.

Interrogative (Simple)

7. Is he playing hockey?
8. Am I reading a book?
9. Are we watching T.V.?

Used to get confirmation whether action is going on or not.

Interrogative (Double)

10. Where is he playing hockey?
11. Which book am I reading?
12. When are we watching T.V.?

Used to make enquiry about an action, going on at the time of speaking.

(b)

In the above examples, 'Is, Am, Are' have been used as Helping Verbs. These verbs are also used as Main Verbs as in the following examples–

Affirmative	*Negative*	*Interrogative*
1. I am a doctor.	I am not a doctor.	Am I a doctor?
2. He is a musician.	He is not a musician.	Is he a musician?
3. We are happy.	We are not happy.	Are we happy?
4. I am a student.	I am not a student.	Am I a student?
5. Raju is a clerk.	Raju is not a clerk.	Is Raju a clerk?
6. Birds are chirping.	Birds are not chirping.	Are birds chirping?

C

Present Perfect Tense

(a)

Affirmative

1. He has called me.
2. I have seen the Taj.
3. They have bought a car.

To show an action completed in the immediate past.

Negative

4. He has not called me.
5. I have not seen the Taj.
6. They have not bought a car.

To show an action that is not completed in the immediate past.

Interrogative (Simple)

7. Has he called me?
8. Have I seen the Taj?
9. Have they bought a car?

To confirm whether an action is completed in the immediate past.

Interrogative (Double)

10. Why has he called me?
11. When have I seen the Taj?
12. When have they bought a car?

To make an enquiry about some action which is completed in the immediate past.

(b)

In the above examples, 'Has, Have' are Helping Verbs. But these verbs are also used as Main Verbs as in the following examples–

Affirmative	*Negative*	*Interrogative*
1. He has a car.	He does not have a car.	Does he have a car?
2. I have a van.	I do not have a van.	Do I have a van?
3. They have a bus.	They do not have a bus.	Do they have a bus?
4. Rekha has a pen.	Rekha does not have a pen.	Does Rekha have a pen?
5. Pintu has a toy.	Pintu does not have a toy.	Does Pintu have a toy?

190

D

Present Perfect Continuous

Affirmative

1. She has been cooking food for four hours.
2. I have been reading a book since morning.
3. They have been playing hokey for three hours.

To show an action, which began at some time in the past and is still in progress.

Negative

4. She has not been cooking food for four hours.
5. I have not been reading a book since morning.
6. They have not been playing hockey for three hours.

Negative of the above action.

Interrogative (Simple)

7. Has she been cooking food for four hours?
8. Have I been reading a book since morning?
9. Have they been playing hockey for three hours?

Confirmation about the above action.

Interrogative (Double)

10. Who has been cooking food for four hours?
11. Why have I been reading a book since morning?
12. Where have they been playing hockey for three hours?
13. Why has he been washing clothes since morning?
14. Where have they been playing chess for two hours?
15. Who has been calling you for five minutes?
16. Why have they been sleeping on the road?

Enquiry about some action which began in the past and is still continuing.

Points to Remember

A 1. With third person, singular noun, s/es is added to the main verb. 2. With rest of the subjects, only 1st form of the main verb is used. 3. To make negative, does not/do not is used with 1st form of the main verb. 4. To make Interrogative, do/does is put before the subject. 5. To make Double Int., question word is put before do/does.

B 1. 'Is, am, are' are used with 'ing form' of the main verb. 'Am' is used with only 'I'. 2. 'Not' is added to is, am, are, to make negative. 3. To make Interrogative, 'Is, am, are' are put before sub. 4. To make Double Int., question words are put even before 'Is, am, are.

C 1. 'Has, Have' are used with 3rd form of the main verb. 'Has' is used with 3rd person singular only. 2. To make negative, 'does not/do not' is used after subject and 'have' is used as Main Verb. 3. To make Int., 'does/do' is put before the sub. 4. To make Double Int., question words are put even before 'Has'/'Have'.

D 1. 'Has been/have been' is used with 'ing form of the main verb'. For 'Point of time' 'Since' is used. For 'Period of time', 'for' is used in the end of the sentence. 2. To make negative, 'not' is used after 'has/have' and before 'been'. 3. To make Int., Has/Have is put before the sub. 4. To make Double Int, question words are put even before 'has/have'.

●●

36th Day

Past Tense

Just as Present Tense is divided into four sub-types, similarly past tense is. The four sub-types of Past Tense are: Past indefinite, Past Continuous, Past Perfect and Past Perfect Continuous. In this chapter, we will discuss them in detail.

A
Past Indefinite Tense

Affirmative
1. He flew a kite.
2. I flew a kit.
3. They flew kites.

To indicate an action completed in the past.

Negative
4. He did not fly a kite.
5. I did not fly a kite.
6. They did not fly kites.

To indicate an action, not completed in the past.

Interrogative (Simple)
7. Did he fly a kite?
8. Did I fly a kite?
9. Did they fly kites?

To confirm an action, completed in the past.

Interrogative (Double)
10. When did he fly a kite?
11. Where does she cook food?
12. How do I play hockey?
13. Who did break this plate?
14. Where did she dance?
15. Who did announce my name?
16. Why did you open the door?
17. How did they finish their work?

To enquire something about an action, completed in the past.

B
Present Continuous Tense

Affirmative

1. He was playing cricket.
2. I was doing my work.
3. They were flying kites.

To indicate an action going on at some time in the past. The time of action may or may not be indicated.

Negative

4. He was not playing cricket.
5. I was not doing my work.
6. They were not offering prayers.

To indicate an action not completed in the negative past.

Interrogative (Simple)

7. Was he playing cricket?
8. Was I doing my work?
9. Were they offering prayers?

Confirmation about an action going on at some time in the past.

Interrogative (Double)

10. How was he playing cricket?
11. How was I doing my work?
12. When were they offering prayers?

Enquiry about some going-on action in the past.

C
Past Perfect Tense

Affirmative

1. He had eaten food.
2. She had cooked food.
3. I had tasted food.

To indicate an action completed before a certain moment in the past.

Negative

4. He had not eaten food.
5. She had not cooked food.
6. I had not tasted food.

To indicate the above situation in the negative.

194

Interrogative (Simple)

7. Had he eaten food?
8. Had she cooked food?
9. Had they distributed food?
10. Had I tasted food?

⎤ To confirm about something or regarding an action in the above situation.

Interrogative (Double)

11. When had he eaten food?
12. Where had she cooked food?
13. How had they distributed food?
14. Why had I tasted food?

⎤ To enquire about an action in the above situation.

D

Past Perfect Continuous Tense

Affirmative

1. He had been ringing the bell for five minutes.
2. She had been singing a song since 2 o'clock.
3. They had been running about for ten minutes.

⎤ To indicate an action that began before a certain point in the past and continued upto that time.

Negative

4. I had not been teaching her since 2015.
5. They had not been living here for two years.
6. The children had not been solving sums since morning.
7. He had not been searching for the job for a month.
8. I had not been playing cricket since 2017.

⎤ Above situation in the negative.

195

Simple & Double Interrogative

9. Had he been playing cricket for
   two hours?
10. What had they been doing
    since morning?
11. How had she been washing
    clothes in cold water for two days?
12. Had you been driving the car
    since last night?
13. Who had been calling you
    for three days?
14. Why had he been writing letters
    to her for a month?
15. Had she been practising cooking
    for a year?

Confirmation and enquiry
in the above situation.

Points to Remember

1. In this tense, only 'had been' is used with all kinds of subjects, belonging to any person or number. Rest points are the same, i.e., 'ing form' of verb and since/for in the end.

2. If two actions happened in the past, it is necessary to show which action happened earlier than the other. The past perfect is for latter action. For the former action, Past Indefinite is used.

   (a) The patient had died before the doctor came.
       Past Perfect   Past Indefinite

   (b) The doctor came after the patient had died.
       Past Indefinite   Past Perfect

••

37th Day

Future Tense

Future Tense is also divided into four sub-types, i.e. Future Indefinite, Future Continuous, Future Perfect and Future Perfect Continuous. Future tense indicates time which is to come.

A

Future Indefinite Tense

Affirmative

1. He will run.
2. She will weep.
3. I shall dance.
4. We shall travel.

> Used to talk about things we think or believe will happen in the coming time.

Negative

5. He will not fly a kite.
6. I shall not fly a kite.
7. They will not fly kites.

> Used to talk about future events in the negative.

Interrogative (Simple)

8. Will he fly a kite?
9. Shall I fly a kite?
10. Will they fly kites?

> Used to confirm events to be taken place in future.

Interrogative (Double)

11. When will he fly a kite?
12. Where will she cook food?
13. How shall I play hockey?
14. Why will you buy a car?
15. Who will purchase your sofa?
16. Where shall we reach in the evening?

> Used to enquire something about an action to be completed in future.

B

Future Continuous Tense

Affirmative

17. He will be running.
18. She will be weeping.
19. I shall be dancing.
20. We shall be travelling.

Used to talk about actions which will be in progress at a time in the future.

Negative

21. He will not be running.
22. She will not be weeping.
23. I shall not be dancing.
24. We shall not be travelling.

Used in the above situation in the negative.

Interrogative

25. Will he be running?
26. Will she be weeping?
27. Shall I be dancing?
28. Shall we be travelling?

Used to confirm or enquire about something in the above situation.

C

Future Perfect Tense

Affirmative

1. He will have run.
2. She will have wept.
3. I shall have danced.
4. We shall have travelled.

Used to talk about actions that will be completed by a certain future time.

Negative

5. He will not have run.
6. She will not have wept.
7. I shall not have danced.
8. We shall not have travelled.

Used in the above situation in the negative.

9. Will he have run?
10. Will he have wept?
11. Shall I have danced?
12. Shall we have travelled?

Used to confirm something in the above situation.

D

Future Perfect Continuous Tense

Affirmative

1. He will have been running since next morning.
2. She will have been weeping by noon.
3. I shall have been dancing by 10 o'clock.
4. We shall have been travelling by evening.

Used for actions which will be in progress over a period of time in future.

Negative

5. He'll not have been running since next morning.
6. She'll not have been weeping by noon.
7. I shall not have been dancing by 10 o'clock.
8. We shall not have been travelling by evening.
9. He will not have been eating food by 12 midnight.
10. I shall not have been doing the job by next month.

Used in the above situation in the negative.

11. Will he have been running since next morning?

12. Will she have been weeping by noon?

13. Shall I have been dancing by 10 o'clock?

14. Shall we have been travelling by evening?

15. Will he have been eating food by 12 midnight?

16. Shall I have been doing the job by the next month?

17. Shall we have been travelling since morning by next week?

Used to confirm about something in the above situation.

Points to Remember

1. In this tense, two helping verbs– will and shall– are used 'Shall' is used only with first person pronouns. With second and third person pronoun, 'will' is used.

2. First form of the main verb is used with 'will' and 'shall' in Indefinite Tense.

3. In continuous of future, 'will be/shall be + ing form' is used.

4. In Future Perfect, 'will have/shall have + 3rd form of the main verb' is used.

5. In Future Perfect Continuous, 'will/shall have been + ing form' is used. 'Since' or 'for' as per the demand.

●●

38th Day

—Can—

Rajni	:	Can you play sitar?
Shashi	:	Yes, I can play the flute as well.
Rajni	:	Can you return my books?
Shashi	:	No, I cannot return them yet.
Rajni	:	Can you read Sanskrit?
Shashi	:	Yes, I can?

—May—

Student	:	May I come in, sir?
Teacher	:	Yes, you may.
Student	:	May I attend Bal Sabha, sir?
Teacher	:	Yes, with great pleasure/of course.
Student	:	May I accompany Suresh?
Teacher	:	No, you better finish your work first.

—Could—

Raju	:	Could you do this work alone?
Suresh	:	No, I couldn't.
Raju	:	Could she help you in time?
Suresh	:	Yes, she could.
Raju	:	Could you bring me a glass of water?
Suresh	:	With pleasure.

—Might, Must, Ought to, Would/Should—

1. Sohan might have helped him.
2. He might have come here.
3. I must attend his marriage.
4. I must reach home by 10 o'clock.
5. We ought to love our youngers.
6. Would you post this letter, please?
7. You should attend the class more regularly.
8. I would go to my teacher's house daily.
9. She might drop in anytime.
10. Children ought to obey elders.

Points to Remember

1. *(a) Can I walk?*   *(a) May I walk?*
   (b) Can you do this job?   *(b) May I do this job?*
   (c) Can you sing a song?   *(c) May I sing a song?*
   In sentences of 'Can', there is a show of power or capacity to do something. In sentences using 'may', there is a sense of permission or will. 'Can' is also used for seeking permission. People sometimes use 'Can' in the sense of 'may'. It is permissible informally only.

2. 'Could' is the past form of 'Can'. 'Could' is generally used in making request or to show politeness. 'Might' is the past form of 'may'. Might is used in showing possibility. 'Would' is the past form of 'will' but is used extensively to show strong obligation, advice or moral value. 'Must' is stronger in meaning than 'Should' and 'Ought to'.

3. To show past of 'must', use 'had to'. Past of 'Should' is 'should have + 3rd form'. Past of 'ought to' is 'ought to have + 3rd form of the main verb'. For example–
   (a) I must go. — I had to go.
   (b) I should go. — I should have gone.
   (c) I ought to go. — I ought to have gone.

39th Day

Sentences of Order and Request

We give below some sentences based on order or request. These types of sentence are called Imperative sentences. No tense, out of the twelve, which we discussed in the earlier days, is used in these sentences. However, these sentences start with first form of the main verb or action words in most of the cases. So, read them carefully and practise them.

Sentences of Order

1. Look ahead.
2. Go straight.
3. Drive slowly.
4. Hold your tongue.
5. Mind your own business.
6. Come here.
7. Shut the door.
8. Open the window.
9. Turn/switch on the fan.
10. Turn/switch off the light.
11. Read the book.
12. Show me your Report Card.
13. Chew you food thoroughly.
14. Be ready.
15. Pack up your luggage.
16. Move a little.
17. Sit down.
18. Wait here.
19. Ring the bell.
20. Clean the room.
21. Wash your hands.
22. Go to bed.
23. Wake up early.
24. Brush your teeth.
25. Tell me a story.

26. Speak the truth.
27. Save your time.
28. Comb your hair.

Prohibitory Sentences

29. Don't play on the road.
30. Don't waste your time.
31. Don't tease your neighbours.
32. Don't look down upon the poor.
33. Don't backbite others.
34. Don't create indiscipline.
35. Don't enter somebody's house without permission.
36. Don't be dishonest in dealings.
37. Don't back down from your promises.
38. Don't make a noise.
39. Don't tell a lie.
40. Don't trust an unknown person.
41. Don't deceive anybody.
42. Don't help the oppressor.
43. Don't insult elders.
44. Don't spit on the wall.
45. Don't beat about the bush.

Request or Suggestion in Imperative Sentences

46. Please bring me a glass of water.
47. Please tell me your address.
48. Please help me.
49. Please tell me the way to the bus stand.
50. Please put your hands together for Mr. Munib.
51. Please check me up.
52. Please sit down.
53. Please open the door.
54. Let him tell his story.
55. Let them cook the food.

56. Let them enjoy in the party.
57. Let bygone be bygone.
58. Let me explain it to you.
59. Let me solve the puzzle.
60. You should serve you parents.
61. Let not anger overcome you.
62. Let not beggars be rebuked.
63. Let not children enter that premises.
64. Let promises be kept.
65. Let water be saved.

Points to Remember

1. You have seen that when 'is, am, are, was, were, will, shall, can, could, may' come in the beginning of a sentence, the sentence becomes interrogative and when these Helping verbs come after subject, the sentence becomes Assertive.

<u>Interrogative</u>	<u>Assertive</u>
Is he a batsman?	*He is a batsman.*
Are you going to market?	*You are going to market.*
Shall we stay here?	*We shall not stay here.*

2. In Imperative sentences, main verb comes in the beginning of a sentence in most of the cases.

   Stand up.   *Sit down.*   *Look here.*   *Be silent.*

3. In Imperative sentences, generally the subject is not mentioned because it is understood. 'Request is made or order is generally given to a person who is before our eyes. And because he/she is in our mind, we don't mention them.

4. Sometimes, 'please' is added before the main verb to make the request polite.

   For example,   *Please come here. Please sit down.*

●●

40th **Day**

You want to be able to speak English fluently and correctly. We also wish you the same. For this purpose, we would like to give you some valuable pieces of advice. Follow them and you would surely be able to speak English fluently, correctly and effectively.

1. Make a friend. Read the sentences given in this book carefully. Also follow the instructions given along. Starting conversation can be made in the form of question-answer. In this stage, there would occur mistakes as well. But don't get disheartened. Tell your friend's mistakes and try to improve them mutually. Gradually, the mistakes become less and your speaking will improve.

2. Sit before a mirror in order to practise. Speak again and again with correct pronunciation and your confidence will boost up.

3. In this chapter, some exercise tables are given for self-test. By doing them, you will find your confidence increased and your knowledge will also enhance. In this way, you yourself can find out what and how much you have gained.

Table-1

1	2	3
He She	is	ready.
I	am	hungry.
They You We	are	thirsty. tired.

Table-2

1	2	3
He She I	was	rich. poor.
They You We	were	pleased. sorry.

(i) With the help of Table-1 and Table-2, form 24 sentences from each. Then speak them and explain their meanings to your friend.

(ii) In the above tables, there are 48 affirmative sentences. Now, you have to change them into negative. How will you do that? For this, add 'not' after verbs 'is, am, are, was, were'. For example–
- He is not ready.
- They are not thirsty.
- She is not ready.
- We are not tired.

(iii) Similarly, you have to change sentences from table-2 into interrogative.

Table-3

1	2	3
The boy His friends	did not can may must not ought should will cannot	use this train. do as I say. go for hunting. enter the cave.

In Table-3, 64 sentences have to be formed. Form them, speak them out to your frined and practise them.

Table-4

	1	2
1.	Be	day after tomorrow?
2.	Go	Sanskrit?
3.	Have you written	Ramesh, Sir?
4.	Did you wake up	this problem?
5.	Will you come	at once.
6.	Can you read	to Radha?
7.	May I accompany	early yesterday?
8.	Could Rana solve	your own business.
9.	Mind	ready.
10.	Don't come	before me.

Match the two columns in Table-4 and form complete sentences.

Exercise for Practice

31st Day

1. There are some mistakes in the following sentences. Remove them and practise sentences.

(a) Good night uncle, how are you? (6 p.m.)

(b) Is he your cousin brother?

(c) She is not my cousin sister.

(d) Good afternoon, my son. (9 a.m).

(e) Good morning, mother. (2 p.m.)

2. Read the following sentences and improve them.

(a) Gandhji was a famous artist.

(b) Pushpaji is a great actor.

(c) Babaji was now 70 years old.

(d) Kumarji lives in Noida last year.

(e) Soniyaji was Italian by birth.

(f) Modiji is our prime ministers.

3. Let us revise some sentences based on manners.

(a) If you visit somebody and they entertain you well, you should say, **"Thanks for your hospitality."**

(b) Now read the following sentences:

"I am very grateful to you." "I shall be very grateful to you." "You have been a great help."

You will find that the above sentences are all different. Now, see which sentence should come where. If you ask for somebody's favour, and he/she does that, you should say, **"I am very grateful."** When you want to thank somebody in advance even when the favour has not been done, then you should say, **"I shall be highly obliged to you"**, or **"I shall be very grateful to you."**

(c) If somebody praises you in your presence, stop him by saying, "Oh, I don't deserve this praise."

4. Look at these words– (a) God, gods; (b) good, goods. These are two pairs. They seem to be identical but they are totally different from each other. 'God' is the divine creator of the universe whereas 'gods' are many human beings endowed with supernatural powers. They are all different in different religions and sects. 'Good' is an adjective which describes the quality of something but 'goods' is lugguage.

Now, you have to consult a dictionary and find out the difference between the following pairs of words:

(a) Artisan, artist   (b) Couple, pair

(c) Farmer, former   (d) Beside, besides

(e) Alter, altar   (f) Affect, effect

5. Try to understand the correct usage of the following words:
Nasty, Woe, Hello, Hurrah, Alas, Bravo, Welldone.

6. Look at these expressions– (a) Well begun, half-done. (b) To err is human; to forgive, divine. (c) Thank you. (d) Just coming. These expressions seem to be incomplete sentences. There is no verb in (a) and (b), no subject in (c) and (d). Such types of sentence are used in spoken language and are called **elliptical** sentences.

7. In the 4th Day, there is an elliptical sentence "Just coming", i.e., I am coming shortly or without delay. Now, this sentence also conveys a different meaning, i.e. "He is coming shortly." How? suppose, a guest visits your house and he asks about you father who is inside. You go to him and informs him that so and so has come and he asks about you. Your father says, "I am just coming". Now you return to the guest and says, "Just coming" meaning "He is just coming."

Read the following sentences carefully–

(i) You speak English. (ii) Do you speak English? The first sentence is positive and the second one is Interrogative. We see that the Interrogative sentence was made by adding a helping verb 'do' before the subject. **Now, by adding 'do' 'does' and 'did', change the following sentences into interrogative.**

(1) You go to school. (2) She cooks tasty food. (3) He dances swiftly. (4) The children play cricket. (5) I like swimming very much. (6) My mother prepared tea for me. (7) The school opened on Monday. (8) The tailor sewed my shirt. (9) She gave me a pen. (10) I love you.

(Note) When we make Interrogative sentence, the main verb always come in the first form in the above sentences. Interrogative sentences always end with Question Mark (?).

There are 24 Helping verbs in English– 'do, does, did, is, am, are, was, were, has, have, had, will, shall, would, should, may, might, can, could, must, ought (to), need, dare, used to.' First 13 verbs are used in Tense. You have used them in standards V, VI and VII. You have studied 'don't' 'would' 'should' 'could' 'might' in standard VIII. Why are these verbs called, Helping verbs? They are called 'Helping verbs' because these verbs help the main verb in different tenses. Helping verbs come before the main verbs. If the affirmative sentences are to be changed into negative, we use 'not' after the helping verb and before the main verb.

Change the following affirmative sentences into negative:

(1) He is playing football. (2) Karina is singing a song. (3) He has completed his work. (4) My mother has ironed the clothes. (5) Ashwini, Natasha and Mohini have shown their projects to me. (6) I shall go to Australia next week. (7) My father will come to see me. (8) We shall go to Shimla in the summer vacations. (9) The principal may go on the round after 2 p.m. (10) Tripti can prepare delicious food in no time.

Answers to questions can be given in two ways – a complete answer and a short answer. For example–

Q. Do you like coffee?

Ans. Yes, I like coffee. (Complete answer)

Yes, I do. (Short answer)

Now read the following questions and answer them in complete and short way:

Q 1. Do you like English?

Q 2. Can you help me?

Q 3. Have you visited the Taj Mahal?

Q 4. Does your brother love photography?

Q 5. Should we follow our elders?

Q 6. Can you solve this sum?

Q 7. Does Ramesh take regular intake of protein?

Q 8. Is your mother quite well now?

Q 9. Can you hear me?

Q 10. May the doctor be available now?

(Note)– In conversation, we should use short answers. The benefit is that we save both time and energy. It also sounds good to ears because in complete answer, some words from the question are repeated, and repetition is not considered to be good.

●●

41st Day

5th Expedition (Grammar Contd...)

You have completed one expedition in 10 days. During this period, you learnt about basic things of spoken English which are very important for every learner to know in order to become a proficient English speaker.

Now, in this second expedition, you will learn some basic knowledge about the English Alphabet and some of its characteristics, pronunciation of words, formation of Negative and Interrogative sentences, etc.

Alphabet of Roman Script

English is written in Roman Script. It has 26 letters in all. These letters are written in two ways– Printing and writing– either in Capitals or Small letters. In this way, the letters can be divided into four–

(a) Printing Capital   (ABCDEFG)

   Printing Small   (abcdefg)

(b) Writing Capital   *(A B C D E F G)*

   Writing Small   *(a b c d e f g)*

Roman script is very stylish in writing. These letters are written within the domain of four lines. Capital letters are written only in the three upper lines and such letters are called Ascenders.

Small letters, on the other hand, are written in different lines. They are divided into four types:

(i)   Ascenders (6)   (ii) Descenders (5)

(iii) X-height (13)   (iv) Full length (2)

213

Ascenders

b d h k l t

Descenders

g j q y z

X-heights

a c e i m n o r s u v w x

Full lengh

f p

Beautiful handwriting is also a good thing to practise. It is said that writing is the mirror of one's personality. In case of English, it is very easy to improve handwriting. The only requirement is a copy of four lines and the 'will' to improve. With regular practice, every thing is possible. Practice makes a man perfect.

Now, we give below the capital letters in writing style. This is also called cursive style.

A B C D E F G H I J K L

M N O P Q R S T U

V W X Y Z

Small letters in printing style.

a b c d e f g h i j k l m n o p q r s t

u v w x y z

Capital letter in printing style

A B C D E F G H I J K L M N O P Q R S T

U V W X Y Z

Points to Remember

1. Capital letters are used in the beginning of a sentence, in abbreviations and acronyms. Proper nouns (names of persons, places or things) are also written with first capital letter.
2. First person singular pronoun 'I' is always written in capital whether it is in the beginning, middle or end of a sentence.
3. Each fresh line of a poem is written with capital letter.
4. Adjectives derived from proper nouns are written with capital letter, e.g., Indian, African, American, Shakespearian, etc.
5. All nouns and pronouns used for Diety, e.g, The Lord, Lord Budha, Lord Krishna, etc.
6. The interjection 'O' or 'Oh' is written with capital letter.
7. A good handwriting makes you attractive. So, practise until your handwriting becomes beautiful and effective.
8. Handwriting reflects your personality. So make your handwriting not only legible but also beautiful with constant practice and patience.

●●

42nd Day

Vowels and Consonants in English

There are five vowels and twenty-one consonants in English. A, E, I, O, U are representatives of vowel sound and the rest are consonants. It is important to know their difference.

Pronunciation of English Letters

Letter	Pronunciation	Example	Letter	Pronunciation	Example
A	/ei/	Apple	N	/en/	New
B	/biː/	Book	O	/əu/	Orange
C	/siː/	Cement	P	/piː/	Parrot
D	/diː/	Doll	Q	/kjuː/	Quality
E	/iː/	English	R	/aː(r)/	Rose
F	/ef/	Fan	S	/es/	Solution
G	/dʒiː/	Gel	T	/tiː/	Tooth
H	/eich/	Horse	U	/juː/	Union
I	/ai/	Ice	V	/viː/	Value
J	/dʒei/	Jug	W	/dʌbljuː/	We
K	/kei/	Kettle	X	/eks/	Xmas
L	/el/	Lemon	Y	/wɑɪ/	Yes
M	/em/	Money	Z	/zed/	Zero

Important combinations: There are certain sounds which take two or more letters but the sound is single.

th = /θ/ and /ð/ as think and then
ph = /f/ as phone and philosophy
sh = /ʃ/ as show and shine

216

gh = /f/ as rough and tough

ck = /k/ as black and back

cae, ce, cy = /si/ as caesarean, cement, cycle

ch = /tʃ/ as church

ge = /dʒ/ as gel and gem

ca, co, cu, = /k/ as camel, coin, cucumber, etc.

In almost all the English words beginning with 'Q', 'U' comes immediately after 'q', e.g., opaque, oblique, etc. However, non-Englsih words don't take 'u'.

Example: Qazi, Qari, Qanoon, Qayamat, etc.

Points to Remember

1. In English, c, k and q are used for the sound /k/. Sometimes 'ck' is also used for /k/ sound. 'C' is also pronounced as /s/.
2. For /g/ sound, 'g' is used whereas for /dʒ/ sound, 'j' is used. But 'g' is also pronounced as /dʒ/, as *germ*.
3. For /vi:/ sound, both 'v' and 'w' are used as – *very, wall*.
4. For /f/ sound, 'f', 'ph' and 'gh' are used as – *fox, phone, rough*.

●●

43rd Day

People are generally heard committing mistakes in the pronunciation of English words. There are some rules and regulations in this regard. So, read the following points carefully.

Pronunciation of 'A'

A /əe/ as in At, An, Lad, Man, Mad, Stand, Ban, etc.
A /ɔ:/ as in All, Wall, Fall, War, Call, Small, etc.
A /a:/ as in Far, Are, Bar, Car, Jar, Small, etc.
A /eə/ as in Ware, Care, Fare, Dare, Share, etc.
A /ei/ as in Pay, Way, Stay, Gay, Brain, Main, etc.
A /ə/ as in About, Around, Arouse, Aside, etc.

Pronunciation of 'E'

E /e/ as in Net, Men, Sell, Well, Beg, Then,Wet, etc.
E /i/ as in He, She, We, Be, etc.
E /i:/ as in Bee, See, Weep, Sleep, Meet, Sweet, etc.
E /i:/ as in Clean, Sea, Heat, Meat, etc.

If 'E' comes in the end of a word, it has no sound of its own. If a word ends with 'e', and before 'e' there is or are any consonants which are preceded by any vowel, that vowel sound is elongated. For example–
Fine, Ripe, Bite, Kite
Rule, Route, Rude, Mute
Nose, Hope, Joke, Smoke, but no sound of 'e' in words Name, Lame, Came, Same, etc.
Ew/ju:/ as in Few, Jew, New, Dew, Mew, etc.

Pronunciation of 'I'

I /i/ as in Ill, Kill, Big, With, Ink, Ship, etc.

I /ai/ as Kind, Behind, Bind, Mind, Mike, Mile, etc.

If I is followed by 'gh', the pronunciation of 'I' will be/ai/, as–Right, Fight, Night, Sight, etc.

I /ə/ as in Firm, First, Irk, etc.

I /aiə/ as in Fire, admire, Dire, Expire, etc.

I /i:/ as in Receive, Conceive, Brief, Siege, etc.

Pronunciation of 'O'

O /ɒ/ as in On, Ox, Fox, Hot, Pot, Spot, Top, Drop, Dot, Soft, Not, God, Got, etc.

O /əu/ as in Open, So, Hope, No, Old, Gold, Home, Most, Joke, Post, etc.

O /u/ as in Look, Book, Took, Foot, Good, Hood, Stood, etc.

O /u:/ as in Room, Roof, Moon, Noon, Boot, Do, Root, etc.

O /ʌ/ as in Son, Come, Canon, None, etc.

O /əu/ as in How, Now, Cow, Bow, Row, Low, Mow, etc.

O /ɔi/ as in Joy, Boy, Toy, Coy, Employ, Destroy, etc.

O /auə/ as in Hour, Our, Sour, etc.

Pronunciation of 'U'

U /ʌ/ as in Up, Cup, Hut, Mud, Fun, Sun, etc.

U /u/ as in Put, Pull, Push, Bush, etc.

U /ju:/ as in Duty, Durable, Duration, Cute, Fume, Huge, Human, Humour, Curious, Mute, etc.

U /uə/as in Sure, Pure, Lure, etc.

Pronunciation of 'Y'

Y /i/ as in Playing, Policy, Felony, Many, Carry, etc.

Y /aiə/ as in Tyre, Byre, Flyer, etc.

In the above examples, you see that the same letter has different sound patterns. This can only be mastered gradually by listening to radio, television and by consulting dictionary.

Silent Letters

Silent letters are written but not ponounced, as 'l' calm/ ka:m/.

Silent 'A'

Caesar: Roman Emperor.

Caecum: A small bag which is part of small intestine.

Caesarean: A medical operation in which an opening is cut is a woman's body.

Haemoglobin: A red substance in the blood that carries oxygen and contains iron.

Haematite: A dark red rock from which iron is obtained.

Encyclopaedia: A book or set of books containting detailed information on a subject.

Aegis: Protection.

Aeolian: Connected with or caused by the action of wind.

Aeon: Extremely long period of time.

Aesthete: A person who has love and understanding of art and beautiful things.

Silent 'B'

Crumbs: Very small pieces of loaf, etc.

Indebted: Grateful to somebody for helping you.

Plumber: One who fits and repairs water pipes, toilets, etc.

Succumb: Unable to fight or attack.

Comb: A flat piece of plastic with a row of thin teeth.

Debt: A sum of money that somebody owes.

Silent 'C'

Science: Knowledge about the structure and functioning of something.

Scenario: Description of how things might happen in future.

Scene: The place where something happens.

Scent: Pleasant smell.

Schedule: A plan of things to be happened.

Scissors: A tool for cutting paper or cloth.

Silent 'D'

Budget: Money that is available and a plan how and when to be used.

Budgie: A small bird of parrot family.

Budge: To move slightly.

Midget: An extremely small person.

Cudgel: A short thick stick used as a weapon.

Edge: Opposite limit of an object.

Edgy: Nervous especially about what might happen.

Fidget: To keep moving your body.

Gadget: A small tool or device.

Silent 'G'

Benign: Gentle and kind.

Design: A general arrangement of different parts of somethings.

Malign: To say bad things about somebody publicly.

Resign: To officially tell somebody that you are leaving your job.

Sign: An event or action that shows that something exists.

Silent 'H'

Honour: Respect.

Honorary: Given as an honour.

Honest: Always telling the truth.

Hour: Period of 60 minutes.

Silent 'K'

Knife: A sharp blade with a handle.

Knock: To hit a door firmly to get attention.

Knight: A man of high social rank.

Knit: To stitch.

Knob: A round switch on a machine or handle.

Knoll: A small round hill.

Knot: A joint made by tying together two pieces of cord or rope.

Know: To have information in your mind.

Knuckle: Any of the joints in the finger.

Silent 'L'

Alms: Money or clothes given to poor people.
Balm: Oil with a pleasant smell.
Calm: Not excited or nervous.
Talk: To speak or converse.
Walk: To move or go somewhere.
Balk: To be unwilling to do something

Silent 'M'

Mnemonik: A word, sentence, poem, etc that helps you remember something.

Silent 'N'

Column: A tall, solid, vertical post.
Autumn: Season when leaves change colour.
Condemn: To express very strong disapproval.
Solemn: Of a person, not happy or similing.
Hymn: Song praising God.

Silent 'O'

Colonel: An officer of high rank in army.

Silent 'P'

Psyche: The mind.
Psoriasis: Skin disease that causes rough red areas where the skin comes off in small pieces.
Psalm: A song or poem that praises God.
Psephology: The study of how people vote in elections.
Pseud: A person who pretends to know a lot about a particular subject.
Corps: A large unit of any army.
Coup: A sudden change of government that is illegal and violent.
Pneumonia: A serious illness affecting one or both lungs that makes breathing difficult.
Receipt: A piece of paper that shows that goods have been paid for.

Silent 'R'

Iron: A chemical element.

Irk: To annoy somebody.

World: The earth with all its countries, peoples and natural features.

Word: A single unit of language which means something.

Turn: To move or make something move around a central point.

Term: A word or phrase used as the name of something.

Terminal: A place where journeys begin or end.

Silent 'S'

Isle: Used specially in poetry, meaning island.

Aisle: A passage between rows of seets in a church, train, etc.

Debris: Pieces of wood, metal, brick, etc that are left after destruction.

Apropos: Concerning or related to sb.

Bourgeois: Belonging to the middle class.

Silent 'T'

Asthma: A medical condition of the chest that makes breathing difficult.

Ballet: A style of dancing that tells a dramatic story with music.

Castle: A large, strong building with thick high walls and towers.

Gourmet: A person who knows a lot about good food and enjoys.

Listen: To pay attention to what somebody says.

Rapport: A friendly relationship in which people understand each other very well.

Ricochet: To hit a surface and come off it fast at a different angle.

Soften: To become or make something softer.

Silent 'U'

Colleague: A person that you work with.

Guess: To try and give an answer.

Guard: A person who protects a person or place.

Guide: A book or magazine or person that gives you information.

Guilt: The unhappy feelings caused by knowing or thinking that you have done something wrong.

Guitar: A musical instrument that usually has six strings that you play with your fingers.

Guinea: A British gold coin.

Tongue: The soft part in the month that moves around when speaking.

Silent 'W'

Answer: Something that you say to a question.

Sword: A weapon with a long metal blade.

Two: Number which comes before three and after one.

Pillow: A square piece of cloth filled with soft material to rest your hand on.

Whole: Complete.

Wrist: The joint between the hand and the arm.

Writ: A legal document.

Write: To make numbers or letters on paper using a pen or pencil.

Silent 'X'

Faux Pas: An action or remark that causes embarrassment because it is socially incorrect.

Faux: Artificial but intended to look or seem real.

Silent 'Z'

Rendezvous: Place where people have arranged to meet.

Points to Remember

The list of silent letters which has been given above is not complete. Some popularly known words with silent letters have been included. By consulting a dictionary, prepare a long list of such words on your own.

●●

44th Day

Pronunciation of English Consonants

Like vowels, there are also differences in English consonants, as–'C' is pronounced both /s/ and /k/; 'G' is pronounced /g/ and /dʒ/; 'S' is pronounced /s/, /z/ and /ʃ/; 'T' is pronounced /ʃ/, /tʃ/, /θ/, /ð/, etc. If you pay attention to the points given below, it will become easy for you to know the difference.

Consonants in English are–

B	C	D	F	G	H	J
K	L	M	N	P	Q	R
S	T	V	W	X	Y	Z

(Total = 21 letters)

Above are the letters which represent consonant sound. But the consonant sounds are the following—

P/p/as in pen   F/f/ as in fall   H/h/ as in hot

B/b/as in bad   V/v/ as in van   M/m as in man

T/t/as in tea   θ/θ/ as in thin   N/n/ as in now

D/d/as in did   ð/ð/ as in this   ng/ŋ/ as in sing

K/k/as in cat   S/S/ as in sir   L/l/ as in leg

G/g/as in get   Z/z/ as in zoo   R/r/as in red

Ch/tʃ/ as in chain   Sh/ʃ/ as in shoe   Y/j/as in yes

J/dʒ/ as in jain   sio/ʒ/ as in vision   W/w/as in wet

(Total = 24 Sounds)

If you listen to radio or T.V., you can better understand the difference in English consonants. Depending on books alone will not serve the purpose fully. 'C' has both pronunciations /s/ and /k/ as in 'cement' and 'cat'. 'G' also has two pronunciations /g/ and /dʒ/ as in 'Got' and

225

'Gem'. 'S' has two pronunciations /s/ and /ʃ/ as in 'subject' and 'sure'. 'Q' is represented by /k/ as in 'Quality'. 'X' is represented by/ks/ as in x-ray. Hindi sounds are represented by some clusters, as bhabhi, dhanyavad, jhadu, achha, kharab, gherao, Hritik, kaksha, Vijnan, etc.

Difference in pronunciations on change of letters

Pronunciation of C

1. If E, I, Y come after the letter 'C', its pronunciation would be /s/. Receive, Cyclon, Icy, Certificate, Forces, Rice, Niece, Celebrate, Circle, Cinema, Piece, Century, Citizenship, etc.

2. If A, O, U, K, R, T come after 'C', its pronunciation would be /k/ e.g., Cot, Cat, Back, Dock, Custom, Cap, Candidate, Cock, Cutting, Cruel, Cow, Cattle, Lock, Curse, etc.

3. If IA or EA come after 'C', its pronunciation would be /ʃ/ e.g., Social, Ocean, Musician, Special, etc.

Pronunciation of G

'G' also has two pronunciations /g/ and /dʒ/.

1. If E comes after 'g', its pronunciation would be /dʒ/, e.g., Gem, Gentle, Gesture, Generosity, General, George, etc.

2. In the following words also, the pronunciation of 'G' is /dʒ/. e.g., Ginger, Pigeon, Imagine, Gist, Germ, Gem, etc.

   In rest of the situations, the pronunciation would be /g/, e.g.,

   Big, Go, Give, Bag, Gold, Finger, Hang, Hunger, Forget, etc.

Pronunciation of S

It has three main pronunciations /z/, /s/ and /ʃ/.

1. If BE, G, GG, GE, IE, EF, Y come after 'S', the pronunciation would be /z/ e.g., Tribes, Bags, Eggs, Ages, Heroes, Stories, Rupees, Toys, Rays, etc.

2. If F, P, KE, GHT, PE, TE come after 'S', its pronunciation would be /s/ e.g., Roofs, Lips, Jokes, Chips, Kites, Nights, Hopes, Ships, etc.

3. If IA, ION come after 'S', the pronunciation would be /ʃ/ e.g., Aggression, Pension, Mansion, Session, Russia, etc.

Pronunciation of T

1. 'T' has the following four pronunciation /ʃ/, /tʃ/, /θ/ and /ð/, e.g. Initial, Patient, Illustration, Portion, Promotion, Ratio, etc.

2. If 'T10' or 'URE' come after 'T' its pronunciation would be /tʃ/ Question, Future, Creature, Culture, Capture, Nature, Picture, etc.

3. If 'H' comes after 'T' its pronunciation is either /θ/ or /ð/. Think, Three, Thin, Thread, This, That, These, Those, etc.

4. Sometimes 'TH' Sounds like 'T', e.g., Thames, Thomas, etc.

Points to Remember

Some people pronounce, 'The' as /ðə/ and some others /ði/. Both are correct. The difference is that when 'The' is followed by vowel sound, it is /ði/ but when it is followed by consonant sound, it is /ðə/. e.g., the orange, the umbrella, the book, the pen, etc.

●●

45th **Day**

Use of 'What', 'Who' and 'How'
in Interrogatives

We had digressed in the middle because of two important topics which were necessary to be covered– Roman script, spelling and pronunciation. From 6th to 8th Days, we learnt how to make Interrogative sentences. For this, we put helping verb before the subject. Now, you will learn that when question words 'Who' 'What' and 'How' are put even before the helping verbs, the questions become more meaningful.

What	**Answers**
1. What do you want?	A glass of milk.
2. What are you writing?	A letter.
3. What do you want to say?	Nothing.
4. What is your name?	Munib Ahmad.
5. What is your profession?	Business.
6. What is your mother?	A housewife.
7. What are you doing these days?	Studying.
8. What have you seen in Agra?	The Taj Mahal.
9. What did you write to your father?	About my visit.
10. What was she doing in Mumbai?	She was teaching in a primary school.
11. What do you intend to do after passing High School?	I will study further.
12. What is the capital of India?	India.
13. What is our national language?	Hindi.
14. What is our national anthem?	Jan-gan-man.
15. What is our national fruite?	Mango.

228

Who

16. Who are you?	I am a businessman.
17. Who are they?	They are relatives.
18. Who sang the song?	Lata did.
19. Who will go to the market?	I will.
20. Who can do this work?	Radha can.
21. Whom does she want to meet?	Her mother.
22. Who is the owner of this house?	My father.
23. Who is the present prime minister of India?	Sri Narendra Modi
24. Who is the chief minister of Delhi?	Sri Arvind Kejriwal
25. Who is the inventor of Computer?	Sri Charles Babbage
26. Who is the chiarman of Pustak Mahal?	Sri Ram Avtar Gupta
27. Who said, "Give me blood I'll give you freedom"?	Sri Subhash Chandra Bose
28. Who is the first Asian to get the Nobel Prize?	Sri Ravinder Nath Tagore
29. Who started Non-cooperation movement?	Sri M.K. Gandhi
30. Who is called 'Human Computer'?	Smt Shakuntla Devi
31. Who established the first atomic research institute in India?	Sri Homi Jahangir Bhabha
32. Who started study of birds for the first time in India?	Sri Saalim Ali
33. Who was the first President of India?	Dr. Rajendra Prasad

How

34. How does he go to school?	By bus.
35. How is you father?	He is not well.
36. How did you go to Simla?	By train.
37. How did you return?	By bus.
38. How was your health in Simla?	It was perfectly alright there.
39. How was the weather there?	It was quite cold.

40. How old is you son? He is twelve.
41. How far is Connaught Place from About six kilometers.
here?
42. How are you feeling now? Much better.
43. How did you master your Englsih? By studying Rapidex
English Conversation.
44. How long is Mumbai from Delhi? About 1384 kms by train.
45. How effective is this medicine Very good.
for cold?
46. How many days are there in a year? 365 days.

Points to Remember

1. Questions, the answers of which come either in 'yes' or 'no'
are called 'Simple Interrogative'.
   (a) *Do you work in Delhi?* *Ans. Yes.*
   (b) *Was your work easy?* *Ans. No.*
   (c) *Have you taken food?* *Ans. Yes.*

2. Questions, the answers of which come in words other than
'Yes' or 'No' are called 'Double Interrogative'.
   (a) *What is your business?* *Ans. Garment Shop.*
   (b) *How old are you?* *Ans. 30 years.*
   (c) *When did you see the Taj?* *Ans. 10 years ago.*

●●

46th Day

Use of 'Which', 'When', 'Where', 'Why', etc.

You have learnt the use of 'who', 'what' and 'how'. In this chapter, you will learn the use of 'which', 'when', 'where', 'what' and 'why'. 'Which' is used for small animals or lifeless objects. 'When' indicates time of action, 'where' indicates the place of action and 'why' indicates the reason of action. After these question words, helping verbs have to be used.

Which	Answer
1. Which song did you prefer— Lata's or Aasha's?	I like what you have liked.
2. Which book are you reading?	It is the novel which I borrowed from you yesterday.
3. Which is your favourite movie?	Sound of Music.
4. Which is the biggest state in India?	Uttar Pradesh.
5. Which state is the most literate?	Kerala.
6. Which is a common capital for two states?	Chandigarh.
7. Which is the shortest month of the year?	February.
8. Which city is called 'Financial Capital of India'?	Mumbai.
9. Which city is called 'Pink City'	Jaipur.
10. Which is the most beautiful city?	Tokyo.
11. Which season do you like most?	Spring.

When	Answer
12. When do you revise your lesson?	In the morning.
13. When are you coming to us?	As soon as I get time.

14. When did you meet Sanjay?	Last Saturday when he came to Delhi.
15. When did India get freedom?	In 1947.
16. When did C.V. Raman get Nobel Prize?	In 1930.
17. When did Mother Teresa die?	In 1997.
18. When was Indira Gandhi assassinated?	In 1984.
19. When did Lal Bahadur Shastri become P.M.?	In 1964.
20. When did Non-coopration Movement start?	In 1920.
21. When did Marco Polo die?	In 1324.
22. When was Tagore awarded the Nobel Prize?	In 1913.

Where	**Answer**
23. Where do you work?	In a government office.
24. From where do you buy books?	From Pustak Mahal.
25. Where do you live?	In Roop Nagar.
26. From where did you buy your suit?	From Cannaught Place.
27 Where is the Statue of Liberty situated?	America.
28. Where did Lord Budha get enlightenment?	Gaya, Bihar.
29. Where did Lenin rule?	Russia.
30. Where was S. Radhakrishnan born?	At Tirutani in Madras.
31. Where did Vasco de Gama born?	At Venice in Itly.

Why	**Answer**
32. Why do you drink milk daily?	To maintain good health.
33. Why is Meenakshi's teacher so strict?	She is strict because she is interested in the progress of her students.

34. Why are you sitting here?	I'm waiting for my friend.
35. Why was Tagore given Nobel Prize?	For Gitanjali.
36. Why did Ambedkar embrace Buddhism?	In protest of caste system.
37. Why is Chanakya remembered?	For being great diplomat.
38. Why is Mandela hailed as a good leader?	For the independence of South Africa.
39. Why is Raja Ram Mohan Roy remembered?	For abolishing the practice of 'Sati'.
40. Why is Shakuntala Devi called 'Human Computer'?	Because of her mental calculations of computer solvable questions.

Points to Remember

1. 'Who' is used for human beings. 'Which' is used for lifeless objects or small animals. 'Which' is used for selection.

2. 'Who' and 'which' are also used as relative pronouns. 'Who' for humans and 'which' for lifeless objects.
   I met the girl who is the monitor.
   I saw a boy who was laughing.
   You liked the book which I gave you.
   We enjoyed the fruit which he brought.

●●

47th Day

Miscellaneous Sentences

Revise interrogative sentences. Also revise the use of 'is, am, are, was, were, has, have, had, will, shall, etc, with who, what, which, when, where, why,' etc.

Practise all these points one by one.

1. What happened?
2. Had you asked for me?
3. May I go?
4. May I accompany you?
5. Are you coming?
6. Should I bring it?
7. How are you?
8. Did you understand the problem?
9. What do you mean?
10. Is the boss in?
11. Who's he?
12. What is the matter?
13. Where is Dinesh?
14. When did you come?
15. Shall we begin?
16. Will you do me a favour?
17. Is it a holiday today?
18. Do you know?
19. Won't you go?
20. What is the trouble?
21. Are you angry?
22. How is the family?

23. What can I do for you?
24. Where are we now?
25. What brought you here?
26. Has he got a car?
27. Do you want me?
28. Who is coming?
29. What is the menu for dinner?
30. Whose telephone number is this?
31. Where shall we meet?
32. How have you come back?
33. Why have you dropped your studies?
34. How is your mother now?
35. How do you do?
36. Which is the best hotel here?
37. Who is this?
38. Where is Rakesh?
39. What is the news?
40. When shall we meet again?
41. How old are you?
42. How much did this coat cost you?
43. For how long have you been here?
44. How long will it take?
45. Why do you trouble yourself?
46. Why is the road closed?
47. What movie is on today?
48. What are you looking for?
49. Why are you so serious?
50. What should I wear in the party tonight?
51. Where should I contact you?
52. Is there any problem?
53. Are you going to be late tonight?

54. May I dance with you?
55. Would you like to join us?
56. What should I do now?
57. Why don't you listen to me?
58. Which of these two dresses will suit me better?
59. Where should I look for him?
60. What can I do for you?
61. May I use your phone?
62. Do you recognize him?

Points to Remember

You see that in all the above sentences, first of all question words have been used. After them, there are helping verbs 'is am, are, was, were, has, had, will, shall, can, may, should, would, etc. And after these verbs is subject.

Now, you have to change these Interrogative sentences into Affirmative and Negative sentences. For making them Affirmative, Helping verb is to be placed after subject, question word is to be removed and, in the end, question mark (?) is to be replaced with full stop.

To make Affirmative sentences into Negative, you have to add 'not' after Helping verb, e.g.,

Affirmative	Negative
(a) He is eating food.	He is not eating food.
(b) I am sleeping.	I am not sleeping.
(c) She is dancing.	She is not dancing.

••

48th Day

Negative Sentences and Question Tags

In the previous days, you learnt how to make Affirmative and Interrogative sentences. To make Interrogative, you put helping verbs in the beginning of the sentence. To make Affirmative, you put helping verb after the subject.

Now, in this chapter, you will learn how to make Negative sentences out of Affirmative. For this purpose, we add 'not' after the helping verb, as– cannot, will not, is not, etc.

Negative Sentences

1. I do not know him.
2. I do not ask anything.
3. She does not come here.
4. She does not know how to make tea.
5. He did not miss the bus yesterday.
6. We have not heard this news.
7. It is not cold today?
8. She is not married.
9. We are not late today.
10. She was not in Delhi.
11. We did not attend the lecture.
12. She does not have a son.
13. I didn't get the letter.
14. They did not have convergence.
15. Don't worry, father wouldn't be angry.
16. Father wouldn't be at home tomorrow.
17. We shall not be late tomorrow.
18. You must not drive the car on the footpath.
19. I couldn't reach in time day before yesterday.
20. You needn't go there.
21. I cannot ride a motorcycle.
22. No problem.
23. Now we should not close our shop, should we?

Question Tag

It is a mini question which is asked after a statement to get confirmation. It is commonly used in conversations, e.g., **It is very cold, isn't it?** In this sentence, the part **'isn't it?'** is a question tag.

1. It is very hot today, isn't it?
2. They are foreigners, aren't they?
3. You were not pleased, were you?
4. It will be Sunday tomorrow, won't it?
5. We will be ready soon, won't we?
6. I cannot forget it, can I?
7. I won't be with you tomorrow, will I?
8. We have met before, haven't we?
9. You had finished your work, hadn't you?
10. You could not find the book for me, could you?
11. Meenakshi should not go to bed late, should she?
12. Amitabh must wait till 2 o'clock, mustn't he?
13. She has not learnt English, has she?
14. You can speak English, can't you?
15. Great men don't waste their time, do they?
16. You should not talk like this, should you?
17. How pleasant it is, isn't it?
18. You think yourself to be very clever, don't you?
19. She will reach here soon, won't she?
20. She reached home late again, didn't she?
21. We never forget our childhood, do we?
22. She dances well, doesn't she?
23. I am the principal of school, aren't I?
24. He worked hard, didn't he?
25. She will call me in the evening, won't she?
26. They go to school, don't they?
27. This book is very easy, isn't it?
28. He likes reading stories, doesn't he?
29. The driver slept while driving, didn't he?
30. It is raining heavily, isn't it?
31. Sheela writes beautifully, doesn't she?
32. They work in the fields, don't they?

33. He is a lier, isn't he?
34. I know him personally, don't I?
35. She loves me, doesn't she?
36. He will not call you, will he?
37. This is not a good decision, is this?
38. Mother does not take time in breakfast, does she?
39. You will not accompany me, will you?
40. He is a good player, isn't he?

Points to Remember

1. Question tag is always opposite to its statement. It means, if the statement is positive, question tag would be negative, e.g., *It is very cold, isn't it?* If the statement is negative, the question tag would be positive, e.g., *It is not cold, is it?*

2. Subject of a question tag is always a pronoun; never a noun.

3. Some peculiar examples of question tag–

   (a) I am right, aren't I?
   (b) Let's go to market, shall we?
   (c) Wait a minute, can you?
   (d) Have some more tea, will you?
   (e) There is a hospital in that street, isn't there?
   (f) Somebody has called, haven't they?

4. Short forms used in Negative sentences and Question Tags:

(a) isn't = is not	*can't = cannot*
(b) aren't = are not	*shouldn't = should not*
(c) I'm not = I am not	*needn't = need not*
(d) amn't = am not (non-standard)	*wouldn't = would not*
(e) wasn't = was not	*couldn't = could not*
(f) weren't = were not	*doesn't = does not*
(g) won't = will not	*don't = do not*
(h) shan't = shall not	*didn't = did not, etc.*

●●

49th Day

In the previous chapter, you learnt about Negative sentences and Question Tags. Now, in this chapter, you would learn about some pronouns, their types and difference among them.

Use of 'He, She, It, This, That, You, I, Each, None,' etc.

1. This is Hameed.
2. That is Anju.
3. This is a book.
4. That is her diary.
5. He is a boy.
6. She is a girl.
7. You are a student.
8. I am a clerk.
9. This is a pen.
10. This is an apple.
11. It is a box.
12. It is my chocolate.
13. This is the camera I need.
14. This is a pencil, and it's mine.
15. These books are mine.
16. I have a car. It is new.
17. He is my nephew.
18. She is my girl friend.
19. He is an honest shopkeeper.
20. She is a very laborious girl.
21. These are my marbles. They are of different colours.
22. India is our country. We are her inhabitants.
23. Mr. Sharma is your teacher.
24. Meeta and Neeta are sisters. Their mother is a teacher.
25. Each of these boys plays games.

26. None of us went there.
27. We enjoyed ourselves during the holidays.
28. Whoever is the best will get the prize.
29. He is not wiser than me.
30. My handwriting is better than that of my brother.
31. What is that? That is a computer.
32. What are those? Those are cassettes.
33. This is a box. These are its corners.
34. Who is that? He is my colleague.
35. Whose notebook is this?
36. It's hers.
37. This cow is ours.
38. Those shops are theirs.
39. This watch is mine.
40. This house is yours.
41. Your painting is the best.
42. I am listening to you attentively.
43. Who is knocking at the door?
44. Whose luggage is this?
45. That's a different matter altogether.
46. She does not know the value of time.
47. You can trust them.
48. I am very thankful to you.
49. His rude behaviour shocked me.
50. I never expected this from you.
51. These books are of no use to me.
52. We have to leave at once.
53. They have their own houses in Delhi.
54. That shop belongs to my uncle.
55. You are a good student?
56. He has taken his share.
57. You write beautifully.
58. She loves me.
59. He is a man of iron will.

60. She is a classical dancer.
61. It is a very interesting book.
62. This story is really heart touching.
63. That is a far-fatched idea.
64. You are not supposed to oppose the cause.
65. I am very enthusiastic about this plan.
66. Each student will get reward.
67. None of them could be present in the function.
68. He encourages people to help the poor.
69. She can work for long hours unstopped.
70. It is a matter of great concern.

Points to Remember

1. 'He, she, it, this and that' are used for third person singular nouns.
2. 'You' is used for second person, singular and plural nouns.
3. 'This' and 'That' are called Demonstrative Pronouns because they indicate towards something.
4. 'This' and 'That' are used for singular nouns, near and far respectively, i.e., 'this' for near objects and 'that' for remote objects.
5. 'These' and 'Those' are also Demonstrative Pronouns but they are used for plural nouns near and far respectively.
6. 'Each' is a Distributive Pronoun which is used for distribution. It is used with singular Noun.
7. 'None' is also a pronoun and is used as the opposite of 'each'.

●●

50th **Day**

From 41st to 44th Day

1. There are main five vowels in English — A,E,I,O,U. Pronounce the following words. While pronouncing them, pay attention to the sound of vowels.

2. There are 156 words given below from (a) to (f). Write their meanings. If you don't know, look up a dictionary. For 150 correct word-meaning, score 'very good'; for 125; good; and for 100, 'Not bad'.

(a) a = /a:/ (as car)

far	star	card	hard	dark	mark
arm	farm	harm	art	part	start
heart	guard	answer	can't	balm	palm
calm	half	craft	draft	graph	laugh

(b) y or i = /ai/ (as my)

by	buy	cry	try	spy	style
die	lie	tie	eye	life	wife
like	strike	high	sight	right	height
fight	light	might	night	tight	bind
find	mind	kind	fine	line	mine
pipe	ripe	five	strive	drive	knife

(c) u or o = /ʌ/ (as cup)

but	cut	rub	bud	dull	run
fun	gum	up	hunt	lunch	luck
rush	sun	vulgar	cutter	butter	hut
front	worry	some	dozen	cousin	Monday
son	govern	nothing	young	tongue	southern
colour	comfort	become	brother	mother	other

243

(d) i = /i/ (as it)

fit	hit	this	fish	wish	him
in	sin	thin	big	bid	kid
lip	ship	trip	pick	sick	trick
kill	still	ill	fill	will	bill

(e) ea, ee = /ia/(as hear)

clear	tear	near	hear	fear	appear
ear	year	dear	rear	pear	gear
sheer	beer	deer	cheer	queer	compere

(f) ea, /i:/ (as seat)

teat	beat	heat	meat	neat	heap
mean	sea	tea	lead	read	meal
each	reach	breach	preach	teach	speak

3. **There are some silent letters in these words. Find them out and make a list. Also, underline the silent letters.**

4. **Spell these words using pronunciation symbols, as beat = /bi:t/, heat = /hi:t/, etc.**

rough	fall	philosophy	forgive	Asia
from	arm	tribe	hopes	page
Russia	thin	then	Age	calm

5. **Write silent letters in the following words:**

calm	debt	folk	half	knoll
lodge	match	villain	reign	stalk
unknown	known	walk	talk	kneel

6. **Write the pronunciation of the following words in Roman script:**
   lie, can, come, policy, chocolate, receipt, received, pierce, off, accept, borne, horn, clothes, morale, moral, island, gnat, known, psychology, written, honesty, psalm, knitting, honour, wrong, hour, deny.

7. **Find out the correct spelling words from the following and match them with dictionary:**

hieght	height	speek	speak	call	calle
proceed	precede	speach	speech	near	nare
excede	exceed	walk	wak	reech	reach

ecspress	express	treat	treet	ocasion	occasion
havy	heavy	tension	tention	attack	atacke
angry	angary	attension	attention	sleep	sleap
new	nue	simpaly	simply	switch	swich
plastek	palstic	tuche	touch	velley	valley
pleese	please	midal	middle	flower	flover
compeny	company	nature	nateur	substract	subtract

From 45th to 49th Days

8. **We give some Interrogative words. Use them in your own sentences:**

'what, who, which, when, where, why, how, how many, how much, how long.

9. **Read the following sentences carefully and write their pronunciation in phonetic symbols.**

1. The shop is closed, ins't it? 2. We are late, aren't we? 3. You came, didn't you? 4. You told her a story, didn't you? 5. We won't go there, will we? 6. You told her story, didn't you? 7. I am not late today, am I? 8. They played well but you did not. They won't reach in time but we will 9. My mother won't attend the meeting, but my father will. 10. I must go but you should not. 11. You must not write in red ink. 12. He is wrong, isn't he? 13. I was with you, wasn't I? 14. You knew him well, didn't you? 15. We have done the work, haven't we? 16. You have learnt a list, haven't you?

245

10. **Below given are some questions and their answers. Ask one of your friends to ask you questions and you try to answer them. Then match your answers.**

Q. 1. What's her dog's name?   **Ans.** It is Tony.

Q. 2. What do they want now?   **Ans.** They want more money.

Q. 3. Whom do you wish to see? **Ans.** Mr. B.N. Kohli.

Q. 4. What do you think?   **Ans.** I think that she will come soon.

Q. 5. Who owns this car?   **Ans.** My cousin does.

Q. 6. What did you say?   **Ans.** I said that I would help her.

Q. 7. Who is coming today?   **Ans.** My uncle.

Q. 8. How can a man make many friends?   **Ans.** By being a good friend himself.

Q. 9. How do you earn so much money?   **Ans.** I work day and night.

Q. 10. Which book do you want now?   **Ans.** The Bhagvad Gita.

Q. 11. What has happened to him? **Ans.** He walked into a lamp-post and hurt himself.

Q. 12. What is your suit made of? **Ans.** Wool.

Q. 13. When do you plan to visit your auntie?   **Ans.** On Monday.

Q. 14. When will you be able to see me?   **Ans.** In a day or two.

Q. 15. Where did you sleep last night?   **Ans.** At my uncle's.

Q. 16. Where did she invest the money?   **Ans.** In book trade.

Q. 17. Why must you work hard? **Ans.** To succeed.

Q. 18. Why did you lend him your cycle?   **Ans.** I lent him my cycle because he wanted to go to market.

Q. 19. Why did you vote for Dr. Mishra?   **Ans.** He is very competent.

Q. 20. Whose telephone number is this?   **Ans.** Mr. Gupta's.

Q. 21. Does Rama know how to prepare tea?   **Ans.** No, he doesn't.

Q. 22. Shall we be late tomorrow?   **Ans.** No, I don't think so.

Q. 23. What is the date tomorrow?   **Ans.** 20th February.

11. Frame questions for the answers given below:

1. I want three hundred rupees as loan. 2. He is known to the Prime Minister. 3. No, not at all. He is a book-worm. 4. No sir, the postman has not come yet. 5. Yes, he is weak but he is good in English. 6. No, it is slow by 5 minutes. 7. Raju, I don't have any appetite. 8. No, this is no thoroughfare. 9. Yes, it is snowing too. 10. Yes, but it gains ten minutes every day. 11. No, I'm not thirsty. 12. I have nothing else to say. 13. No, he had a headache. 14. It takes me half an hour. 15. She has gone to her school. 16. I have been working here for the last five years. 17. Don't give up. 18. No, he is an author. 19. The shop is closed. 20. My mother has gone to attend the meeting. 21. He is finishing his homework. 22. I want to visit Dehradun. 23. Sunita is preparing bed for me.

12. We use 'It' in the beginning of those answers the questions of which end with 'this' or 'that', for example–

Question			Answers		
What is	that? this? it?	It is	a an	book pen table chair umbrella bus car

13. **When 'shall' 'will' 'should' and 'would' are used in Interrogative sentences, they show politeness.**

Shall	I	stop	walking	now?
Should	we	begin	to do it	soon?
Will	you	like	to see it	at once?
Would	they	try	the other way	tomorrow?

14. **Complete the following sentences by filling in suitable pronoun:**

	is	my brother.
	am	... teacher.
	are	naughty boys.
?	was	in the class.
	were	at...uncle's.
	will be	...fiance.
	shall be	... neighbours.
	has	to leave...hostle.
	have	to contact...office.

He	—
I	Your
They	—
He	—
They	their
He	my
We	their
He	his
They	their

51st Day

6th Expedition (Grammar Contd...)

In this expedition, we are going to give you some basic but important knowledge of Grammar which will help you in a general way. The main topics which have been covered from 51st to 59th day are: Prepositions, Co-relatives and Temporals, Phrasal Verbs and Phrase Prepositions, Active and Passive Voice, Transformation of Sentences, Countable and Uncountable Nouns, use of 'It' and 'There' as subject, some structures of sentences, Idiomatic sentences and Drill Tables.

Use of On, At, Into, In, Of, By, With, Beside, Besides, Between, etc

1. The book is on the box.
2. The computer is on the table.
3. The clerk is at the seat.
4. There is green paint on the door.
5. Father is standing at the door.
6. I'll see you at home.
7. Neha is coming into the room.
8. I'll pour some more water in the room.
9. Rishabh and Richa both are in the room.
10. People bathe in the river.
11. We sit on the bench, but father sits in the arm chair.
12. Why don't you sit at the tables?
13. Insert the floppy into the computer.
14. He went into his office.
15. The letter was sent by Courier.
16. Please translate from Hindi into English.
17. Himachal Pradesh is in northern India.
18. Nepal is to the North of India.
19. Don't judge a person by his clothes.
20. I filled the bottle with milk.
21. The tiger was killed by the hunter.
22. He stood beside his brother.

23. I play football besides hockey.
24. Divide the sweets between Karan and Suman.
25. Simla is situated among the hills.
26. He is a man of principle.
27. There is a bridge over Yamuna river.
28. Throw the ball over the wall.
29. Birds are flying over the bridge.
30. Boats are under the bridge.
31. Amar is standing between Raj and Vikas.
32. Rama is in front of Sita. Sitaji is standing behind him.
33. We are in confusion. The money is in my pocket.
34. Fishes are in the sea.
35. I saw birds flying in the sky.
36. She is sitting among her friends.
37. What comes between ten and twelve?
38. Distribute the sweet among the children.
39. The student came running into the class.
40. The thief broke into the shop.
41. He passed the salt on to me.
42. Please turn over the page.
43. The policeman was shouting with mic.
44. I went around the school building.
45. They are sitting against a tree trunk.
46. Air is fresh on mountains.
47. Sunita kissed me on the forehead.
48. Love children without prejudice.
49. I saw a huge snake inside the cave.
50. Lions are in great number in Africa.
51. An owl is sitting on the banyan tree.
52. Who is present at the gate?
53. He came running into my room.
54. The spectacles are in the drawer.
55. This table is made of wood.
56. We shall reach Mumbai by 8 in the evening.
57. He came here with all his belongings.
58. I sat beside the president.
59. Who else is going to America besides me?
60. Distribute the sweet between Raju and Rani.
61. Please switch on the heater.

62. I was surprised at his remarks.
63. Don't look into the matter.
64. Please come in.
65. Of which material is your plate?
66. You can get fish by the riverside.
67. Come with your family.
68. Keep this cup beside the kettle.
69. I took mangoes besides bananas.
70. Hold the pen between two fingers.
71. This discussion is on Independence.
72. The car ran at a speed of 80 km/hr.
73. Put your books in the bag.
74. Throw the garbage into the bin.
75. I am a man of respect.
76. The letter was posted by Rakesh.
77. Open the lid with opener.
78. Who is standing beside father?
79. Besides grammar, mathematics is also a good subject.
80. Who is elder between Rama and Shyama?
81. He is on his duty.
82. I shall invite him in the party.

Points to Remember

1. 'In' and 'on' indicate static position, whereas 'into' and 'onto' or 'upon' show motion.
2. 'Between' is used for two, whereas 'among' for more than two.
3. Some prepositions are used after verbs. This combination is called 'phrasal verb'.
   Meaning of phrasal verb keeps changing with the change of preposition; so, learn them by heart.

●●

52nd Day

There are certain words in English which are used in combination. For example, no sooner...than, scarcely... when, hardly...when, not only...but also, etc. Today, you will learn about these words. Study carefully and practise them. The more you practise, the more perfect you will become.

A

(Co-relatives)

as soon as ——	as long as ——	unless ——
as far as ——	—— until	—— till
—— so that	no sooner—— than	hardly —— when
not only —— but also	either —— or	neither —— nor
although ——	scarcely —— when	rather —— than
no less —— than	the —— the	

1. As soon as we reached the station, the train left.
2. No sooner did he get up to deliver his speech, than the hall began resounding with cheers.
3. We had scarcely reached the school when the bell rang.
4. He had hardly left his house when it started raining.
5. Unless you run fast, you will not be able to catch the train.
6. Please wait for me until I return.
7. As long as I am here, you needn't worry about anything.
8. Although he is poor, he is honest.
9. As far as I remember, he was here yesterday.
10. Get the roof repaired before it should leak.

11. What to speak of standing first, he cannot even pass the examination.

12. He would rather fail than copy.

13. No less a person than the Chief Minister of the state hoisted the National Flag.

14. He is so ill that he cannot rise from the bed.

15. He works hard so that he may win the prize.

16. The higher you go, the colder it is.

17. Either you or your brother is guilty.

18. She is too weak to walk.

19. She is so weak that she cannot walk.

20. I study not only English but also French.

21. Neither Sameer nor his brother Adeeb abuses.

(Temporals)

'Temporals' are words or phrases connected with Time.

22. It is January nineteen hundred and seventy-seven.

23. You will receive his letter in three days.

24. We left for Mumbai on 20th February.

25. You came at half past three.

26. The shop remains open from 9:30 a.m. to 7 p.m.

27. She was here till 5 p.m. yesterday.

28. The boys play every day for one hour.

29. He has been staying here since yesterday.

30. She has been living here since 1970.

31. How long have you been learning English?

32. I have already written to her/him.

33. She has not come yet.

34. The show is about to start.

35. I shall finish my work by next Friday.

36. He will finish his work in about four hours.
37. I reached there around 3 o'clock.
38. When Radha came, Madhav left.
39. He was breathing his last at dawn.
40. I will meet her next month.
41. He has been working here since 1970.
42. The journey took five hours to complete.
43. She will come out of the airport around 2 p.m.
44. How long will it take to reach Rajasthan?
45. The food will be served within half an hour.
46. He visited Agra thrice a year.
47. Come to me whenever you feel like.
48. They scored a century in just two hours.
49. Their operation took 3 hours each.
50. Sushmita keeps phoning me in the morning.

Points to Remember

1. No sooner, No only, Hardly, Scarcely, Both are such conjunctions which always come in pairs.
2. Either, Neither, Rather, Till, Until are such prepositions which may come single or in pair.
3. 'In' is used before the names of months, as in April, in October, 'on' is used before the names of days as– on Monday, on Saturday, 'at' is used before time, as– at 2 o'clock, at 3:50 p.m. Similarly, 'in' is used before 'morning' and 'evening' whereas 'at' is used before 'noon' and 'night', as– in the morning, in the evening, at noon, at night, etc.
4. 'Since' is used before the 'point of time' and 'for' is used before 'period of time', as – since 2 o'clock, since Friday, since 1988 and for 2 hours, for two days, for 3 years, etc.

53rd Day

Prepositions with Verbs and Other Words

(From, by, with, in, of, for, in, into,
against, on, our, about)

There are certain rules in English which require 'Prepositions' with verbs and other words. In each case, there is a certain principle working. Read the following sentences and know about them.

About

1. The mother is **worried about** her son's health.
2. She was **enquiring about** Seema.

Against

3. I always **warn** you **against** our enemies.
4. The doctor **warned** him **against** working too hard.

By

5. His company is progressing **by leaps and bounds.**
6. I was **accompanied by** my father.
7. Please don't get **disturbed by** this news.
8. He was highly **amused by** my story.
9. This packet should **reach** Mumbai **by** Monday.

For

10. Is she **preparing/studying for** the test?
11. I always **care for** him.
12. He **apologised** to me **for** his misbehaviour.
13. He will have to **account for** the money.

From

14. The boy was **absent from** school.
15. You must **abstain/refrain from** smoking. You must **avoid** smoking.

255

16. My uncle has come **from** Assam.
17. He **prevents/stops** me **from** going there.

In

18. He was **absorbed/busy in** his work.
19. Sheela is **deaf in** one ear.
20. You must be **polite in** your behaviour.
21. He is **well-versed in** music.

Into

22. The police **enquired/looked into** the matter.
23. We **put** our books **into** our bags.
24. He **went into** the room.

Of

25. He was **sure of** success.
26. He is fully **aware of** his weakness.
27. He is **fond of** mangoes.
28. He **reminds** me **of** his brother.
29. It's a **matter of** great honour for me.

On

30. His criticism is not **based on** facts.
31. Why are you **bent on** going there?
32. We cannot **rely on** him.
33. My mother **insisted on** my carrying an umbrella.

Over

34. His tenure as a clerk **spanned over** two decades.
35. The bridge is **over** the river.

To

36. He is **addicted to** smoking.
37. He acted **contrary to** the rules.
38. Some people **prefer** wealth **to** health.
39. He **referred** the matter **to** the higher authorities.

With

40. You don't know how to **deal with** others.
41. We should be **acquainted with** the English language.
42. He was **gifted with** a talent for painting.
43. We got **fed up with** his behaviour.
44. My boss was **pleased with** me.

Phrase prepositions

45. I was **about to** go.
46. He succeeded **by dint of** hard work.
47. We should be prepared to sacrifice everything for the **sake** of our country.
48. We must work **in order to** live.
49. I tried to get **rid of** him.
50. My friend came to see me **in spite of** being very ill.
51. Can you give me your bicycle **in exchange for** my match.
52. He had to leave suddenly **in the midst of** meeting.
53. Pankaj had to **give up** studies **for want of** money.
54. I topped college **due to** hardwork.
55. He did come **in spite of** ill-health.

Points to Remember

1. 'From' is generally used with 'abstain', 'refrain', 'present', 'recover', etc; 'with' is used with 'pleased' 'accompany', 'satisfy'; 'for' is used with 'prepare' 'care', 'apologise'; 'to' is used with 'rely' and 'based'.
2. Some prepositions are fixed with their respective verbs. They always come together, as—
   'by dint of', 'for the sake of', 'in order to', 'in the midst of', 'on the eve of', 'on account of', etc.

●●

54th Day

Active Voice and Passive Voice

There are two ways of saying something. By stressing on the subject and by stressing on the object. For example (a) Tinku learnt a lesson. (b) A lesson was learnt by Tinku. The first way is called 'Active voice' and the second way is called 'Passive voice'. Now study the following sentences and practise them.

Active Voice	Passive Voice
1. He sings a song.	A song is sung by him.
2. I delivered the message.	The message was delivered by me.
3. They will play cricket.	Cricket will be played by them.
4. Are you writing a letter?	Is a letter being written by you?
5. Labourers were digging a canal.	A canal was being digged by labourers.
6. Have you finished this job?	Has this job been finished by you?
7. Will you have packed your luggage before the trains arrival?	Will your luggage have been packed by you before the train's arrival?
8. Help him.	He should be helped.
9. I have taken food.	Food has been taken by me.
10. You had rung the bell.	The bell had been rung by you.
11. He was washing clothes.	Clothes were being washed by him.
12. Children make a noise.	A noise is made by children.
13. They collected stamps.	Stamps were collected by them.
14. I called him.	He was called by me.
15. He is playing hockey.	Hockey is being played by him.
16. They drew a picture.	A picture was drawn by them.
17. You wrote a complaint.	A complaint was written by you.

Some Other Examples of Passive Voice

1. The Taj was built at an enormous cost.
2. Maize is sown in the rainy season.
3. You will be punished for your negligence.
4. He was accused of theft.
5. All the papers will have been marked.
6. Have you been cheated?
7. Has he been informed?
8. He was killed fighting the Chinese aggression.
9. Gandhiji was born on 2nd October 1869.
10. The Nauchandi fair is held every year in Meerut.
11. Many dailies are published from Delhi.
12. He will be pleased to see you.
13. I was surprised to see the fury of the floods.
14. It is said that Shivaji was an incarnation of Shiva.
15. Let this work be done by you.
16. He should be asked to sit down.
17. He should be punished.
18. Let the post be advertised.
19. You are requested not to smoke.
20. Indiscipline should not be encouraged.

Points to Remember

1. There are twelve tenses in Active Voice but in Passive Voice, there are only eight tenses. It means four tenses cannot be changed into Passive Voice. These four tenses are: Present Perfect Continuous, Past Perfect Continuous, Future Perfect Continuous and Future Continuous.

2. In Passive Voice, main verb is always used in the 3rd form.

3. In Passive Voice, the object is stressed upon. So, the object of Active Voice becomes subject in Passive Voice and the Subject of Active Voice becomes object in Passive Voice. If the subject and object are in the form of pronoun, their form also gets changed accordingly, for example–

   A. V. *I called him.*
   P. V. *He was called by me.*
   A. V. *She helped me.*
   P. V. *I was helped by her.*

4. In Passive Voice, 'by' is generally used before the object.

5. In Passive Voice, 'Helping verb' is also used with the main verb. The helping verb keeps changing as per the tense of the Active Voice.

In Present Indefinite, the Helping verb 'Is, Am, Are, are used, in Present Continuous– is being, are being, am being; in present Perfect– has been, have been; in Past Indefinite– was, were; in Past Continuous– was being, were being; in Past Perfect– had been; in Future Indefinite– will be and shall be; and in Future Perfect 'will have been' and 'shall have been' are used.

6. To change Imperative Sentences particularly those which consist of a direct object or a noun as object into Passive, 'Let' is used before the object. Thereafter 'be' is used and then 3rd form of the main verb. For example–

   A. V. *Open the door.*
   P. V. *Let the door be opened.*

7. Passive Voice is used when the subject is not known or is not important, for example–

   1. *The meeting has been postponed.*
   2. *The road has been repaired.*
   3. *The thief has been killed.*

••

55th Day

Transformation of Sentences

We can say the same thing in more than one way. And in doing that, the form of the sentence gets changed. This change of form is called Transformation. In Transformation, only the form of a sentence is changed whereas the meaning remains unchanged. Active and Passive Voice is also an example of Transformation. Other examples of Transformation include– change from Interrogative into Assertive, from exclamatory to Affirmative; from Imperative to Interrogative; from Positive to Comparative and from Negative to Affirmative. Study these examples and practise them.

From	To
Interrogative	**Assertive**
1. Can anybody bear such an insult?	Nobody can bear such an insult.
2. Is not health more precious than wealth?	Health is more precious than wealth.
3. Did they not enjoy at the party?	They enjoyed at the party.
4. Shall we ever forget these good days?	We shall never forget these good days.
5. Did you ever steal something?	I never stole anything.
6. Can't you read out this letter?	I can read out this letter.
7. Is time not precious?	Time is precious.
8. Can you ever count the stars?	I can never count the stars.
Exclamatory	**Affirmative**
9. What a beautiful sight it was!	It was a very beautiful sight.
10. What a cold night it is!	It is a very cold night.
11. What a hard life we live!	We live a very hard life.

261

12. What a tragic scene it is!	It is a very tragic scene.
13. How beautiful the Taj is!	The Taj is very beautiful.
14. What an excellent performance it is!	It is an excellent performance.
15. How charming you are!	You are very charming.
16. What a disgusting idea it is!	It is a very disgusting idea.

Imperative (Request)	**Interrogative**
17. Please open the door.	Will you please open the door?
18. Please have a cup of milk.	Will you please have a cup of milk?
19. Please keep quiet.	Will you please keep quiet?
20. Please help me.	Will you please help me?
21. Please lift my bag.	Will you please lift my bag?
22. Please listen to him.	Will you please listen to him?
23. Please inform me.	Will you please inform me?
24. Please take your seat.	Will you please take your seat?

Positive	**Comparative**
25. Amit is as tall as Sanjay.	Sanjay is not taller than Amit.
26. Very few cities in India are as big as Mumbai.	Mumbai is bigger than most other cities in India.
27. No other man was as strong as Bhima.	Bhima was stronger than any other man.
28. Very few Indian saints were as popular as Vivekananda.	Vivekananda was more popular than most other Indian saints.
29. He is as witty as I am.	I am not wittier than him.
30. Very few cases are as complicated as hers.	Her case is more complicated than most other cases.
31. No other playwrite is as great as Shakespeare.	Shakespeare is greater than any other playwrite.
32. She is not as smart as I am.	I am smarter than her.

Negative	Affirmative
33. No man is immortal.	Man is mortal.
34. She is not as beautiful as my wife.	My wife is more beautiful than her.
35. There is no gain without hard work.	Where there is hard work there is gain.
36. She never neglects her daily routine work.	She always pays attention to her daily routine work.
37. No sooner had I reached the station than the train left.	Scarcely had I reached the station when the train left.
38. He is not lazy.	He is active.
39. My handwriting is not ugly.	My handwriting is beautiful.
40. I am not old.	I am young.

Points to Remember

1. Transformation is the change of form, not the meaning of a sentence. So, Active and Passive, Direct and Indirect speech, conversion of the degrees of Adjective, etc. all are different ways of transforming sentences.

2. It needs some amount of practice. So, study this chapter carefully and try to practise it.

●●

56th Day

A

(Countable Nouns)

1. There are some/a few **students** in the class.
2. Is there any **girl** in the hall?
3. There is no **boy** in the playground.
4. None of these **girls** was present there.
5. Did any of you play **football**?
6. Many of the **boys** had not come to school yesterday.
7. How many **mangoes** are there in the basket?
8. Hardly would any **girl** like him.
9. That **book** has more pages than this book.
10. Many a **man** has suffered at his hands.
11. Neither **man** has come.
12. He gets a small **salary**.
13. I have many **dictionaries** of English.
14. How many **brothers** and sisters do you have?
15. He ate ten **chapatees** in the competition.
16. Please give me four **mangoes**.
17. He delivered a total of twenty **lectures**.
18. They have visited fifteen **countries** of the world.
19. We have four **seasons** in India.
20. There are twelve **months** in a year.

21. I saw a **lion** in the forest.
22. He has four **bikes**.
23. Please give me a **pen**.
24. **Mangoes** are very sweet.
25. His **books** are very costly.
26. Fifty **students** is a big class.
27. This **stapler** is very strong.
28. Take your **seat**.
29. Give me the key of the drawer.
30. I am a helpful **friend**.
31. Eat an **apple** a day.
32. Where is your **turban**?
33. This **box** is too heavy.
34. Don't **tease** children.
35. **Mother** is a gift from God.

B

(Uncountable Nouns)

36. Is not there any **milk** in the bottle?
37. Get me some **water**.
38. This chair is made of **wood**.
39. **Honesty** is the best policy.
40. **Pride** goes on horseback but returns on foot.
41. **Truth** always prevails.
42. How much **water** is there in the jug?
43. **Gold** is a precious metal.
44. **Time** waits for none.
45. Be bold in **adversity**.
46. Coconut **oil** is good for burns.
47. **Smoking** is injurious to health.
48. **Health** is wealth.
49. He is a man of good **character**.
50. **Tea** and coffee are beneficial in cold.
51. **Beauty** is discipline.
52. Blowing **air** is called wind.
53. **Laughter** is the best medicine.

54. **Experience** is the best teacher.
55. **Hatred** begets hatred.
56. He takes five cups of **tea** a day.
57. We should drink about 10 glasses of **water** a day.
58. Give me two kilograms of **sugar**.
59. I need five metres of **cloth** for bedsheet.
60. Three jars of **paints** was purchased yesterday.
61. Goat **milk** is very costly.
62. **Water** is life saver.
63. **Discipline** is a good virtue.
64. **Cruelty** is hated everywhere.
65. **Army** of India is very powerful.
66. The **team** won the match.
67. **Petrol** is getting costly day by day.
68. Some **cattle** are grazing in the field.
69. **Time** and tide wait for none.
70. **Sincerity** pays in the long run.

Points to Remember

1. Generally, Proper noun is not used in plural.
2. Collective nouns are used in plural if they are taken as a unit.
3. Material nouns are uncountable. But to show their quantity, we have to use a countable noun before them as a measurement, e.g., five cups of tea. 'Tea' is uncountable, so we cannot say five teas. Similarly, piece of advice, item of news, litre of milk, kilogram of sugar, metre of cloth, etc.

●●

57th Day

There are some expressions in English which start with 'It' and 'There'. Study them carefully and try to understand them through their usage and practice.

A
(Examples of sentences starting with 'It')

1. It is kind of you to help us.
2. It was clever of Rajeev to reach the station.
3. It was foolish of her to touch hot pan.
4. It is fortunate of me to see you here.
5. It is unwise of you to stay here alone.
6. It was wicked of her to blame me.
7. It is easy to learn English.
8. It was tough to climb the mountain.
9. It will be hard to solve the sum without practice.
10. It is not good to borrow money from anybody.
11. It is cruel to treate animals badly.
12. It was nice to accompany you.
13. It is strange that he accuses you baselessly.
14. It is possible that it rains in the afternoon.
15. It is not sure whether he will come or not.
16. It was fortunate that you escaped the accident.
17. It is pity that you didn't try harder.
18. It would be nice that you sleep now.
19. It takes me ten minutes to reach home.
20. It took him an hour to finish the job.
21. It takes us five minutes to eat food.
22. It will take you half an hour to reach here.
23. It took an hour to contact him.

24. It has taken me two days to write the article.
25. It is Monday today.
26. It is very cold outside.
27. It is the 4th of October today.
28. It is 2017.
29. It is very pleasant today.
30. It was very humid yesterday.
31. It is good to talk to you.
32. It is a very famous detective story.
33. It was a ferocious dog.
34. It will rain soon.
35. It will cost you rupees five hundred.
36. It is the most interesting point.
37. It will be very hot after two months.
38. It is nice to meet you.
39. It will open at 9 a.m.
40. It is scheduled to arrive at 5 p.m.

B

(Examples of sentences beginning with 'There')

41. There is a boy in the classroom.
42. There are twelve months in a year.
43. There was a thunder five minutes ago.
44. There will be enough noise after interval.
45. There can be a big crowd in his funeral.
46. There is a book on the bench.
47. There will be a buzzing sound after ten minutes.
48. There is no bus for Jaipur after 10 p.m.
49. There is a possibility of his coming back.
50. There may be cancellation of match due to rain.
51. There should be a train for Kolkata tonight.
52. There are lots of blooming flowers in the spring.
53. There was not a single doctor in the clinic.
54. There are frequent landslides in the rainy season.
55. There cannot be any prejudice in my office.
56. There are many short stories in this book.
57. There used to be kind people in the olden days.

58. There was a well in the village.
59. There was a very handsome prince in a city.
60. There used to be fights with wild animals in the Mughal period.
61. There is a difference between the rich and the poor.
62. There was a king in Delhi.
63. There are crores of stars in our galaxy.
64. There cannot be a holiday in his office.
65. There were many tourists in the van.
66. There is a concensus on this point.
67. There was an uproar on this issue.
68. There will be a fine of rupees one hundred.
69. There are a lot of options before you.
70. There is a big tea stall in our locality.
71. There shall never be riots if we want.
72. There is a hero in every person.
73. There were twenty students in the mess.
74. There is no possibility of the publication of this magazine.
75. There is no qualified doctor in your neighbourhood.
76. There was a shortage of money in 2016.
77. There cannot be a person in the bus.
78. There are few lions left in our country.
79. There is no example of his bravery.
80. There is always love in parents for children.

Points to Remember

1. Any tense can be used in structures starting with 'It' and 'There'.
2. The verb is generally singular after 'It'.
3. The verb may be singular or plural on the basis of noun coming afterwards in structure beginning with 'there'.

●●

58th Day

C
(Adverb 'Too' + Adj + Infinitive)

1. He is too weak to run fast.
2. She is too lazy to finish the work in time.
3. The wind is too strong for me to maintain balance.
4. The tea is too hot to be sipped.
5. The teacher was too busy to listen to me.
6. She speaks too fast to be understood.
7. You are too young to go to school.
8. The water was too cold to take bath.
9. He is too stupid to solve the easiest problem.
10. I am too busy to attend the party.
11. My mother is too active to sit idle.
12. I am too enthusiastic to withdraw.

D
(Adj/Adv + Enough + Infinitive)

13. He is strong enough to carry the box.
14. She is wise enough to handle the situation.
15. They are powerful enough to settle the matter.
16. We are clever enough to understand you.
17. My father is old enough to lead us.

18. The principal was angry enough to hear anything.
19. You are bold enough to face the storm.
20. He is hard enough to be bent.
21. She is tall enough to touch the bulb.
22. I am wise enough to understand the matter.
23. She is beautiful enough to charm anybody.
24. I am bold enough to withstand her protest.

E
(So + Adj/Adv + that-clause)

25. It is so dark that I cannot see anything.
26. She is so wise that you cannot befool her.
27. You are so strong that nobody can frighten you.
28. We are so tired that we cannot walk now.
29. He was so confused that he could not talk.
30. The cat was so fast that the rat could not hide.
31. The day was so cold that she could not go outside.
32. Father was so angry that the children could not see them.
33. They are so busy that you cannot see them.
34. I am so happy that I cannot hide my joy.
35. He is so proud that he cannot walk on foot.
36. I am so energetic that I cannot stop in the middle.

F
[(What + (Adj) + Noun + Sub + (Verb!)]

37. What a fool he is!
38. What a beautiful girl she is!
39. What an idea!
40. What a lovely garden it is!
41. What a nice game he is playing!
42. What a nonsense it is!
43. What a lame excuse it is!
44. What a brilliant idea!

271

45. What a powerful protest it was!
46. What a nasty planning they made!
47. What a childish talk you do!
48. What a rosy face it is!

G
(How + Adj/adv + Sub + Verb!)

49. How fool he is!
50. How bold you are!
51. How sweet she sings!
52. How fast the time passed!
53. How intelligent you are!
54. How absurd the sketch is!
55. How sluggish his walk was!
56. How merciful Mother Teresa was!
57. How affectionate his parents are!
58. How kind of you!
59. How wonderful your speech was!
60. How witty you are!

Points to Remember

1. Every structure has a definite meaning. Don't be confused. Guess their differences.
2. Sentences under C and E are identical in meaning.
3. Sentences under F and G are also identical in meaning but the style is different.
4. Sentences under D show the capability of a person to do certain task. Practise all of them. Best luck!
5. Sentences coming under F and G end with mark of exclamation (!)

●●

272

59th Day

1. I **backed up** (supported) your claim.
2. The problems will soon **below over** (pass off).
3. I produced evidence to **bear out** (strengthen) the charge of robbery.
4. He must not have **built** his hopes **upon** (rely upon) her promises.
5. The problem has been **cleared up** (explained).
6. He quickly **closed with** (accepted) my offer.
7. I am ready to **dispose of** (sell) the used furniture.
8. Rust has **eaten away** (corroded) the door.
9. He **fixed upon** (chose) me to finish the job.
10. My behaviour **gained on** (won the favour of) the boss.
11. Your habits should not **grow upon** (become stronger) you.
12. I request you to **hear** me **out** (listen to the end).
13. I saw a thief **hanging about** (loiter about) my house.
14. They **hit upon** (found) a good idea to solve the problem.
15. The revolution **led up to** (culminated) the freedom from the British rule.
16. I **lighted upon** (chanced to find) a golden bowl in the cave.
17. Disheartened people **long for** (desire) death.

273

18. He was caught **red handed** (on the spot).

19. It took him three months to **shake off** (get rid of malaria).

20. Why have you threatened him to **show up** (expose)?

21. We all can **stave off** (prevent) war from happening.

22. She is **sticking out** (persist in demand) for increased salary.

23. **Think over** (consider) the matter.

24. I **trained up** (educated) my child how to eat food and walk on the road.

25. I am an expert in **trumping up** (fabricating) stories.

26. Bad habits should be **nipped in the bud** (stopped in the beginning).

27. Mohan lives from **hand to mouth** (in poverty).

28. He is still **at large** (not caught).

29. The murderer was caught **red handed** (on the spot).

30. His **days are numbered** (about to die).

31. **Building castles in the air** (imaginary planning) would not help.

32. We should not **lose our temper** (get furious) over trifles.

33. He has seen many **ups and downs** (fluctuations) in his life.

34. I can work for twelve hours **at a stretch** (continuously).

35. He wants to reach the top **by hook** or **by crook** (at any rate).

Proverbial Expressions

Besides the idiomatic expressions, proverbial expressions are also sometimes used. These expressions are nothing but sayings of the wise and experienced people which are handed down to us for centuries and they still hold good. Some proverbial expressions are given as sample. Learn them by heart.

36. While in Rome do as Romans do. (*Act as per the need of the hour*).

37. As you sow so shall you reap. (*Our reward or punishment is according to our deeds*).

38. To the good, the world appears good. (*If you are positive, everything seems to be positive*).

39. An empty vessel makes much noise. (*A person who knows nothing boasts of his knowledge*).

40. Health is wealth. (Health is valuable).

41. No pain, no gain (*To get something, we have to sacrifice something*).

42. Time once lost can never be regained. (*Time is a precious gift. Value it*).

43. Society moulds man. (*Outside society, man becomes wild*).

44. Union is strength (*We are powerful if we are united*).

45. Penny wise, pound foolish. (*Spending too much for saving little*).

Points to Remember

Practice makes a man perfect. The only success *mantra* is practice, practice and practice. All the exercises and material, you have gone through so far, need your practice and sincerity. Remember, practice leads to perfection!

●●

60th Day

51st Day

1. **Fill in the blanks with appropriate prepositions in the following sentences:**
   (a) The book is —— the table.
   (b) The clerk is —— the seat.
   (c) Father is standing —— the door.
   (d) People bathe —— the river.
   (e) Feed the floppy —— the computer.
   (f) The letter was sent —— the courier.
   (g) Translate —— Hindi —— English.
   (h) Nepal is —— the north —— India.
   (i) I filled the bottle —— milk.
   (j) He stood —— his brother.
   (k) Simla is situated —— the hills.
   (l) Pour some water —— the room.

52nd Day

2. **Complete the following sentences by filling in suitable conjunctions:**
   (a) —— we reached the station, the train left.
   (b) —— did he stand up, —— he fell down.
   (c) He had scarcely seen me, —— the door closed.
   (d) —— you run fast, you will miss the train.

276

(e) Please wait for me —— I come back.

(f) —— I am here, you need not worry at all.

(g) —— he is poor, he is honest.

(h) —— I remember, he was here yesterday.

(i) Get the roof repaired —— it should leak.

(j) I would rather like coffee —— tea.

(k) Wait here —— the bus arrives.

(l) Work hard —— you may succeed.

(m) Don't call me —— you get message.

(n) —— he is poor —— honest.

(o) He is —— rich —— honest.

3. Fill in the following sentences with suitable Temporals:

(a) He gets up early ——.

(b) We should go to bed ——.

(c) Walking barefoot —— is useful for health.

(d) We should walk after dinner ——.

(e) Don't go outside —— in summer.

(f) The patient is in the ICU for ——.

(g) He has been in Mumbai ——.

(h) —— I am here, you needn't worry.

(i) She has not come ——.

(j) The show is —— to start.

(k) I shall finish the job by —— weak.

(l) It took him —— to finish the letter.

(m) There is darkness —— in villages.

(n) We went to him —— , but he left earlier.

(o) Flowers bloom —— .

53rd Day

4. Supply with suitable prepositions.

(a) The boy was absent —— school.

(b) You must refrain —— smoking.

(c) I was accompanied —— my father.

(d) He was highly amused —— my story.

(e) You don't know how to deal —— others.

(f) He was gifted —— a talent for painting.

(g) Sheela is deaf —— one ear.

(h) He must be polite —— behaviour.

(i) I am sure —— success.

(j) He apologised —— me for his misconduct.

(k) The police enquired —— the matter.

(l) I always warned you —— your enemies.

54th Day

5. **Change the following Active Voice into Passive Voice:**

   (a) He sings a song.

   (b) I delivered the message.

   (c) They will play cricket.

   (d) Are you writing a letter?

   (e) Have you finished the job?

   (f) Help him.

   (g) I have taken food.

   (h) You had rung the bell.

   (i) He was washing the clothes.

   (j) Children make a noise.

   (k) Open the window.

   (l) Call the peon.

55th Day

6. **Change the following sentences as per the instructions given against each sentence:**

   (a) Can anybody bear such an insult? **(Assertive)**

   (b) Shall we ever forget these good days? **(Assertive)**

   (c) What a beautiful sight it is! **(Affirmative)**

278

(d) We live a very hard life. **(Exclamatory)**

(e) Please open the door. **(Interrogative)**

(f) Will you please keep quiet? **(Assertive)**

(g) Very few cities in India are as big as Mumbai. **(Comparative)**

(h) Bhima was stronger than any other man. **(Positive)**

(i) No man is immortal. **(Affirmative)**

(j) He is not lazy. **(Affirmative)**

(k) Where there is hard work, there is gain. **(Negative)**

(l) My wife is more beautiful than her. **(Negative)**

7. **There are some sentences given here. Tell which noun has been used in them —— countable or uncountable?**

(a) I have some **friends** in Mumbai.

(b) Tell me which **coffee** do you like most?

(c) He has much **water** in his tank.

(d) She has four **dogs**.

(e) I like **mangoes** very much.

(f) You need **help**.

(g) They have a **car** and two elephants.

(h) We should not tell a **lie**.

(i) Always speak the **truth**.

(j) They are my **roommates**.

(k) You have enough **rice**.

(l) Shall we get any **data?**

8. **Supply with suitable word for subject.**

(a) —— is kind of you to help us.

(b) —— was foolish of her to touch hot pan.

(c) —— is a boy in the classroom.

(d) —— is a possibility of his coming back.

(e) —— is unwise of you to stay here alone.

(f) —— should be a train for Kolkata tonight.

279

(g) —— was nice to accompany you.
(h) —— are lots of blooming flowers in the spring season.
(i) —— are many short stories in this book.
(j) —— is pity that you didn't try harder.
(k) —— was a very handsome prince in a city.
(l) —— has taken me two days to write the article.

58th Day

9. **Complete the following sentences with appropriate words:**
   (a) He is —— weak to run fast.
   (b) They are powerful —— to handle the situation.
   (c) The tea is —— hot to be sipped.
   (d) It is so dark —— I cannot see anything.
   (e) He was —— confused that he could not talk.
   (f) You are —— young to go to school.
   (g) —— an idea!
   (h) —— beautiful the Taj is!
   (i) —— a lovely flower it is!
   (j) She is tall —— to touch the bulb.
   (k) He is —— stupid to solve the sum.
   (l) I am so happy —— I cannot hide my joy.

59th Day

10. **Write the meanings of the underlined words:**
    (a) The problems will soon blow over.
    (b) I produced evidence to bear out the charge of robbery.
    (c) The problem has been cleared up.
    (d) I am ready to dispose of my old furniture.
    (e) He fixed upon me to finish the task.
    (f) My behaviour gained on my boss.
    (g) I request you to hear me out.
    (h) I saw a thief hanging about my house.
    (i) They hit upon a good idea to solve the problem.
    (j) Disheartened people long for death.
    (k) I stick out to him to accompany me.
    (l) We should not lose our temper over trifle things.

Answers

1. (a) on   (b) at   (c) at
   (d) in   (e) into   (f) by
   (g) from, into   (h) to, of   (i) with
   (j) beside   (k) among   (l) into

2. (a) As soon as   (b) No sooner, than   (c) When
   (d) Unless   (e) till   (f) As long as
   (g) Though   (h) So far as   (i) lest
   (j) to   (k) till   (l) so that
   (m) unless   (n) Not only, but also   (o) both – and

3. (a) in the morning   (b) early at night   (c) in the morning
   (d) at night   (e) at noon   (f) 2 hours
   (g) since 1998   (h) As long as   (i) yet
   (j) about   (k) next   (l) 2 hours
   (m) after sunset   (n) in the morning   (o) in the morning

4. (a) from   (b) from   (c) by
   (d) by   (e) with   (f) with
   (g) in   (h) in   (i) of
   (j) to   (k) into   (l) against

5. (a) A song is sung by him. (b) The message was delivered by me. (c) Cricket will be played by them. (d) Is a letter being written by you? (e) Has the job been finished by you? (f) Let him be helped. (g) Food has been taken by him. (h) The bell had been rung by you. (i) The clothes were being washed by him. (j) A noise is made by children. (k) Let the window be opened. (l) Let the peon be called.

281

6. (a) Nobody can bear such an insult. (b) We shall never forget these good days. (c) It is a very beautiful sight. (d) How hard life we live! (e) Can you please open the door? (f) Please keep quiet. (g) Mumbai is bigger than most of the cities in India. (h) No man is as strong as Bhima. (i) Man is mortal. (j) He is active. (k) No pain, no gain (l) She is not as beautiful as my wife.

7. (a) Countable (b) Uncountable (c) Uncountable (d) Countable (e) Countable (f) Uncountable (g) Countable (h) Uncountable (i) Uncountable (j) Countable (k) Uncountable (l) Uncountable.

8. (a) It (b) It (c) There (d) There
   (e) It (f) There (g) It (h) There
   (i) There (j) It (k) There (l) It

9. (a) too (b) enough (c) too (d) that
   (e) so (f) too (g) what (h) how
   (i) what (j) enough (k) too (l) that

10. (a) pass off (b) strengthen (c) explained (d) sell (e) chose (f) won the favour (g) to listen to the end (h) loitering about (i) found (j) desire (k) to persist in demand (l) get furious

••

SECTION-3

Word Power

1. One-word Substitute

Sometimes it so happens that certain words are on the tip of our tongue but we are unable to recollect them exactly. To overcome this problem, one-word substitute is of great help. Given below is an alphabetical list that would help you choose the exact word you are looking for.

To formally relinquish power or authority esp. by a monarch	-	**Abdication**
The original inhabitants of a country	-	**Aborigines**
To do away with a rule	-	**Abrogate**
To accustom oneself to a foreign climate	-	**Acclimatise**
To break off proceedings of a meeting for a time	-	**Adjourn**
Stage between boyhood and youth	-	**Adolesence**
Voluntary sexual intercourse between a married person and a person who is not his or her spouse	-	**Adultery**
A list or program of things to be done or problems to be addressed	-	**Agenda**
The place where public, government or historical records are kept	-	**Archives**
Words used in ancient times but no longer in general use at present	-	**Archaic**
Public building where weapons and ammunition are made or stored	-	**Arsenal**
A sea abounding in island	-	**Archipelago**
Not identified by name; of unknown name	-	**Anonymous**
Commencement of words with the same letter	-	**Alliteration**
Regard for others as a principle of action	-	**Altruism**
A story in which ideas are symbolized as people	-	**Allegory**
Allowance due to a wife from her husband on separation	-	**Alimony**
The school or college in which one has been educated	-	**Alma mater**
A raised place on which offerings and religious ceremonies are made	-	**Altar**
The cessation of warfare before a treaty is signed	-	**Armistice**
A thing or person behind time	-	**Antiquated**
Anything which destroys the effect of poison	-	**Antidote**

285

A short, usually amusing story about some real person or event	- Anecdote
Medicine which lessens pain	- Anodyne
Deviation or departure from common rule or standard	- Anomaly
A pioneer of a reform movement	- Apostle
A life history written by oneself	- Autobiography
A voice loud enough to be heard	- Audible
One who is desirous of getting money	- Avaricious
Place where birds are kept	- Aviary
Open to more than one interpretation	- Ambiguous
Animals living on land and in water	- Amphibian
A general pardon of political offenders	- Amnesty
Strong and settled dislike between two persons	- Antipathy
Lack of enough blood	- Anaemia
Yearly celebration of a date or an event	- Anniversary
A room leading into a large room or hall	- Anteroom
Science of bodily structure	- Anatomy
Constant effort to achieve something	- Attempt

B

Simplest and smallest form of plant life, present in air, water and soil; essential to life but which may cause disease	- Bacteria
Poem in short stanzas narrating a story	- Ballad
Gentle; kindly	- Benign
Nation engaged in war	- Belligerent
To surround with armed forces	- Besiege
Part of a church in which bells hang	- Belfry
A life history written by somebody else	- Biography
Practice of having two wives or husbands	- Bigamy
To talk without respect of something sacred or holy	- Blasphemy
Clumsy or ill-bred	- Boor
A small shop that sells fashionable clothes, cosmetics, etc.	- Boutique
Likely to break or crack	- Brittle
A small house with all rooms on one floor	- Bungalow
Shelter for cow	- Byre

C

That which makes it difficult to recognise the presence of real nature of somebody or something	- Camouflage
A flesh eating animal	- Carnivorous
Tending to move away from the centre or axis	- Centrifugal

A small piece of potato	-	**Chip**
An extremely deep crack or opening in the ground	-	**Chasm**
Unreal and visionary	-	**Chimerical**
To talk much without coming to the point	-	**Circumlocution**
Place where bankers exchange cheques and adjust balances	-	**Clearing house**
A small, named group of fixed stars	-	**Constellation**
An associate in an office or institution	-	**Colleague**
Gradual recovery from illness	-	**Convalescence**
A disease which spreads by contact	-	**Contagious**
Careful preservation and protection	-	**Conservation**
Opposed to great or sudden change	-	**Conservative**
People living at the same time	-	**Contemporaries**
Joint sovereignty exercised over a country by two or more countries	-	**Condominium**
Relationship by blood or birth	-	**Consanguinity**
Which can be easily believed	-	**Credible**
A low area storm with high winds rotating about a centre of low atmospheric pressure	-	**Cyclone**

D

To send an unwanted person out of the country	-	**Deport**
To cause troops, etc. to spread out in readiness for battle	-	**Deploy**
To transfer one's authority to another	-	**Delegate**
To deprive a thing of its holy character	-	**Deseret**
The rule of a person who is tyrant	-	**Despotism**
A song sung at a burial	-	**Dirge**
A book containing summarised information on all branches of knowledge, numbers, etc.	-	**Directory**
A large sleeping-room with many beds	-	**Dormitory**
Extreme old age when a man behaves like a fool	-	**Dotage**
A game in which no one wins	-	**Draw**
Time after twilight and before night	-	**Dusk**

E

Not conforming to ordinary rules of behaviour	-	**Eccentric**
Study of environment	-	**Ecology**
A poem written on the death of someone loved and lost	-	**Elegy**
A place of ideal peace and happiness	-	**Elysium**
A persuasive and fluent speech	-	**Eloquence**
Run away from home with lover	-	**Elope**

Mental weariness for want of occupation	-	**Ennui**
A speech by an actor at the end of a play	-	**Epilogue**
Words written on the tomb of a person	-	**Epitaph**
A verse letter	-	**Epistle**
Having no beginning or end to its existence	-	**Eternal**
Bringing about gentle and painless death from incurable disease	-	**Euthanasia**
Leave or cause the occupants to leave	-	**Evacuate**
Willing to take a definite stand	-	**Evasive**
A short journey made by a group of persons together	-	**Excursion**
To free somebody from all blame	-	**Exonerate**
Large scale departure of people	-	**Exodus**
To atone for one's sins	-	**Expiate**
Forcing out (blood, etc.) from its vessel	-	**Extravasate**
Speech delivered without previous preparation	-	**Extempore**

F

An animal story with a moral	-	**Fable**
A disease which ends in death	-	**Fatal**
One filled with excessive and mistaken enthusiasm in a cause	-	**Fanatic**
To congratulate someone in a formal manner	-	**Felicitate**
Continuing fight between parties, families, clans, etc.	-	**Feud**
Bring to an end	-	**Finish**
To issue a thunderous verbal attack	-	**Fulminate**
The plants and vegetation of a region	-	**Flora**
Counterfiet certificates and documents	-	**Forgery**
The line which a plough cuts in the ground	-	**Furrow**

G

A building or house for storing grains	-	**Granary**
The branch of medical science which deals with the problems of the old	-	**Geriatrics**
A fixed orbit in space in relation to earth	-	**Geo-stationary**
A list of explanation of words, especially unusual ones at the end of a book	-	**Glossary**
A sudden rush of wind	-	**Gust**

H

A loud talk or speech	-	**Harangue**

The part of a Muslim household reserved for wives, concubines, etc.	-	Harem
A perception without objective reality	-	Hallucination
Two-wheeled cab for two to ride inside with driver mounted up behind	-	Hansom
Wicked to a high degree	-	Heinous
A place for the collection of dry plants	-	Herbarium
Belief or opinion contrary to what is generally accepted	-	Heresy
A grass-eating animal	-	Herbivorous
Having superior or intellectual interests and tastes	-	Highbrow
Parts of a country behind the coast or a river's banks	-	Hinterland
Course for chariot races	-	Hippodrome
Line at which the earth or sea and sky seem to meet	-	Horizon
A post without remuneration	-	Honorary
Seat on elephant's back	-	Howdah
An exaggerated statement	-	Hyperbole
A song embodying religious and sacred emotions	-	Hymn

A statement which cannot be understood		-Incomprehensible
Short descriptive poem of picturesque scene or incident	-	Idyll
Incapable of being explained or accounted for	-	Inexplicable
That which is against the law	-	Illegal
A handwriting that cannot be read	-	Illegible
The policy of extending a country's empire and influence	-	Imperialism
Free from infection	-	Immune
That is sure to happen	-	Imminent
Exemption from punishment	-	Impunity
That which cannot be described	-	Indescribable
A formal written charge against a person for some crime or offence	-	Indictment
That which cannot be done without	-	Indispensable
That which cannot be avoided	-	Inevitable
That which cannot be corrected	-	Incorrigible
A story that can hardly be believed	-	Incredible
Travelling under the name other than one's own	-	Incognito
Soldiers on foot	-	Infantry
Incapable of making a mistake	-	Infallible
Something that cannot be imitated	-	Inimitable
That which cannot be satisfied	-	Insatiable

Unable to pay off one's debts	-	**Insolvent**
To examine one's own thoughts and feelings	-	**Introspection**
That cannot be touched	-	**Intangible**
To mediate between two parties in a dispute	-	**Intercede**
Interval between two events or two periods of time of different character	-	**Interlude**
The period between two reigns	-	**Interregnum**
Hint or signal by the mind without reasoning	-	**Intuition**
That cannot be won	-	**Invincible**
Incapable of being wounded	-	**Invulnerable**
Place which provides both board and lodging	-	**Inn**
A list of goods sent with their prices	-	**Invoice**
Interested mainly in a small group, country, etc.	-	**Insular**
That which cannot be rectified or made good	-	**Irreparable**

J

Language difficult to understand because of bad form	-	**Jargon**

K

A constantly changing pattern or sequence of objects or elements	-	**Kaleidoscope**
A home for dogs	-	**Kennel**
The place where bricks are baked	-	**Kiln**
A school for infants and young children	-	**Kindergarten**

L

A place where a wild animal lives	-	**Lair**
Room with toilet facilities	-	**Lavatory**
A medicine used to loosen the stuff in the bowels	-	**Laxative**
A book of accounts showing debits and credits	-	**Ledger**
Gift left by will	-	**Legacy**
Stories of old time gods or heroes	-	**Legend**
Responsible according to law	-	**Legitimate**
That which is lawful	-	**Legal**
The part of government which is concerned with making of rules	-	**Legislature**
Cutting for stone in the bladder	-	**Lithotomy**
Science of reasoning	-	**Logic**

M

A person's first speech	-	**Maiden**
Ridiculous use of words	-	**Malapropism**
Policy of a political party	-	**Manifesto**
An instrument for measuring gaseous pressure	-	**Manometer**
A paper written by hand	-	**Manuscript**
Morning prayer in the church	-	**Matins**
A dramatic performance	-	**Masque**
Part-song for several voices without instrumental accompaniment	-	**Madrigal**
Informal business communication with a personal signature	-	**Memorandum**
One who is neither intelligent nor dull	-	**Mediocre**
The list of courses at a meal or of dishes that can be served in a restaurant	-	**Menu**
Careful and particular	-	**Meticulous**
Life history of a person written by another	-	**Memoir**
A place where money is coined	-	**Mint**
Design made by putting together coloured pieces of glass or stones	-	**Mosaic**
A place where monks live as a secluded community	-	**Monastery**
Practice of having one wife or husband	-	**Monogamy**
Of outstanding significance	-	**Monumental**
Open rebellion of soldiers and sailors against lawful authority	-	**Mutiny**

N

A medicine for producing sleep	-	**Narcotic/Opiate**
Giving undue favours to one's own kith and kin	-	**Nepotism**
Just punishment for wrong doing	-	**Nemesis**
Use of new words	-	**Neologism**
A hollow place in a wall for a statue	-	**Niche**
Home sickness or sentimental longing for the past	-	**Nostalgia**
The loop of rope with a running knot used to hang a person	-	**Noose**
Having an evil reputation	-	**Notorious**
Collection of coins	-	**Numismatic**

O

A word no longer in use, outdated	-	**Obsolete**
Printed notice of somebody's death	-	**Obituary**
A style in which a writer makes a display of his knowledge	-	**Oligarchy**

In a state of tension or anxiety or suspense	-	**On tenterhooks**
That through which light cannot pass	-	**Opaque**
A place where orphans live	-	**Orphanage**
A field or a part of a garden where fruit trees grow	-	**Orchard**
Correct spelling	-	**Orthography**
Dungeon entered by trapdoor	-	**Oubliette**

P

To walk with slow or regular steps	-	**Pace**
To bring peace and end violence	-	**Pacify**
Loss of power to move in any or every part of the body	-	**Paralysis**
A funny imitation of a poem	-	**Parody**
A temporary release allowed on certain conditions	-	**Parole**
Property inherited from one's father or ancestor	-	**Patrimony**
Study of ancient writing	-	**Paliography**
A remedy or cure for all diseases, troubles, etc.	-	**Panacea**
Very pleasing to eat	-	**Palatable**
Story told to illustrate a moral or spiritual truth	-	**Parable**
Thing that can be felt or touched	-	**Palpable**
Government by all	-	**Pantisocracy**
Belief of God in nature	-	**Pantheism**
Biological entity which lives on another organism	-	**Parasite**
Be the embodiment or perfect example of	-	**Personify**
A style in which a writer makes a display of his knowledge	-	**Pedantic**
Equal in rank, merit or quality	-	**Peer**
To remove the skin of a potato or an orange	-	**Peel**
That which is everlasting	-	**Perennial**
Land so surrounded by water as to be almost an island	-	**Peninsula**
The science of judging a person's character, capabilities, etc. from an examination of the shape of his skull	-	**Phrenology**
To take secretly in small quantities	-	**Pilferage**
A ride on someone else's back or shoulders	-	**Piggyback**
A commonplace remark	-	**Platitude**
Practice of borrowing ideas and words from others and using them as his own	-	**Plagiarism**
Decision made upon a political question by the votes of all qualified persons	-	**Plebiscite**
Use of more words than are needed to express the meaning	-	**Plenasm**
Practice or custom of having several wives	-	**Polygamy**
Anything written in a letter after it is signed	-	**Postscript**

Occurring or appearing after the death of the originator	-	**Posthumous**
Books, pictures etc. intended to arouse sexual desire	-	**Pornography**
That which can be carried	-	**Portable**
Something which can be taken for granted	-	**Postulate**
A book or picture produced merely to bring in money	-	**Pot-boiler**
The custom of having more than one husband at the same time	-	**Polyandry**
A figure with many angles or sides	-	**Polygon**
Explicit undertaking to do something	-	**Promise**
A child of unusual or remarkable talent	-	**Prodigy**
A forecast of the result of a disease or illness	-	**Prognosis**
Code of diplomatic etiquette and precedence	-	**Protocol**
Woman who offers the use of her body for sexual intercourse to any one who pays for it	-	**Prostitute**
To write under a different name	-	**Pseudonym**
Careful in performing duties	-	**Punctilious**

Q

Confinement to one place to avoid spread of infection	-	Quarantine

R

People in a rowdy scene	-	**Rabble**
A means of raising money by selling numbered tickets; lottery	-	**Raffle**
Sharp disapproval or criticism	-	**Rebuke**
Present opposing arguments or evidence	-	**Rebut**
Paying back injury with injury	-	**Reprisal**
An expression of mild disapproval	-	**Reproof**
Shining, brilliant and magnificent	-	**Resplendent**
Asking everyone for an opinion	-	**Referendum**
A place for improving one's health	-	**Resort**
Give tit for tat	-	**Retaliate**
A lady's small handbag or workbag	-	**Reticule**
Give back to the users, their youthful vigour and appearance	-	**Rejuvenating**
Too much official formality	-	**Red-tapism**
A person who lives alone and avoids other people	-	**Recluse**
Witty and clever retort	-	**Repartee**
Atonement for one's sins	-	**Repentance**
The art of elegant speech or writing	-	**Rhetoric**

S

An act of violating or profaning religious things	-	**Sacrilege**
Deriving pleasure from inflicting pain on others	-	**Sadism**
A place with a good climate for invalids	-	**Sanatorium**
A very private place	-	**Sanctum or Sanctorium**
A government in which no distinction is made between persons of different religion. / A person who believes in no religion	-	**Secular**
A place adjoining kitchen for washing dishes, etc.	-	**Scullery**
An instrument for detecting earthquakes	-	**Seismograph**
A religious discourse	-	**Sermon**
Acutely affected by external expressions	-	**Sensitive**
Music sung or played at night below a person's window	-	**Serenade**
A case in which sword is kept	-	**Sheath**
One who despises persons of lower social position	-	**Snob**
Walking in sleep	-	**Somnambulism**
A short stay at a place	-	**Sojourn**
Applicable to widely scattered groups of people	-	**Sporadic**
A place where horses are kept	-	**Stable**
A heavy unnatural slumber	-	**Stupor**
Indifference to pleasure or sin	-	**Stoicism**
A government by the military class	-	**Stratocracy**
Walk in a vain, self-important way	-	**Strut**
The short remaining end of a cigarette	-	**Stub**
A short walk for pleasure or exercise	-	**Stroll**
Income just sufficient to live on	-	**Subsistence**
Something which is not thorough or profound	-	**Superficial**
Below the surface	-	**Subterranean**
A person's last utterance	-	**Swansong**
To slap with a flat object	-	**Swat**

T

A list or table of duties payable on exports or imports	-	**Tariff**
The act of preserving skin	-	**Taxidermy**
That which is perceptible by touch	-	**Tangible**
The power of reading the thoughts of others	-	**Telepathy**
An instrument for viewing objects at a distance	-	**Telescope**
The foolish belief for self to be God	-	**Theomania**

The art of cutting trees and bushes into ornamental shapes	-	**Topiary**
A group of three novels or plays, each complete in itself	-	**Trilogy**
The doctrine that human souls pass from one body to another at the time of death	-	**Transmigration**
A drawing on transparent paper	-	**Transparency**
That through which light can partly pass	-	**Translucent**
Those who pass through this gate without permission	-	**Trespassers**
Plain or self-evident truth	-	**Truism**
Science of printing	-	**Typography**

U

That which cannot be understood	-	**Unintelligible**
Something that relates to everyone in the world	-	**Universal**
An imaginary ideal state	-	**Utopia**

V

Changing one's mind too quickly	-	**Vacillation**
Word for word/word by word reproduction	-	**Verbatim**
A style full of words	-	**Verbose**
Able to adopt oneself readily to many situations	-	**Versatile**
A state of complete continence on part of a woman	-	**Virginity**

W

A place where clothes are kept	-	**Wardrobe**
An unexpected stroke of good luck	-	**Windfall**
To move along with quick, short twisting	-	**Wriggle**

Y

A light sailing boat built especially for racing	-	**Yatch**

●●

2. Foreign Words and Phrases

English is one of the most widely used languages of the world. Its vocabulary is not entirely its own. It has embraced words from different languages, like Greek, French, Latin, German, Spanish, Japanese, etc. Not only this, words from Indian languages have also been incorporated into it from time to time. Latin words are the maximum in number. Such words or phrases are called foreign words and phrases.

a bas	(*French*)	down
ab initio	(*Latin*)	from the beginning
a bon marche	(*French*)	cheap, a good bargain
ab origine	(*Latin*)	from the origin
a cheval	(*French*)	on horseback
ad finem	(*Latin*)	to the end
ad hoc	(*Latin*)	for a particular purpose
ad infinitum	(*Latin*)	endlessly; forever
ad interim	(*Latin*)	for time being, temporarily
ad libitum	(*Latin*)	at pleasure
ad nauseam	(*Latin*)	to the point of disgust
ad rem	(*Latin*)	to the purpose
adsum	(*Latin*)	I am present, I am here!

Sometimes, your ignorance of foreign words and phrases can prove dangerous!

A man visits his Chinese friend in a hospital. "Li kai yang qi guan," says the Chinese friend. The man doesn't understand a single word and becomes desperate about what to say next. "Li kai yang qi guan!" says the patient, as his face becomes red.

After a few weeks, the man goes on a business tour of China. There he learns the meaning of "Li kai yang qi guan": "Get off my oxygen tube."

ad valorem	(*Latin*)	according to value or custom.
aide memoire	(*French*)	a memorandum summarizing the items of an agreement
alter ego	(*Latin*)	intimate friend
alter ipse amicus	(*Latin*)	a friend is another self
a'maximis ad minima	(*Latin*)	from the greatest to the smallest
ambiance	(*French*)	(literally: surroundings): mood, character, atmosphere
amcus humani generis	(*Latin*)	a friend of humanity
amicus curiae	(*Latin*)	a friend of the law-court
an attendant	(*French*)	in the mean while
anglice	(*Latin*)	in English
anima mundi	(*Latin*)	the soul of the world
animo et jide	(*Latin*)	by courage and faith
annus mirabilis	(*Latin*)	year of wonders
apologia	(*Latin*)	a formal apologetic writing
a priori	(*Latin*)	based on theoretical deduction rather than empirical observation
apropos	(*French*)	with reference to, concerning
avant-garde	(*French*)	new, experimental
ante bellum	(*Latin*)	before the war
ante meridiem	(*Latin*)	before noon; morning (a.m.)
antiquarium	(*Latin*)	collection of antiquities
arbitrium	(*Latin*)	power of decision
arcana imperii	(*Latin*)	state secrets
au fait	(*French*)	well-versed; an expert

B

bandolero	(*Spanish*)	a dacoit or bandit
bella donna	(*Latin*)	a pretty woman
bella, horrida bella	(*Latin*)	wars, horrible wars
bellum lethale	(*Latin*)	deadly war
biennium	(*Latin*)	period of two years
bon enfant	(*Fench*)	a good fellow
bon voyage	(*French*)	an enjoyable journey, especially abroad

297

bête noire	(*French*)	an object of dislike
bon appetite	(*Spanish*)	enjoy your meal
bona fides	(*Latin*)	in good faith; honesty and sincerity of intention
bona mobilia	(*Latin*)	movable goods

C

carte blanche	(*French*)	a free hand, full freedom
cause célèbre	(*French*)	a controversial issue that attracts a great deal of public attention
cadeau	(*French*)	a present, a gift
cadre	(*French*)	official status; list of officers
caeca est invidia	(*Latin*)	envy is blind
canard	(*French*)	a hoax or rumour
casus belli	(*Latin*)	involving a war
caveat actor	(*Latin*)	let the doer beware
centum	(*Latin*)	a hundred
charge d'saffaires	(*French*)	a diplomat or an ambassador
cito	(*Latin*)	quickly
compos mentis	(*Latin*)	of sound mind, sane
compte rendu	(*French*)	a report or review; an account rendered
con spirito	(*Latin*)	with spirit
confer	(*Latin*)	compare
consilio et animis	(*Latin*)	by wisdom and courage
contra bonos mores	(*Latin*)	against good manners or morals
coram popula	(*Latin*)	in the presence of the public
corpus delicti	(*Latin*)	the substance of an offence.
corrigendum	(*Latin*)	correction made in a book after printing
coup d'etat	(*French*)	a swift stroke of policy; to change government by rebellion.
coup de grace	(*French*)	a death blow
coup de hasard	(*French*)	a lucky chance
coup de main	(*French*)	a bold attempt
crimen falsi	(*Latin*)	crime of perjury
cuisine	(*French*)	speciality dishes.

culpa levis	(*Latin*)	a slight fault
cul-de-sac	(*French*)	a street or passage closed at one end
currente calamo	(*Latin*)	with a running pen

D

de facto	(*Latin*)	in fact, whether legally or not
de jure	(*Latin*)	by right; legally
de rigueur	(*French*)	required by etiquette
detente	(*French*)	release from tension
data et accepta	(*Latin*)	expenses and receipts
de bon augure	(*French*)	of good omen
de die in diem	(*Latin*)	from day to day
de integro	(*Latin*)	afresh, anew
de novo	(*Latin*)	anew; again; afresh
de trop	(*Latin*)	too much; superfluous
dei gratia	(*Latin*)	by the grace of God
deo favente	(*Latin*)	with God's favour
deo gratias	(*Latin*)	thanks to God
deus avertat!	(*Latin*)	god forbid!
deus det	(*Latin*)	god grant!
domine, dirige nos!	(*Latin*)	god, direct us!
dum spiro, spero	(*Latin*)	while I breath, I hope

E

élan	(*French*)	energy; style; enthusiasm
enfant terrible	(*French*)	a person of outrageous behaviour
en masse	(*French*)	all together; in a body
en route	(*French*)	on the way
entente	(*French*)	friendly understanding
espirit de corps	(*French*)	pride and honour shared by the members of a group
exempli gratia (e.g.)	(*Latin*)	for example
ex officio	(*Latin*)	by virtue of one's office
ex post facto	(*Latin*)	after a happening
editio princeps	(*Latin*)	original edition (of a book)
elite	(*French*)	the best; superior

emeritus	(*Latin*)	one retired from active service (professor)
en bloc	(*French*)	taken all together; in a body
en effet	(*French*)	in effect; reality
en train	(*French*)	under progress or process
eo nomine	(*Latin*)	by that name
erenata	(*Latin*)	according to the exigencies of the case
esprit de corps	(*French*)	spirit of comradeship
et hoc genus omne	(*Latin*)	everything of this or that sort
ex curia	(*Latin*)	out of court
ex delicto	(*Latin*)	owing to crime
ex dono	(*Latin*)	as a gift
ex gratia	(*Latin*)	as an act of grace; payment made in favour or free
ex parte	(*Latin*)	one sided judgement
ex tacito	(*Latin*)	silently
ex tempore	(*Latin*)	without preparation; especially a speech made without preparation
ex utraque parte	(*Latin*)	on either side
ex voto	(*Latin*)	according to one's prayer
expressis verbis	(*Latin*)	in express terms

F

faux pas	(*French*)	a false step
faber est quisque	(*Latin*)	everyone fashions
forunae suae	(*Latin*)	his own fortune
facsimile	(*Latin*)	a perfect copy
facta non verba	(*Latin*)	deeds, not words
factum est	(*Latin*)	it is done
fadaise	(*French*)	a silly talk
fait accompli	(*French*)	a thing already done
fata obstant	(*Latin*)	the fate opposes it
faux pas	(*French*)	a false step or social blunder
fecit	(*Latin*)	made or executed
festina lente	(*Latin*)	make haste slowly; careful
fiat justitia, ruat clelum	(*Latin*)	let justice be done though the heavens

fide et amore	(*Latin*)	by faith and love
fidus et audax	(*Latin*)	faithful and bold
fillius nullius	(*Latin*)	a bastard

G

gaillard	(*French*)	lively
garcon	(*French*)	a boy, bachelor a lad
gloria in excelsis	(*Latin*)	glory to God is the highest
gratis	(*Latin*)	free of charge

H

hoi polloi	(Greek)	the common people (derogatory)
honoris causa	(*Latin*)	degree awarded as a mark of esteem
hoc age	(*Latin*)	attend to what you do
hoc anno	(*Latin*)	in this year
hoc loco	(*Latin*)	in this place
hoc tempre	(*Latin*)	at this time
hominis est errare	(*Latin*)	to err is human
honoris causa	(*Latin*)	honorary

I

ibidem (ibid)	(*Latin*)	in the same source (used for reference)
idem	(*Latin*)	the same
impasse	(*Latin*)	hang-up
impromptu	(*Latin*)	unplanned; unrehearsed
in camera	(*Latin*)	in the private room
incognito	(*Italian*)	concealing one's identity
in extenso	(*Latin*)	in full
infra dignitatem	(*Latin*)	below one's dignity
in limine	(*Latin*)	in the beginning
in re	(*Latin*)	with regard to; in the case of
in situ	(*Latin*)	in the original position
in toto	(*Latin*)	in the whole; entirely
ipso facto	(*Latin*)	virtually; really

in abstracto	(*Latin*)	in the abstract
in aeternum	(*Latin*)	eternal for forever
in curia	(*Latin*)	in court
in equilibris	(*Latin*)	in equilibrium
in esse	(*Latin*)	in fact
in initio	(*Latin*)	in the begining
in pace	(*Latin*)	in peace
in status quo	(*Latin*)	in the former state
in terrorem	(*Latin*)	as a warning
in toto	(*Latin*)	completely or entirely
infra dignitatem	(*Latin*)	below one's dignity
inter alia	(*Latin*)	among other things
ipso jure	(*Latin*)	by the law
inter se	(*Latin*)	among themselves

J

jure divino	(*Latin*)	by divine law
jure humano	(*Latin*)	by human law

L

laissez faire	(French)	complete freedom
lingua franca	(Italian)	a common or mixed language spoken by the Europeans
locus standi	(Latin)	place for standing, right to appear in a court
labor ipsev oluptas	(Latin)	labour itself is pleasure.
lacuna	(Latin)	a gap; shortcoming
lapsus calami	(Latin)	a slip of the pen
lapsus linguae	(Latin)	a slip of the tongue
lapsus memoriae	(Latin)	a slip of the memory
lese majeste	(French)	high treason
lucri causa	(Latin)	for the sake of gain
lusus naturae	(Latin)	a freak of nature

M

magnum opus	(Latin)	a great work of art/literature
mala fides	(Latin)	in bad faith; faithlessly

memoralia	(Greek)	things worth remembering
mon ami	(French)	friend (male)
mon amie	(French)	a female friend
modus operandi	(Latin)	mode of operating
mutatis mutandis	(Latin)	with necessary alterations
magnum bonuni	(Latin)	a great good
mandamus	(Latin)	a writ issued by a higher court to a subordinate court
materia medica	(Latin)	material used for medicine; in current use pharmacology is included
matinee	(French)	an afternoon performance; usually cinema artists
me judice	(Latin)	in my opinion
memento mori	(Latin)	remember that thou shalt die
Memorabilia	(Latin)	things to be remembered
mirabile dictu	(Latin)	wonderful to tell
mirabile visu	(*Latin*)	wonderful to see

N

née	(French)	a married woman's maiden name; originally called
nom de plume	(French)	an assumed name
non sequitur	(Latin)	an inference or conclusion that does not follow from the premises or evidence
nouveau riche	(French)	newly rich
nolens volens	(Latin)	willing or not willing, whether he will or not
noli me tangere	(Latin)	don't touch me
nota bene	(Latin)	abbr. N.B take notice, mark well nulli
secundus	(Latin)	unparalled, second to none
nunc est bibendum	(*Latin*)	now is the time for drinking

O

obiter dictum	(Latin)	something said by the way; an incidental remark
omnia bona bonis	(Latin)	all things are good to the good
onus probandi	(*Latin*)	the burden of proof

P

par excellence	(French)	extra excellence
pari passu	(Latin)	together, side by side
par exemple	(French)	for example
pari passu	(Latin)	with equal pace; together
particeps criminis	(Latin)	an accomplice
per annum	(Latin)	per year; annually
per capita	(Latin)	for each person
per diem	(Latin)	daily; per day
per se	(Latin)	by itself
persona grata	(Latin)	a welcome guest
piece de resistance	(French)	the most remarkable or important feature of a creative work
prima facie	(Latin)	on the first view
primo	(Latin)	In the first place
pro bono	(Latin)	for the public good
pro forma	(Latin)	according to form
pronto	(Spanish)	without delay; quickly
pro tempore	(Latin)	for the time being
pro rata	(Latin)	in proportion
per centum	(Latin)	by the hundred
per mensum	(Latin)	per month
populus vult decipi	(Latin)	the people wish to be fooled
post meridiem	(Latin)	afternoon (p.m.)
post mortem	(Latin)	an examination of dead body to find cause of death; after death
post obitum	(*Latin*)	after death

Q

quid pro quo	(Latin)	something given or taken as equivalent to another
qui tacet consentit	(Latin)	he who keeps silence consents

R

raison d'être	(French)	important reason or purpose for something
re	(Latin)	about; again

résumé	(*French*)	biodata, summary
repondez, s'il vous plait	(French)	reply, if you please (R.S.V.P.)
res gestae	(Latin)	exploits
res judicata	(French)	in law; already decided

S

sanctum sanctorum	(*Latin*)	holy of holies
sangfroid	(French)	composure or coolness in danger
sine qua non	(Latin)	absolutely essential
status quo	(Latin)	existing state of affairs
status quo ante	(Latin)	previous state of affairs
stet	(Latin)	let it stand; an instruction to the printer or typist
sine die	(Latin)	indefinitely; without a day
sine odium	(Latin)	without hatred
sine qua non	(Latin)	an indispensable condition
sobriquet	(French)	a nickname
sponte sua	(Latin)	of one's own accord
sub judice	(Latin)	under judicial consideration
sub poena	(Latin)	a writ ordering a person to attend a court

T

tete- a- tete	(French)	private conversation between two people
terra incognita	(Latin)	an unknown country
tout a coup	(French)	suddenly
tour de force	(French)	A feat demonstrating brilliance or mastery in a field

U

ultimatum	(Latin)	a final demand of terms
ultimo	(Latin)	of the last month
ultima thule	(Latin)	the utmost limit
ultra vires	(*Latin*)	beyond one's legal power

V

vale	(*Latin*)	farewell
verbatim	(*Latin*)	using exactly the same words
versus	(*Latin*)	against
veni, vidi, vici	(*Latin*)	I came, I saw, I conquered
versus	(*Latin*)	against, via, by way of; en route
via media	(*Latin*)	a middle course; solution
vice	(*Latin*)	in place of; a substitute
vice versa	(*Latin*)	the terms being exchanged
vide	(*Latin*)	look at, refer to, see, consult
vis-a-vis	(*French*)	opposite facing
viva voce	(*Latin*)	oral examination, by word of mouth, orally
voila	(*French*)	behold; there it is
volente Deo	(*Latin*)	god willing
vox populi, vox Dei	(*Latin*)	the voice of the people is the voice of God

X

xystum	(*Latin*)	a shaded walk in a garden

Z

zonam perdidit	(*Latin*)	who lost his wealth, in need of money

●●

3. British vs American Words

Difference between British English and American English does not lie only in the pronunciation of words; their vocabulary, spelling and grammar also differ on many counts. In India, British English is most commonly used in personal and professional spheres. However, increasing American influence has started attracting youths towards it. Therefore, it becomes necessary to acquaint our youths with this difference at least in vocabulary at this stage if not in all aspects.

Acknowledgement	Acknowledgment
Aeroplane	Airplane
Aesthetic	Esthetic
Aesthetician	Esthetician
Ageing	Aging
All right	Alright
Aluminium	Aluminum
Analyse	Analyze
Anti-clockwise	Counterclockwise
Appendix	Appendixes/ Appendices
Authorise	Authorize

Behaviour	Behavior
Biscuits	Cookies
Bun	Muffin
Bottom/Bum	Butt

British and American English are two major varieties of English

Bernard Shaw once said that America and England were two great nations separated by the same language.

Boot (car)/dickey	Trunk
Bonnet (car)	Hood

Calliper	Caliper
Cancel (Cancelled/Cancelling)	Canceled/ Canceling
Cancellation	Cancelation
Candour	Candor
Catalogue	Catalog
Centralise	Centralize
Centre	Center
Characterise	Characterize
Cheque	Check
Chips	Fries
Cinema	Movie
Civilisation	Civilization
Civilise	Civilize
Colour	Color
Conceptualise	Conceptualize
Cooperate	Co-operate
Coordinate	Co-ordinate
Cosy	Cozy
Counselling	Counseling
Customise	Customize

Datable	Dateable
Defence	Defense
Dial (Dialled/Dialling)	Dialed/ Dialing
Dialogue	Dialog
Diarrhoea	Diarrhea
Dicey	Dicy

What has become very evident over the years is that the language is merging between all the various countries. In the UK, people have adopted 'Americanism' into everyday language and some British terms are now being used in the USA. This is probably due to travel and the wide exchange of TV programmes.

Disc	Disk
Discolour	Discolor
Dishonour	Dishonor
Disorganised	Disorganized
Dispatch	Despatch
Disrupter	Disruptor

E

Economise	Economize
Emphasise	Emphasize
Enamour	Enamor
Encyclopaedia	Encyclopedia
Enquiry	Inquiry
Endeavour	Endeavor
Equal (Equalled/Equalling)	Equaled/ Equaling

F

Familiarise	Familiarize
Fantasise	Fantasize
Favour	Favor
Favourite	Favorite
Fertilise	Fertilize
Fibre	Fiber
Film	Movie
Flat	Apartment
Flavour	Flavor
Fuel	Fueled/ Fueling
Fulfil	Fulfill
Full stop	Period

G

Glamour	Glamour
Globalise	Globalize
Grill	Broil
Grey	Gray

H

Harbour	Harbour
Harmonise	Harmonize
Handbrake	Emergency Break
Honour	Honour
Hospitalise	Hospitalize
Hosteller	Hosteler
Humour	Humor
Hypnotise	Hynotize

I

Icying	Frosting
Idealise	Idealize
Idolise	Idolize
Immovable	Immoveabie
Immunise	Immunize
Individualise	Individualize
Industrialisation	Industrialization
Instalment	Installment
Install, instal	Install
Interrupter	Interruptor
Italicise	Italicize
Itemise	Itemize

J

Jail, gaol	Jail
Jeopardise	Jeopardize
Jewelled	Jeweled
Jewellery	Jewellery
Judgement	Judgment

K

Kerb	Curb

L

Label (Labelled/Labelling)	Labeled/ Labeling
Labour	Labor

Labourer	Laborer
Lady finger	Okra
Legalise	Legalize
Legitimise	Legitimize
Licence	License
Lift	Elevator
Likable	Likeable
Liquefy	Liquify
Liveability	Livability
Localise	Localize
Loveable	Lovable
Liquefy	Liquify
Liveability	Livability
Lorry	Truck

Magnetise	Magnetize
Manoeuvre	Maneuver
Marginalise	Marginalize
Maths	Math
Meagre	Meager
Mechanise	Mechanize
Mediaeval	Medieval
Memorise	Memorize
Mesmerise	Mesmerize
Metre	Meter
Minimise	Minimize
Misbehaviour	Misbehavior
Mobile	Cellphone
Mobilise	Mobilize
Model (Modelled/Modelling)	Modeled/ Modeling
Modernise	Modernize
Moisturise	Moisturize
Monopolise	Monopolize
Mould	Mold

N

Nationalise	Nationalize
Neighbour	Neighbor
Normalise	Normalize

O

Ochre	Ocher
Offence	Offense
Organisation	Organization
Organise	Organize

P

Panel (Panelled/Panelling)	Paneled/ Paneling
Parlour	Parlor
Parcel	Package
Pavement	Sidewalk
Penalise	Penalize
Personalise	Personalize
Philosophise	Philosophize
Phoney	Phony
Postman/Postwoman	Mailman/ Mailwoman
Practice	Practice
Pressurise	Pressurize
Prioritise	Prioritize
Programme	Program
Prologue	Prolog
Protester	Protestor
Publicise	Publicize

Q

Queue	Line
Quarrel (Quarrelled/Quarrelling)	Quareled/ Quareling

R

Rationalise	Rationalize
Realise	Realize
Recognise	Recognize
Routeing	Routing
Rubber	Eraser
Rubbish	Garbage
Rumour	Rumor

S

Saleable	Salable
Sanitise	Sanitize
Savour	Savor
Scandalise	Scandalize
Sceptic	Skeptic
Sensationalise	Sensationalize
Sensitise	Sensitize
Serialise	Serialize
Shoelace	Shoestring
Socialise	Socialize
Sombre	Somber
Speciality	Specialty
Spiritualise	Spiritualize
Stabilise	Stabilize
Standardise	Standardize
Sterilise	Sterilize
Storey	Story
Summarise	Summarize
Sweets	Candy
Synchronise	Synchronize
Synthesise	Synthesize
Systematise	Systematize

T

Tantalise	Tantalize
Theatre	Theater
Timbre	Timber
Tranquillity	Tranquility
Travelling	Traveled/ Traveling/ Traveler
Travelogue	Travelog
Trivialise	Trivialize
Tyre	Tire

U

Uncivilised	Uncivilized
Unfavourable	Unfavorable
Unpractised	Unpracticed

313

Unrecognised	Unrecognized
Urbanise	Urbanize
Utilise	Utilize

V

Valorise	Valorize
Valour	Valor
Vaporise	Vaporize
Vapour	Vapor
Video Recorder	VCR
Vendor	Vender
Veranda	Verandah
Verbalise	Verbalize
Victimise	Victimize
Visualise	Visualize

W

Wardrobe	Closet
Warrantor	Warranter
Westernise	Westernize
Wilful	Willful

Y

Yogurt	Yoghurt

●●

4. Cliches

> Chiche is a phrase or idea which becomes stale or uninteresting due to its overuse in due course of time. Mostly used in fiction for creating comic effect, they do have some amount of truth in their meaning. They are not always false or inacurate.

A rose by any other name would smell as sweet
If you call something by another name, it doesn't change its origin.

Abandon ship
To leave a project or quit a job

About face
To change directions means to change one's mind

Absence makes the heart grow fonder
When you are not with your loved one, you miss him/her even more

Absolute power corrupts absolutely
People with power are usually corrupt

Above board
Legal or legitimate

Ace in the hole/Ace up your sleeve
A hidden tool or supply that others don't know about

Acid test
A decisive test to see if something is correct or valid

Actions speak louder than words
What people do, gives you a better idea of what they are thinking as opposed to what they say

All bets are off
Any agreement which is not being considered

Annoying Movie Cliché
The just-in-time bomb disabling
In this scene, the protagonist finds the bomb while it's ticking down its last minute to detonation, and he always cuts the wire and disables the bomb with exactly one second left on the timer, even though you're watching about ten minutes pass between him finding the bomb and disabling it.

All bent out of shape
Upset or angry

Airing dirty laundry
Talking about private matters in public

After my own heart
Being very friendly and likeable

Ah, to be young and foolish...
Immature

All dressed up and nowhere to go
When something looks good but has no purpose

All ears
Listen intently

All for one, and one for all
Everyone should work for the team and not for themselves

All hands on deck
Everyone needs to help

All in a day's work
Part of the daily routine

All in due time
Things will happen when they are scheduled for

All over the map
Not focused or clear in one's thinking

All paled in comparison
To seem much serious or important when compared with someone or something else

All talk and no action
When someone says to do something with much discussion but no action or result finally

All that glitters is not gold
Something that appears good is not always good

All the bits and pieces
Including everything

All thumbs
Not well coordinated

All's fair in love and war
When it comes to love or war, no one wants to follow the rules

Already got one paw on the chicken coop
Someone caught in the act of doing something wrong

All's well that ends well
Even though something did not go well, it is ok if it ended well

Altitude is determined by attitude
Your attitude will affect how far you will go in life

Always a bridesmaid, never the bride
To be close to success but never manage it

Always look on the bright side
Be optimistic.

An apple a day keeps the doctor away
If you behave in a healthy way everyday, you will not get sick

An arm and a leg
Extremely expensive or costly

An idle mind is the devil's workshop
When you don't have anything to think about, you will probably do something bad

An oldie, but a goodie
Something from the past makes you feel good; nostalgic

Prevention is better than cure
Keeping a problem from happening is much better than fixing it afterwards

Another day another dollar
Poorly paid or unimportant job

Ants in his pants
The inability to sit quietly

Any friend of yours is a friend of mine
This person is trustworthy because you think he or she is trustworthy

Any port in a storm
When in a desperate situation, the quickest and easiest resolution is welcome

Anything goes
Without any rules or regulations

Apple of my eye
A person who is favourite of someone

Are you a man or a mouse?
Are you strong enough or weak?

Around the horn
To give each person a chance in a discussion

As all get out
As much as something can be

As beautiful as the day is long
To describe someone who is very beautiful

As far as the eye can see
A very long distance

As good as gold
Authentic or Worthy

As honest as the day is long
Back when days were considered long, this was used to describe an honest man

As horny as a three balled tomcat
Full of sexual desire

As luck would have it
When something good happens without planning

As plain as the nose on your face
To be very obvious

As tender as a mother's heart
Very kind

As you sow, so shall you reap
Everything that you do has repercussions/what goes around comes around

Ashes to ashes, dust to dust
Everything will die and when it does, it will dissipate into nothing

Ask me no questions and I'll tell you no lies
If you ask me that question, I will not be able to tell you the truth

Asleep at the wheel
Not seeing and understanding what is happening

Ass backwards
Doing something in the wrong order

At the crack of dawn
Early in the morning

At the drop of a hat
Very quickly and suddenly

At the end of my rope
Desperate

At the end of the day
When all things have been considered

At the last minute
Happening at the last possible moment

At wits' end
Incomplete despair

Baby blues
Friendly blue eyes

Back against the wall
Having no options

Back from the dead
When someone or something becomes healthy again after being close to dying

Back in a sec
Back in a very short amount of time

Back stabber
Someone who is deceitful or who cannot be trusted

Back in the saddle
When someone has regained stature or a position he/she had previously lost

Backhanded compliment
Ridicule; making fun of someone

Bad blood
When two people or parties have an unsettled dispute between them

Bad to the bone
A person with no good qualities

Bag and baggage
Everything (as a whole)

Balls out
Fast and with all the effort possible

Ball is in your court
When opportunity is in your hand

Banging your head against a brick wall
To try to do something that is very difficult to achieve and causes you to feel annoyed

Barn burner
A very well contested game that consists of a lot of scoring

Bat the idea around
Discuss the idea with others

Be in the same boat
To be in the same set of circumstances as someone else

Be there or be square
If you are not there, you are nobody

Bear down
To force into a lower place; to depress or sink, to overthrow or crush by force

Beats me
When we don't know the answer to a specific question

Beat around the bush
To talk indirectly about something

Beat it!
Go away or leave

Beat the street
When a company reports earnings better than the expectations

Beauty lies in the eyes of the beholder
What may not be beautiful to one person may be very beautiful to another

Before you were the gleam in your father's eye
Meaning your father's interest in your mother that lead them becoming parents

Beggars can't be choosers
If you request something to be given, you should not question what you are given

Bells and whistles
To have every option or accessory available, avail the extras possible

Bend over
Get prepared to endure pain

Bet the farm
To bet a large sum of money

Better half
Your spouse

Better late than never
It is better to conclude something late than never to conclude it

Better safe than sorry
It is better not to take chances

Big as a house
Very big

Big as life
Very big or large

Big mouth
Someone who talks a lot or someone who says things that are hurtful to others

Big wig
The boss or leader

Bigger they are, the harder they fall
Big companies or people are more noticeable when they are beaten

Bite me
An expression of anger or disgust

Bite the bullet
Endure something unpleasant

Black as pitch
Very black or dark

Bite your lip
If you have to bite your lip, you have to make a conscious effort not to react

Black eye
A bad or undesireable reputation

Blast from the past
Something or someone from your past. Used often when referring to nostalgic music

Blew him away
When someone does something that is very unexpected

Blood money
Money made at the expense of someone's life

Blind as a bat
Lacking the ability to understand something

Blood is thicker than water
A tie to a relative is stronger that a tie to a wife or husband

Blow chow
Describes the act of vomiting or regurgitating

Blow it
Make a mistake

Body slam
An easy sale for full price

Bone chilling cold
Intensely cold, penetrating cold

Born with a silver spoon in his mouth
Born to a rich family

Bottom line
The essence of something

Boys will be boys
All boys are the same; they can be noisy; they can act childishly or misbehave

Bragging rights
To boast after winning a game

Bring it
To perform at or above the level expected

Brush off, To (The)
To disregard as not important or serious

Bury the hatchet
To stop fighting

Business as usual
When things go in routine way

Business at hand
What is important now, not what may be important in the future

Busted
Caught doing something wrong or illegal

Busy as a bee, As
Very busy and always working

Butterflies in your stomach
Anxious

Buy in to
Agree with; Believe in

By the book
Follow the rules

(To) Call it a day
Time to quit for the day; to stop working

(You) Can't have your cake and eat it too
You have to choose between one or another

Can't judge a book by its cover, (you)
Don't make a judgement on appearance

Can't learn to swim without getting in the water
You have to experience things to learn them

Can't say enough about him
Someone who is very good at what he does

Can't teach an old dog new tricks
As people get older, they are less likely to change the way they do things

Cash cow
A product or service that regularly produces a large amount of money

Cast a very long shadow
The ability to influence or intimidate someone from far away

Cat nap
A short nap or sleep

Cat's meow
The subject of admiration

Caught with his pants down
Caught in the act of doing something illegal or immoral

Caught with your hand in the cookie jar
Caught in stealing something

Change your tune
To say something different from what you have said in the past

Changes hands
Passed back and forth between two people or teams

Cheap date (A)
A person who requires a small amount of alcohol to get drunk

Cheap trick
Something that, although it may be legal, deceives someone

Chew the fat
To have discussions about nothing and waste time

Child's play
Something that is easy to do or understand

Chill out
Relax

Chip on your shoulder
Not friendly, Arrogant

Clean sweep
To win every game of a series

Clean your clock
To knock you out

Clear as a bell
Often used to describe the highest level of understanding

Clear as mud
Not clear or easy to understand

Climbing the walls
Making me angry, frustrated and/or irritated

Close call
A near accident

Close early and often
When selling something, ask the customer for the order early in the sales process and often throughout the sales process

Close ranks
To strengthen a group's unity and like-minded thinking usually when confronted by an adversary

Cock and bull story
A lie

Cool as cucumber
Laid back and relaxed, especially in a difficult situation

Cold feet
To decide not to do something that you had agreed to do

Cold shoulder
To ignore someone

Come hell or high water
Intending to do something in particular no matter what obstacles get in the way

Come in under the wire
Happening at the last possible moment

Complete picture, The
Including all options

Crack the nut
Solve the problem

Crazy as a loon
Someone who does not appear to be in control of their mental abilities

Crime doesn't pay
If you think that commiting a crime is an easy way to make money, but it will get you into trouble and will not leave you

Crocodile tears
To cry fake tears

Cross the line, To
To break a rule or law

Cry all the way to the bank, To
To gloat over making money

Cry over spilled milk, To
To cry or lament over an irreversible situation

Cry wolf
To raise a false alarm or warning

Curiosity killed the cat
It is often a mistake to be too curious

Cut off your nose to spite your face
To disadvantage yourself in order to do harm to an opponent or adversary

Cuts like a knife
Words that hurt you so bad that you feel like someone has stabbed you

Cuts to the core
Something that goes directly to the most important part of a thought or idea

Dances to the beat of a different drum
Someone who does things differently than other people

Dangle a carrot in front of him
To motivate someone by providing a reward

Dark horse
The competitor that could surprise us and win

Dead as a doornail
When something is not working or dead

Dealt a fatal blow
An act that leads to death

Diamond in the rough
Something good that is yet undiscovered

Dig yourself into a hole, To
To leave yourself with no options

Dip your toe in the water
To proceed with an activity at a slow, cautionary pace

Do or die
A situation in which you must take a big risk in order to avoid failure

Do what it takes
To do everything possible to get something done

Doesn't stand a chance
Have no hope or chance to succeed

Dogs bark, but the caravan moves on
When many characters may create chaos, but the main idea will continue to progress

Don't count your chickens before they're hatched
Don't assume that you will get something. Wait until you actually have it

Don't get your knickers in a knot
Acting mysterical or emotional; upset or angry

Don't rock the boat
To aggravate a situation

Don't make a fuss
To waste a lot of time or energy

Dressed to kill
Dressed very nicely, extravagantly or elaborately

Drop in the bucket
A very small amount or unimportant amount

Dry as a bone also (bone-dry)
Extremely dry

Dumb as a stump
An expression to describe someone who is not very smart or who is dumb

Early bird catches the worm, The
If you start something early, you stand a better chance of success

Early to bed, early to rise, makes a man healthy, wealthy and wise
Sleeping early and getting up early will help you be healthy and successful.

Easy as ABC
Very easy

Eat like a horse, To
To eat large amounts of food

Elephant in the room, The
A large issue with influence over a discussion ; a major controvertial problem that is not discussed

Emotional roller coaster, An
Something that causes you to feel many kinds of emotions from happiness to sadness

Empty flattery
False praise

Every dark cloud has a silver lining
Some good things can happen even when things appear to be bad. Every bad situation has some good aspect to it

Every dog has his day
Everyone, regardless of wealth or previous luck, will have good things happen to them at some point o; time

Fair weather friend
A person who is your friend only when things are going well

Face like a bulldog chewing on a wasp, A
Unattractive because of the ugly expression on the face

Family affair, A
Things that should be dealt with, within a family

Fan the flames
To do something to make a bad situation worse

Feather in one's cap, A
A special achievement or acknowledgement of one's work or effort

Fight like cats and dogs
To fight often and ferociously

Fine wine, A
Something that gets better with the years

Fine line
A very slight difference

Fish out of water, A
Being in a place or situation that you are not suited for

Fit as a fiddle
Very good in shape

Following in his footsteps
A situation when someone does the same things as his father or predecessor

Free as a bird
Not confined either physically, emotionally, or spiritually

From day one
From the beginning, ab initio

Full of mischief
Always getting into trouble

Game is on the line, The
The game, at a point when what happens next will determine the winner

Get an earful, To
To get a scolding

Get out of my hair
Stop bothering me

Get over the hump
To get to a point where the task has been passed

Give a hoot, To
To show a concern for something

Give me a hand
To help someone

Give them an inch, and they'll take a mile
When you offer something to someone, they will want much more of it

Go against the grain, To
To choose a difficult path

Go back to the well
To return to specific resource

Go head to head
To confront or engage an opponent directly

Gold digger, A
Someone who is wealthy

Good beginning makes a good ending, A
Planning is the key to success

Good fences make good neighbours
As long as neighbours mind their own business, they will get along well

Good man is hard to find, A
Finding a good husband or a man is not easy

Good things come to the one who waits
Good things happen to people who are patient

Got under my skin
Which irritates and makes you angry

Grinning from ear to ear
A very pronounced grin or smile

Half-baked idea, A
A scheme that has'nt been thought over or planned well

Hang on every word
To listen intently and wait expectantly for what is said next

Hard-headed
A critical way of saying that someone is stubborn

Hard to swallow
Difficult to believe

Haste makes waste
If you try to do something too quickly, you may not do it well and hence it goes waste

Have a heart
A polite way of asking someone to show kindness

Have the last laugh
When others realize that you have won or succeeded after thinking that you had initially failed

Have egg on the face
Feel embarrassed

He who cannot dance, blames the drum beater
When one looks to blame someone else for their own weakness

Head over heels
To fall down wildly

Heart breaker
Loosing a close game

Hell raiser
Someone who makes a lot of trouble

High hopes
A strong belief that something good will happen

History repeats itself
Things that happened in the past, will happen again in the future

Hit below the belt
To commit an act that is against the rules

Hot as hell
Very, very hot

Hot water, In
In deep trouble

In cold blood
Without the feeling of remorse

I wasn't born yesterday
To say, I'm not dumb or stupid.

Idle hands are the devil's workshop
When you don't have anything to do, you will probably do something bad.

If wishes were horses, beggars would ride
Wishing for something or wanting, is not the same as getting it or having it

If you can't stand the heat, get out of the kitchen
If you can't handle a particular situation, you should get out of that situation

If you chase two rabbits, both will escape
Two tasks together, you will not even complete one

If you don't have anything nice to say, don't say anything at all
Don't say bad things, if you cannot speak good

Ill-fated idea, An
A bad idea

Journey of a thousand miles begins with the first step, A
To reach a goal, you have to take action; To progress at anything, you first need to get started

Just the tip of the iceberg
Only a small fraction or piece of the whole thing

Justice is blind
The idea that laws are enforced without biases of race, gender, or sexuality

Keep something at bay, To
Not letting something get close to you

Keep your eyes open
Concentrate on something.

Kick back, To
To relax.

Kick the bucket, To
To breakdown; cannot be repaired (machine etc)

Knock off, A
To describe poorly made imitation of an expensive item

Last, but not least
Although something may be the last one presented, it is not a representation of its quality or importance

Leave no stone unturned
If you try to achieve everything, you leave no stone unturned

Licking one's wounds
Repairing and rejuvenating oneself after a defeat or loss

Lightning never strikes the same place twice
You may get very lucky once, but don't count on getting lucky twice

Like father, like son
Having the same characteristics as one's parent

Like there is no tomorrow
To do something to an extreme

Lion's share, The
The majority of the reward

Looking for a needle in a haystack
Trying to find something that is very difficult to find

Love is blind
Lovers do not see bad results or consequences in their love

More we learn, the less we know, The
The more we experience life, the more we learn what we don't know

Make a long story short, To
To provide the essential information so that the message gets communicated

Make or break, To
To succeed at something or face dire consequences

Man for all season's, A
A man who is very well-rounded and refined

Money can't buy you happiness
Even if you have a lot of money, you may not be happy

Money doesn't grow on trees
Used to illustrate to someone the value of money and hard work

Money is the root of all evil
To get money, people sometimes do things that are illegal or immoral

Monkey business
Unethical behaviour or behaviour that is deceitful

Necessity is the mother of invention
Most inventions are created to fill needs

Nip it in the bud
Fixing a small problem before it becomes a larger one

No pain, no gain
Everything worthwhile takes effort

None of your business
Of no concern

On the cutting edge
New

On the tip of my tongue
When you know something, but are not able to remember exactly what that was

Out of sight, out of mind
If you don't see someone or something enough or at all, they are easy to forget

Out of the woods
To be past a difficult or complicated problem

Over and over again
Happening repeatedly

Penny saved is a penny earned, A
It is smart to save every penny you can

Pay lip service, To
To talk about doing something, but not actually do it

People who live in glass houses shouldn't throw stones
If you have weaknesses, you should not point out the weaknesses of others

Poor as a church mouse
Having no money

Quick buck, A
Getting money for little or no effort

Reopen an old wound, To
To bring up a subject that causes pain or anger

Rolling stone gathers no moss, A
An ambitious person is more successful than a person not trying to achieve anything.

Rome wasn't built in a day
Large projects take a lot of time to complete

Rub salt in the wound
To make something that is painful or difficult even more painful or difficult

Rub your nose in it
To bring repeatedly and forcefully to another's attention

See the glass as half empty, To
To be pessimistic

See eye to eye, To
Agree on an issue

Separate the wheat from the chaff
An act of determining what is good and what is bad

Shape up or ship out
Behave correctly or leave this location

Shoestring budget, A
Being very frugal or financially conservative

Short pleasures are often long regretted
Doing something that doesn't last very long may have bad consequences

Shot in the dark, A
A guess

Silence is golden
It is often better to say nothing than to talk, so silence is golden

Slow and steady wins the race
Consistency, although progress may be slow, will eventually be more beneficial than being hasty with getting nothing in the end

Stitch in time saves nine, A
If you address problems when they first happen, you will save time and prevent trouble in the future

Stone faced
To show no facial expressions

Swallow one's pride
To set aside one's pride so that they can fix a problem or difficult situation

Swim against the tide
To take a difficult route or path

Take the bull by the horns
Accept a challenge with enthusiasm

Take your life in your own hands
Do something dangerous

There's no place like home
Nothing compares to the comfort of being in your own house

Think outside the box
To be creative

Those who do not look back from where they come from, will not reach their destination
Respect the circumstances you started from

Through thick and thin
Staying together through adversity or tough times

Time is money
The time is precious

Time heals all wounds
Given enough time, disputes between people will go away

Tongue tied, To be
Confused

Too many cooks spoil the broth
When too many people try to manage a job, they will cause it to turn out poorly

Two heads are better than one
When more than one person works on a problem, they will be more successful

Ugly as sin
Very ugly

Under the table
To receive payment illegally

Variety is the spice of life
Different things and different people keep life from being boring and boring is bad

Waiting for the dust to settle
Waiting for things to calm down

Walls have ears, The
People can hear what is being said

Water water everywhere, and not a drop to drink
Having an abundance of something that you can't use

Wear many hats
Perform many different tasks

What goes up, must come down
Anything that has risen or been raised must eventually fall down

When life gives you lemons, make lemonade
Take the struggles that you get and turn them into opportunities

When you lie with dogs, you catch fleas
When you deal with wrong people, your integrity will become questionable

You can lead a horse to water, but you can't make him drink
You can force certain things on people, but you can't make them like it

You have to break a few eggs to make an omelette
Some things may have to be broken or torn down in order to build something better

You must crawl before you can walk
You must learn before going to learn or do more complex things

You scratch my back, and I'll scratch yours
You do me a favour and I'll do you one

Zip your lip
Used as a directive to instruct someone to stop talking or to be quiet immediately

5. Idioms and Phrases

> Idiom is a group of words whose meaning is different from the meaning of the individual words. Used to make the language impressive, they are used extensively especially in formal usage. Phrase is, on the other hand, a group of words which does not consist of verb. Both are an essential part of good knowledge of the language.

Act

Act by (adhere) *They don't act by the norms of their religion.*
Act upon (follow) *Sona is acting upon my advice.*
Act up to (put into practice) *She likes to act up to her principles.*
Act on (affected) The medicine **acted on** his illness.

Back

Back up (support or favour) *Back up your requests with some facts.*
Back out (to withdraw from a promise) *She promised to support me but she backed out suddenly.*
Back down (from), (to give up a claim) *He has backed down from the race of presidentship.*

Bear

Bear down (to overcome, suppress) *He was trying to bear down the opponent.*
Bear away (to win) *She bore away the prize in the recitation of a poem.*
Bear out (to confirm) *The sample reports bear out the claims.*
Bear with (to tolerate) *When the lights went out in the hall, the speaker told the audience, 'please bear with us', lights will be back soon.*
Bear a grudge against (to feel hatred for) *Monika bears a grudge against her divorced husband.*

World's most famous writers often have a lot of hidden surprises!!!

Agatha Christie worked as a nurse in a military hospital during the First World War. Later she worked at the pharmacy; that is why she is good in poisons and a lot of murders in her books have been committed with the help of the poison.

She suffered from dysgraphia, that is almost unable to write by hand. All of her famous novels have been dictated.

Bear a hand (give assistant) *He could **bear** me **a hand** when I was in trouble.*
Bear up against (to sustain) *Seema **bore up against** all odds confidently.*
Bear down upon/on (to attack quickly) *The hurricane **bore down on** the town fiercely.*
Bear through (to support) *Courage can **bear** us **through** the difficulties.*
Bear in mind (remember) ***Bear in mind** that healthy outlook is the key to success.*
Bear the brunt (to face utmost fury) *The centre of the army has to **bear the brunt** of the battle.*
Bear hard upon (to press heavily upon, to oppress) *This new law will **bear hard upon** the consumers.*

Break

Break away (go away abruptly, leave suddenly) *The captive **broke away** from his guards.*
Break down (to collapse) *There was a **breakdown** in the power house leading to the failure in the supply of electricity.*
Break forth (burst out) *When shall the light **break forth** as the morning?*
Break into (to enter forcibly) *A neighbour **broke into** his house last week.*
Break open (to open by force) *The thief **broke open** the lock and made away with the cash.*
Break with (to cut off connection) *I have **broken** all ties **with** him.*
Break loose (to get free) *The angry bull **broke loose** from its rope.*
Break news (to convey a news suddenly) *I did not have the heart to **break the news** of his son's accident.*
Break out (to spread) *Dengue fever has **broken out** in the town.*
Break off (to stop suddenly)*The leader **broke off** his speech in the middle.*
Break up (come to pieces) *The ship **broke up** on the rocks.*
Break in (to train or adapt) *The boss has asked the office staff to **break in** the new assistant.*

Bring

Bring about (to cause) *Welfare schemes **brought about** a qualitative change in the lives of the common people.*
Bring home to (to convince a person) *The teacher **brought home to** me the importance of discipline.*
Bring to book (to bring to justice) *The robber was **brought to book** by the police.*
Bring forth (to bear) *An honest action **brings forth** good results.*
Bring out (publish) *I am going to **bring out** a new book.*
Bring to light (to disclose) *The murder was **brought to light** after all.*
Bring to bear on (to use force) *His strength was **brought to bear on** the table which broke.*
Bring down (cause to fall) *Heavy supply **brought down** the price.*

Bring up (to rear) *The mother **brings up** her children with love and care.*
Bring to mind (to recall) *I could not **bring to mind** when I had met the girl.*
Bring round (to induce) *We **brought** him **round** to agreeing my views.*
Bring on (to cause) *Dirty hands often **bring on** diseases.*
Bring under (to capture) *The robbers were easily **brought under** by the police.*

Beat

Beat about the bush (to digress) Do not **beat about the bush,** but come to the point.
Beat back (to compel to retire) *The flames **beat back** the firemen.*
Beat into (to install sense in a dull mind by repeated instructions) *Can you **beat** some sense **into** him?*
Beat out (to remove by striking with a hammer, stick etc.) *Take a stick and **beat out** the seed from these pods.*
Beat upon (to strike upon repeatedly) *The rain descended, and the floods came, and the winds blew, and **beat upon** that house, and it fell.*
Beat down (to crush) *The Indian Army **beat down** the Pakistani forces.*

Call

Call on (to pay a visit) *I will **call on** my cousin tomorrow.*
Call at (to visit) *Rozy will **call at** my house in the evening.*
Call out (summon) *The fire brigade was **called out** twice.*
Call upon (to appeal to do something) *The President **called upon** the chief guest to address the meeting.*
Call in (request or order the return of) *The government **called in** the gold coins.*
Call to mind (to recall) *I cannot **call to** my **mind** when I called the girl.*
Call forth (to bring into action) *This work will **call forth** courage.*
Call in question (to doubt) *His honesty was **called in question**.*
To call to account (to take to task) *He will be **called to account** for his carelessness.*
To call names (to abuse) *When he **called me names** I too abused him.*
Call for (demand) *Success in life **calls for** hard work.*
Call into play (to bring plainly) *The task should **call into play** all your powers of concentration.*
Call off (to withdraw) *The show was **called off** because of bad weather.*
Call up (to phone) *I will **call** you **up**, when I need your help.*

Carry

Carry off (to win) *Karan **carried off** all the school prizes.*
Carry on (to continue) *Haider **carried on** his work and did not stop.*
Carry through (to support) *Her courage **carried** her **through** all difficulties.*
Carry a thing too far (to go beyond certain limit) *If you **carry a joke too far**, your friend will not like.*
Carry into effect (to put into practice) *You **carry** a plan **into** execution.*
Carry away (to be influenced by) *He was **carried away** by her beauty.*

Carry sth away (to be lost by breaking) *The ship's mast was **carried away** during the storm.*

Carry weight (to be influenced) *I think your arguments **carry no weight**.*

Carry one's point (to gain one's point) *Despite opposition, I **carried my point**.*

Carry something on (manage) *Rising costs made it hard for him to **carry on the business**.*

Come

Come about (to happen) *How did this **come about**?*

Come after somebody (to follow in a line) *which ruler **came after** Shahjahan?*

Come after something (to chase) *The police **came after** the thief with a pistol in hand.*

Come along (make haste) ***Come along** else we'll be late for the show.*

Come apart (break into pieces) *The new glass set just **came apart** in her hands.*

Come round (to agree) *The family **came round** to our way of thinking.*

Come off (take place) *His entrance test will **come off** in January.*

Come of (to belong to) *Rahul Gandhi **comes of** a noble family.*

Come on (follow) *You go first, I'll **come on** later.*

Come by (to get) *How did you **come by** this book?*

Come before sb/st (to be more important than sth else) *Kavish feels his family **comes before his career**.*

Come to blows (to fight) *From hot words they **came to blows**.*

Come across (to see accidentally) *I **came across** my old friend near my office.*

Come forward (to offer help to someone) *The police appealed for witnesses to **come forward** with information.*

Come into force (to operate) *The policy **came into force** last month.*

Come to pass (to happen) *We need to be prepared to fight, but hopefully it won't **come to pass**.*

Come round (to become conscious again) *Mahak fainted in the classroom but soon she **came round**.*

Come true (to be true) *My prediction has **come true**.*

Come through (something) (to continue to live, be strong, or succeed after a difficult or dangerous time) *It's been a tough time, but I'm sure you'll **come through** and be all the wiser for it.*

Come to light (to be known) *After search, the police **came to light** about the murder.*

Come up to (to be equal to) *His presentaion has not **come up to** my expectations.*

Come to terms (to settle a bargain) *We will reduce the prices if they do not **come to terms**.*

Cut

Cut back (to reduce something) *They are planning to **cut back** on public spending.*

Cut down (to decrease or shorten) *We must try to **cut down** our expenses.*

Cut out for (to be suited for) *You are not **cut out for** this job.*

Cut a person dead (to pretend not to notice) *Sameer deceived her but she has cut him dead.*

Cut short (to interrupt) *His work was cut short by their conversation.*

Cut in (to interfere) *She kept cutting in on our discussion.*

Cut a figure (to attract attention) *He always cut a figure in the public meeting.*

Drop

Drop in (to come unexpectedly) *While we were chatting he just dropped in.*

Drop a line (to write a letter) *Please drop me a line when you reach home.*

Drop off (to fall into a short sleep) *I dropped off in front of the television.*

Drop out (to leave or retire) *His injury forced him to drop out at the last minute.*

Do

Do away with (to abolish) *Let us do away with the evil customs.*

Do a good turn (to be kind) *He did me a good turn when I needed.*

Do without (to dispense with) *I cannot do without a servant.*

Do for (to serve the purpose of) *This paper will do for noting the points.*

Done for (to be ruined) *I am done for because I have lost in business.*

Done up (to be exhausted) *He is totally done up, he cannot move further.*

Do up (to fasten something in a particular way) *Do up your coat or you'll get cold.*

Fall

Fall off (to decline or separate) *A button had fallen off her jacket.*

Fall into the hands of (to be caught) *The thief fell into the hands of the policeman.*

Fall in with (to accept someone's ideas) *She explained but I couldn't fall in with her logic.*

Fall foul of (to quarrel) *He is worried that his teenage kids will fall foul of the law.*

Fall back upon (to depend on) *She has no relatives to fall back upon.*

Fall back (to retreat) *The rebels fell back to defence.*

Fall through (to fail) *The planning fell through for lack of advertisement.*

Fall to (to start eating) *A fat man just fell to dish.*

Fall on or upon (to attack) *We fell on the robbers to overpower them.*

Fall flat (to be unsuccessful) *My advice fell flat on him.*

Fall out (to quarrel) *The two girls fell out over a triffle matter.*

Fall short of (to be deficient) *The patients fell short of medical facilities in the hospital.*

Get

Get through (to pass) *I finally got through my final examination.*

Get at (overtake) *The policeman ran after the thief and got at him.*

Get on (to make progress) *I am getting on with my new project.*

Get on with (to make progress in) *My sister is getting on with her new job quite well.*

Get rid (to be free from) *I want to get rid of my maid.*

338

Get off (to escape) *When the dacoits saw the police van, they managed to **get off.***

Get hold of (to seize) *They **got hold of** his factory.*

Get into (to be involved) *Sohan **got into** trouble yesterday.*

Get over (to overcome) *We have to **get over** all our problems to stay happy.*

Get around (to prevail upon) *News of the train accident soon **got around.***

Get up (to rise) *We should **get up** early in the morning to keep fit and healthy.*

Give

Give vent to (to express) *The writer has **given vent to** his feelings in his autobiography.*

Give rise to (to cause) *Her bad conduct has **given rise to** ill feelings.*

Give up (to stop) *That man has **given up** smuggling.*

Give in (to finally agree to accept something that you had at first opposed) *Eventually I **gave in** and accepted the job on their terms.*

Give way (to fall) *The building **gave way** due to poor construction.*

Give away (to distribute) *The Principal announced to **give away** the prizes.*

Give ear (to listen) *Please **give ear** to what your child says.*

Give out (to announce) *It was **given out** that the government was to enter into negotiations with the rebels.*

Give over (to abandon) *He has **given over** the project because of financial crisis.*

Give effect (to fulfil) *The terrorist tried to **give effect** to his mission.*

Give up the ghost (to die) *After prolong illness he **gave up the ghost** in the hospital.*

Given to (to be in the habit of) *He has **given to** smoking.*

Give over (to hand over) *Her mother **gave over** the charge of the household to her daughter.*

Go

Go down (fall in price) *The prices of petrol don't seem to **go down.***

Go off (to explode) *His gun did not **go off.***

Go on (to continue) *We are **going on** with our new assignment.*

Go through (to read) *Have you **gone through** my new book?*

Go in for (to enter as competitor) *I suppose I could **go in for** advertising.*

Go astray (to wander from the course) *It was hard to follow the lecturer's gist, since he kept **going astray.***

Go out (to extinguish) *Suddenly the light **went out.***

Go up (to increase) *The air fares have **gone up** considerably.*

Go by (to follow) *You should **go by** your mother's advice.*

Go off (to pass) *I am sure every thing will **go off** smoothly.*

Go into (to investigate) *The police will **go into** the matter.*

Go hard with (to be in real danger) *If this case gets to a jury, it will **go hard with** the defendant.*

Hold

Hold the stage (to attract attention of the audience) *Sona **held the stage** with her brilliant performance.*

Hold out (to offer resistance, to offer) *It is an alternative method which **holds out** the promise of her health.*

Hold water (to be well-grounded) *Your lame excuse does not **hold water**.*

Hold good (to remain valid) *Your offer **holds good** for 2 days.*

Hold back (to delay) *The plane was **held back** due to fog.*

Hold over (to postpone) *The examinations have been **held over** because of the curfew.*

Hold to (to stick to) *Saba still **holds to** her communal views.*

Keep

Keep away (to keep aloof) *We should always **keep away** from bad company.*

Keep back (to deliberately not tell someone all that you know about something) *I got the feeling he was **keeping** something from me **back**.*

Keep pace with (to go abreast) *I had done my best to **keep pace with** time.*

Keep an eye on (to attend to) *The watchman **kept an eye on** him because he looked suspicious.*

Keep back *(to conceal)* *I was struggling to **keep back** the tears.*

Keep sth down (used to ask someone to make less noise) *Can you **keep it down**, I'm studying.*

Keep up (to maintain) *Teenagers try to **keep up** the reputation of their family.*

Keep aloof (to avoid) *She **keeps** herself **aloof** from society.*

Lay

Lay bare (to expose) *She **laid bare** all her secrets to me.*

Lay by (to save for future) *You must **lay by** something for the future.*

Lay down (to die) *Manish made up his mind to **lay down** his life for the sake of his country.*

Lay heads together (to consult) *My parents are **laying their heads together** to solve my problem.*

Lay hands on (to manage) *He couldn't seem to **lay his hands on** last year's sales figures.*

Lay up (to be confined to bed) *Tarun is **laid up** in the bed.*

Lay out (to grow) *He has **laid out** a plant in his garden.*

Lay waste (to destroy or ruin) *The enemy **lay waste** to the countryside after the invasion.*

Look

Look down upon (to scorn) *Do not **look down upon** the poor.*

Look forward to (to wait anxiously) *I am **looking forward to** your next visit.*

Look daggers (to look angrily at someone) *I do not know why he is **looking daggers** at me.*

Look after (to take care of) *My daughter is mature enough to **look after** herself.*

Look into (to enquire) *I want you to **look into** the matter seriously.*

Look up to (to regard with respect) *All of my friends **look up to** Rohit as our leader.*

Look for (to search) *She is **looking for** a job.*

Look out for (to be on the watch) *I am **looking out for** a big house.*

Look over (to examine) *The officer is **looking over** the letter.*

Look through (to understand thoroughly) *The magistrate will **look through** the case.*

Look upon (to regard) *I **look upon** him as my brother.*

Look sharp (to lose no time) *Please **look sharp**; we are getting late.*

Look to (be careful of or about) *Our government must **look to** the country's defences.*

Make

Make away (to run away) *She decided to **make away** with him.*

Make good (to fulfil, to make for the loss) *You must try to **make good** the loss.*

Make out (to understand clearly) *She couldn't **make out** the riddle.*

Make up (to compensate) *She has **made up** her lodging condition with her friend.*

Make up (to determine) *She has **made up** her mind to be a doctor.*

Make for (to go in the direction of) *The ship **made for** the Eastern islands.*

Make it up with (to settle one's differences) *Till they **make it up with** each other, their kids will suffer a lot.*

Make the most of (to get the best advantage) *Try to **make the most of** your time or your business will not prosper.*

Make up for (to compensate) *I will **make up for** damaging your car.*

Make up one's mind (to decide) *I have **made up my mind** to go to London.*

Make off (to run away with) *The girl **made off** with her boyfriend.*

Make over (to improve the appearance or change the image) *She did a complete **make over** for the Independence Day.*

Make away with (to kill) *A man **made away with** his landlord.*

Pull

Pull together (to work in harmony) *They cannot **pull together** as they have differences of opinion.*

Pull through (to recover) *She will soon **pull through** after her long sickness.*

Pull down (to demolish) *Many slums were **pulled down** by the government officials.*

Pull up (to rebuke) *The boy was **pulled up** for abusing an old man.*

Put

Put on (to wear) *Sohan **put on** his jacket and went out.*

Put forth (to exert) *Khali **put forth** his power to defeat a Korean wrestler.*

Put by (to save) *My mother is **putting by** some money for future security.*

Put down (to suppress) *India is struggling hard to **put down** terrorism.*
Put up with (to tolerate) *She could not **put up with** his remark.*
Put up (to stay) *Sita will **put up** at her uncle's flat.*
Put off (to postpone) *Do not **put off** your programme to go to Agra.*
Put out (to extinguish) *Please **put out** the candle.*
Put in (to submit) *I have **put in** my leave application.*

Run

Run after (to pursue) *Do not **run after** him. He is a liar.*
Run down (to criticize) *She is always **running down** her daughter.*
Run down (to become weak) *I am **running down** on fever since a few days.*
Run into (to be involved) *Mona will **run into** debt if she does not curtail her expenditures.*
Run over (to be crushed) *A motorbike was **run over** by the speeding truck.*
Run short of (to be exhausted) *The lamp **ran short** of oil.*
Run through (to waste) *He **ran through** all his fortune in gambling.*
Run risk (to incur danger) *We are to **run the risk** of losing our private job.*
Run out (to expire) *The time has **run out** very fast.*
Run high (to be violent) *Party spirit usually **runs high** at election time.*

Set

Set apart (to reserve) *I am going to **set apart** some money for the party.*
Set aside (to reject) *The lawyer has **set aside** all the evidences.*
Set in (to start) *Summer has **set in**, it is quite hot.*
Set up (to start business) *Asif has **set up** a new leather factory.*
Set upon (bent or adamant upon) *My friend is **set upon** being an engineer.*
Set about (to begin happily) *I **set about** my work passionately.*
Set off (to go) *He **set off** in search of his lost cow.*
Set out (to start) *He **set out** on his journey for Kanyakumari.*
Set on (to incite) *She **set** her dog **on** me.*

Take

Take after (resemble) *Her daugther **takes after** her grandmother.*
To be taken up (to be occupied) *I am **taken up** with the preparations of her marriage.*
Take down (to record) *His secretary **took down** the dictation.*
Take for (to mistake for) *The police-inspector **took him for** a robbery.*
To be taken in (to be deceived) *She was **taken in** by his dual personality.*
Take to (to adopt a profession) *Anant has **taken to** engineering.*
Take over (to take charge) *Huma will **take over** from her friend.*
To take ill (to feel offended) *Don't **take it ill**. This advice is for your good.*
Take up cause (to support) *Rich people must **take up the cause** of the poor.*
Take off (remove) ***Take off** your shoes before entering the room.*

342

Turn

Turn up (to appear) *We were scolded badly for **turning up** late at night.*

Turn out (to prove) *About 70% of the population **turned out** for the election.*

Turn away (to stop looking at sb/sth) *She **turned away** in fear at the sight of the bloodshed.*

To turn turtle (to capsize) *The bus **turned turtle** as it collided against the tree.*

To turn one's head (to fill with pride) *Sudden increase in income has **turned his head**.*

Turn off (to dismiss) ***Turn off** this boy as he is not sincere.*

To turn one's hand to (to apply oneself to) *I would like to **turn my hand to** Mughlai cooking.*

Turn down (to reject) *Mini **turned down** the proposal of marriage.*

Work

Work up (to excite) *He **worked up** the demonstrators into anger.*

Work out sth (to solve) *He **worked out** the sum in minutes.*

Work out (to develop or progress favourably) *I am sure things will **work out** in our favour.*

Work sb out (to understand sb) *My boss is whimsical and so I have never been able to **work him out**.*

Work wonders (to bring about good results, surprise)*The new coat of paint **works wonders** with my bedroom.*

●●